ALEXANDER SOLZHENITSYN

AN INTERNATIONAL BIBLIOGRAPHY OF WRITINGS BY AND ABOUT HIM

Compiled by

DONALD M. FIENE

ARDIS   ANN ARBOR

Alexander Solzhenitsyn
An International Bibliography of Writings by and about Him, 1962-1973

Introduction

This bibliography is intended to be as complete as is technically feasible for materials by and about Solzhenitsyn in Russian and English. All of the standard reference works known to me were consulted and many periodicals and books were searched individually, including most of the pertinent holdings in Slavic studies at Indiana University, the New York Public Library and the consortium of a dozen or so libraries centered in the metropolitan area of Louisville, Kentucky and southern Indiana. For the other thirty-six languages listed the bibliography is less complete, owing to more limited availability of sources, but it should not be regarded as selective; everything found which mentions Solzhenitsyn was listed except for some news items duplicating entries in English or Russian. The bibliography is selective only insofar as it attempts to categorize many of the items by type and relative importance. Most of the entries are in chronological order; sections devoted only to book reviews are alphabetical according to the title of the reviewing periodical. The format chosen attempts to combine maximum usefulness with minimum repetition. The entries are liberally cross-indexed. In addition, an index of names is provided in three sections: authors; editors, translators and compilers; and persons referred to in titles and descriptive notes. Since full names are given in the name index, the main entries give only first initial and last name of persons referred to.

Though research was begun in the fall of 1971, most of it was conducted during December and January, 1972-73. Items through May of 1973 are included (together with notes on several forthcoming publications in 1973 and 1974), but the practical cut-off date was November or December of 1972. Several of the annual bibliographies consulted, however, were a year or more behind schedule (so noted in the list below).

Standard Reference Works Consulted[*]

English language and international: <u>American Bibliography of Russian and East European Studies</u> (through 1966); <u>Biography Index</u>; <u>Book Review Digest</u>; <u>Book Review Index</u>; <u>British Humanities Index</u>; <u>Cumulative Book Index</u>; <u>Education Index</u>; <u>Essay and</u>

[*] I have chosen to list these in full since it appears that some have been overlooked by other bibliographers of Solzhenitsyn; at the same time I have probably missed some important sources myself and would be grateful for information about them.

General Literature Index; Dissertation Abstracts International; Index to Book Reviews in the Humanities; Index to Religious Periodical Literature; Index Translationum (through 1970); Library of Congress National Union Catalogue; M[odern]L[anguage] A[ssociation] International Bibliography (through 1971); Philosophers' Index; Readers' Guide to Periodical Literature; Social Sciences and Humanities Index.

Indexes to particular periodicals: Christian Science Monitor; Current Digest of the Soviet Press; New York Times; Times (London) Literary Supplement (through 1971) [Note: Index to daily and Sunday London Times not consulted; however, many articles from the Times are listed].

Other: Encyclopaedia Britannica Year Book; Current Biography; Portraits of Prominent USSR Personalities; Prominent Personalities in the USSR; various lists of books in print.

Russian: Bibliography of Russian Émigré Literature, 1918-1968 (L. Foster, comp.); Ežegodnik knigi SSSR; Letopis' gazetnyx statej; Letopis' recenzij; Letopis' žurnal'nyx statej.

Other European: Annual bibliography in Cahiers du Monde Russe et Soviétique (through 1970); Répertoire des thèses de doctorat européennes (through 1970); Jahresverzeichnis des deutschen Schrifttums (through 1971); Bibliographie der Zeitschriftenliteratur aus allen Gebieten des Wissens (through 1971); Bibliografia zawartości czasopism (Poland); Bibliografija Jugoslavije; Članky v českých časopisech (Czechoslovakia); Magyar Folyóiratok Repertoriuma (Hungary; 1965-70 only). Note: Other national reference works similar to the above were consulted by persons who sent me information from abroad; but the only such source named for me is Leket Divret Bikoret al S'farim Hadashim (Israel).

After I had conducted my own research I compared my data with that given in some twenty or more other bibliographies devoted exclusively to Solzhenitsyn. After investigating and resolving all discrepancies noted, I incorporated into my own list all the items that I did not have. The following bibliographies provided me with at least a few entries each:

Thompson Bradley. "Selected Bibliography," 1967. (See item no. 583 in my bibliography, pp. 338-39.)

Peter A. Rolland. "Alexander Isaevič Solženicyn: An Attempt at Complete Bibliography, 1963-1965," 1968. 8 pp. (See 701)

"Solzhenitsyn: A Bibliographic Note," Oct. 2, 1968. 12 pp. (Radio Liberty; see 1349)

"A. I. Solzhenitsyn (A Bibliography)," Nov. 24, 1969. 7 pp. (Radio Liberty; see 1382)

A. N. Artemova. "Bibliografija proizvedenij A. Solženicyna," 1970. (See 428, pp. 369-385)

Stokkeby Nielsen. "Bibliographie," 1970. (See 1958, pp. 170-171)

"Bibliografija proizvedenij Solženicyna," 1971. (See 431, pp. 161-174)

Giovanni Grazzini. [Bibliografia], 1971. (See 2233, pp. 303-11)

Abraham Rothberg. "Bibliography," 1971. (See 569, pp. 203-210)

James G. Walker. "A Selected Bibliography," 1971. (See 694, pp. 181-87)

François d'Argent. "Essai de Bibliographie d'Alexandre Sol-jénitsyne," 1971. (See 1918, pp. 493-519; about 700 items)

Ludmila Havrlant. "A Solzhenitsyn Selected Bibliography, December 1962-October 1970," 1971. (See 642, pp. 243-252)

Leo Carl Moody. "Bibliography," 1971. (See 695, pp. 124-30)

Hans Björkegren. "Bibliography," 1971. (See 570, pp. 181-182; have not seen original Swedish)

Stanley R. Radosh & Laszlo M. Tikos. "Aleksandr Isayevich Solzhenitsyn: A Selected Bibliography," 1972. (See 674, pp. 1-6; about 350 items)

A. N. Artemova. "Bibliografija," 1973. (See 429; have seen this in proof only; about 1200 items)

Harold Hatfield. [Working bibliography], 1973. (See 699; several pages of bibliography from dissertation-in-progress, sent to me by the author)

The lists compiled by d'Argent in 1971 and Artemova in 1973 were especially helpful to me, the former providing about 100 of my entries in the French language and the latter a total of about 200 items in French, German, Russian and English. D'Argent included in his list a number of minor news items that I decided not to copy out into mine. Likewise, Artemova's list contains considerable information that I chose not to carry over, chiefly relating to translations of Solzhenitsyn's works. Artemova's bibliography appears in the appendix of volume 6 of the revised edition (dated 1972 except for volume 6) of the collected works (Sobranie sočinenij) of Solzhenitsyn published by Posev Verlag (Frankfurt a/M), of which Artemova is chief editor. Though she lists several hundred articles about Solzhenitsyn, her main interest is translations and reprintings of his works. She gives very complete data on each book, listing each new edition separately; and she notes size, cost and occasionally the number of copies printed--data which I do not provide in my list. In addition she supplies an index to translations of Solzhenitsyn's fiction. (I do not have such an index, though I do list all the translations; on the other hand, Artemova does not have an index to critical articles as I do; furthermore, her selected list of articles about Solzhenitsyn is limited primarily to French, German, Russian and English publications.) In general, Artemova's list is more useful in the area of translation, mine in literary criticism and biography. Beyond that, her edition of Solzhenitsyn's works, with its supplementary volume of documents, is not merely useful but indispensable to anyone seriously interested in Solzhenitsyn. She was kind enough to send me the proofs of her bibliography, giving me permission to use what I needed, even though there was no chance for her to include in her book the 300 or more items that I sent her in exchange. I am very grateful to her for this generosity, which has resulted in the present bibliography of Solzhenitsyn being more complete by far than any other published up to the present time.

Among the Solzhenitsyn bibliographies that I was unable to consult, I judge the following to be most likely to contain at least some information that I lack:

Ljudmila Torn. "Bibliografija proizvedenij A. Solženicyna," 1970. (See 430, pp. 182-193; but Havrlant, 1971 [see 642] mentions that she had consulted Torn [or Thorn?] in preparing her own list--which I have seen.)

"Bibliographie der Werke von A. Solshenizyn," 1970. (See 1959, pp. iii-xxiv; probably this is a reprinting, more or less, of Artemova's first bibliography [see 428, pp. 369-385].)

R. Pletnev. [Bibliografija], 1970. (See 319, pp. 145-46)

G. Casolari. [Bibliografia], 1970. (See 2219; d'Argent mentions [see 1918, p. 510] that Casolari's article is important and that it includes a bibliography; however, d'Argent presumably carried Casolari's entries over into his own bibliography.)

Gôsuke Uchimura. So[lženicyn] noto. Tôkyô, 1971. (See 2255; probably this book has a brief bibliography; even if it does not, the author very likely refers to the work of other Japanese critics in his text. My bibliography is deficient in the area of Asian criticism of Solzhenitsyn, Japanese in particular.)

J. A. Mezz. [Bibliography], 1971. (See 696; the bibliography in Mezz's dissertation is concerned mainly with articles and reviews relating to Olen' i šalašovka and its world-premier performance in Minnesota, 1970.)

Michael Scammell. [Bibliography], 1973. (See 573; Scammell's forthcoming book on Solzhenitsyn has a bibliography.)

[Bibliographie], 1973. (See 2119; forthcoming collection of articles and documents edited by F. P. Ingold and Ilma Rakusa, Alexander Solschenizyn: Kirche und Politik, has a bibliography.)

[Samizdat publications], 1973. (See 574; forthcoming collection of articles about Solzhenitsyn edited by J. B. Dunlop, Richard Haugh & Alexis Klimoff has a list of samizdat items relating to Solzhenitsyn.)

Inevitably there are other bibliographies that I have not seen; it should be noted, however, that I have not attempted to list here all of the brief check lists known to me--usually of just the main works of Solzhenitsyn in Russian and English, such as that provided by Burg and Feifer, 1972 (see 571). The present introduction, incidentally, is the only place where I list bibliographies of Solzhenitsyn as a special category.

Another important source of information for me was the letters I received from one hundred or more editors, translators and critics around the world in response to several hundred queries mailed out. Most of these respondents do not expect formal acknowledgment of their help; however, I would like to thank individually all those persons and institutions who went to the trouble of doing actual research for me, who made files and documents available to me, or who provided me with detailed information rather beyond the call of ordinary duty, often requiring protracted correspondence:

Esa Adrian, Finnish translator of Solzhenitsyn; sent me a list of 20 items selected from 200-300 reviews, articles and news items on Solzhenitsyn published in Finland through 1971.

Jose Ferrer Aleu, translator of Solzhenitsyn into Spanish; detailed letter, Dec. 18, 1971.

A. N. Artemoff.[Artemova],editor of Posev editions of Solzhenitsyn's works; sent me not only the proof sheets of her forthcoming bibliography, but much other information in several letters, January-March 1973.

C. G. Belousow, Association of Russian-American Scholars in U.S.A.; detailed letter.

Hans Björkegren, Swedish translator of Solzhenitsyn and author of book on him; sent me a list of some 20 items in Swedish selected from a much larger number known to him (end of 1971).

Patricia Blake, author of forthcoming book on Solzhenitsyn; several letters.

Judith Borsuk, American student in Israel; sent me a list of about 20 items on Solzhenitsyn in Hebrew, based on research conducted by her in the Jewish National and University Library, Jerusalem.

Ingvild Broch, University of Oslo, translator of Solzhenitsyn; sent me numerous items on Solzhenitsyn published in Norway, based on selective research done in January and December 1972 and January 1973.

Edward J. Brown, Stanford University; letter.

Karin Busch, Press Department of Luchterhand Verlag, Darmstadt; sent me clippings of reviews of German translations of Cancer Ward and August 1914.

Francisco del Carril, Emecé Editores, Buenos Aires; detailed letter.

Theun de Vries; translator of Solzhenitsyn into Dutch; sent me copies of 150 clippings of brief articles, reviews and news items published in the Netherlands, from which I selected about 20 items.

Donald Fanger; Harvard University; detailed letter.

Farrar, Straus and Giroux, Inc.; Public Relations Department allowed me to examine clipping file containing about 200 brief articles and reviews, chiefly of August 1914.

Harold Hatfield, working on dissertation about Solzhenitsyn for University of Colorado; sent me rough draft of bibliography and much additional information, January-February 1973.

Richard Haugh, Iona College, one of the editors of forthcoming book about Solzhenitsyn; several detailed letters.

Felix Philipp Ingold, University of Basel, editor of several books about Solzhenitsyn; detailed letter.

Helene Iswolsky, Slavic scholar now working with Dorothy Day at Tivoli Farm in New York; detailed letter.

R. C. Kenedy, England, author of article on Solzhenitsyn; letter.

Hak-Soo Kim, Hankuk University, Seoul, translator of Solzhenitsyn into Korean; detailed letter with information about Korean and Japanese translations of Solzhenitsyn.

France Klopčič, Ljubljana, translator of Solzhenitsyn; sent me a detailed list of items by and about Solzhenitsyn published in Slovene.

George Kolodziej, Indiana University; spent several hours of his time helping me do research at Indiana University library.

Elisabeth Koutaissoff, Victoria University of Wellington, New

Zealand; detailed letter.

Helen N. Lunt, Centre for Information on Language Teaching, London; detailed letter.

Mariano Orta Manzano, Barcelona, translator of Solzhenitsyn into Spanish; detailed letter.

Harrison T. Meserole, Bibliographer of the Modern Language Association; sent me uncorrected page proofs of the entries on Solzhenitsyn from the MLA International Bibliography for 1971.

Johnathan A. Mezz, author of dissertation on Solzhenitsyn for University of Minnesota; detailed letter.

Mauceri Mirella, Press Department, Giulio Einaudi Editore, Torino; sent me clippings of reviews and articles on Solzhenitsyn published in Italy (through 1971).

L. Carl Moody, author of dissertation on Solzhenitsyn for Ohio State University; sent me copy of his bibliography, detailed letter.

Israel Naamani, University of Louisville; advised me on transliteration of Hebrew into Latin alphabet.

Alexander P. Obolensky, State University of New York at Albany; sent me copies of articles and a letter.

Tatiana A. Ossorguine, Paris; sent me information about several items published in Russian émigré periodicals.

N. V. Pervushin, University of Ottawa; detailed letter.

Robert Porter, University College of Wales, Aberystwyth; detailed letter.

William Putnam, Research Associate, Slavic Bibliographic and Documentation Center, Association of Research Libraries, Washington, D. C.; sent me several detailed letters with much useful information about research in progress on Solzhenitsyn.

Radio Liberty Committee, Information Division, New York; sent me several Radio Liberty publications which had not had wide distribution, including "A Serial Register of the Arkhiv Samizdata".

Charles Raad, Dar An-Nahar Publishers, Beirut; detailed letter.

Peter Rolland, Indiana University; gave me a copy of his unpublished bibliography on Solzhenitsyn.

Abraham Rothberg, author of book on Solzhenitsyn; letter.

Laszlo M. Tikos, University of Massachusetts, Amherst; detailed letter.

Unipub Distributors, New York; made available to me a copy of latest volume of Index Translationum, just after shipment was received from Paris.

Lionel von dem Knesebeck, Press Department, S. Fischer Verlag, Frankfurt a/M; sent me a list of reviews of German translation of First Circle.

James G. Walker, St. Olaf College; gave me a copy of his translation, Six Etudes.

Kate B. Webb, New York; detailed letter.

László Wessely, translator of Solzhenitsyn into Hungarian; detailed letter about criticism of Solzhenitsyn in Hungary.

Krzysztof Zarzecki, Warszawa; looked up information for me about early translations of Solzhenitsyn into Polish.

Gleb Žekulin, University of Toronto; detailed letter.

Many of the above persons are mentioned again as special sources

in my introductory notes to various sections of the bibliography.
In this frankly collaborative effort, mistakes due to lack of
familiarity with esoteric foreign languages have probably been
held to a minimum. Nevertheless, my typescript must inevitably
contain numerous errors and omissions, for which I alone am to
blame. To reduce the harm done by miscopying bibliographical data, I have tried to include as much basic information as possible for each entry: volume number, issue number, full date and
page numbers--so that the item may still be found if part of the
information is wrong. Most of the items lacking any part of this
information (except for certain newspaper articles) are ones that
I took from secondary sources without verification. My listings
in English and Russian, which comprise two-thirds of the entries,
are most likely to be complete and accurate.

In spelling Russian words and names using Latin letters, I
have consistently used the international system of transliteration employed by linguists and literary scholars (as in Index
Translationum, the MLA International Bibliography and the Slavic and East European Journal). This system is as follows:

А а	a	З з	z	П п	p	Ч ч	č
Б б	b	И и	i	Р р	r	Ш ш	š
В в	v	Й й	j	С с	s	Щ щ	šč
Г г	g	К к	k	Т т	t	Ъ ъ	"
Д д	d	Л л	l	У у	u	Ы ы	y
Е е	e	М м	m	Ф ф	f	Ь ь	'
Ё ё	ё	Н н	n	Х х	x	Э э	è
Ж ж	ž	О о	o	Ц ц	c	Ю ю	ju
						Я я	ja

The only exception I have made is in using the spelling Solzhenitsyn (rather than Solženicyn), which is the way the author's
name is spelled on all of his books in English. However, I usually abbreviate this name in the bibliography with the letter S.,
even when it occurs in the title of an article. Unfortunately,
the Russian name Солженицын has been spelled thirty or more different ways in transliteration:

Solgenitsin   Italian
Solgenitsyn   Italian
Solǧenitsyn   Italian
Soljenichin   Secondary transliteration of Korean:
    쏠제니쯔인
Soljénitsyn   French
Soljénitsyne   French
Solschenitzin   Spanish
Solschenizyn   German
Solshenizyn   German
Solsjenitsyn   Danish, Norwegian, Swedish
Solyenitsin   Spanish, Turkish
Solyenitzin   Spanish
Solzenicyn   Italian; secondary transliteration of Arabic
Solzenitsyn   Italian; secondary transliteration of Greek:
    Σολζενίτσυν
Solzenitzin   Secondary transliteration of Hebrew
Solzenitzyn   Secondary transliteration of Hebrew

xiii

Solženicin	Slovene
Solženicyn	Czech, Slovak, International
Solženitsyn	Italian
Solženjicin	Serbocroatian
Sołżenicyn	Polish
Solzhenitsin	Italian, Spanish, secondary transliteration of
סולדזני'צין ←	Hebrew
Solzhenitsyn	English, Finnish, Spanish, others
Solzhenitzin	Portuguese
Solzjenitsin	Dutch
Solzjenitsyn	Danish, Dutch, Norwegian, Swedish
Sorujenitsuin	Secondary transliteration of Japanese:
ソルジェニツイン [kata-kana form]	
Szolzsenyicin	Hungarian
Szolzsenyicün	Hungarian
鶴 秀	Chinese-Japanese ideograms

The abbreviation S. may therefore be taken to stand for the most common transliteration in any given language (but it will be noted that the Italians have used at least seven different spellings!). Further remarks on this problem are given in introductory notes to the various sections of the bibliography.

Other abbreviations: Al. = Aleksandr (or any transliteration of this name); Is. = Isajevič (or any transliteration of this patronymic). The initial A. or the initials A. I. indicate that these initials were used in the original. Thus: A. I. S. = A. I. Solzhenitsyn; Al. S. = Aleksandr Solzhenitsyn. When the name Solženicyn is inflected, as in the Slavic languages, this is sometimes indicated explicitly with such abbreviations as S-na or S-nu. References to Solzhenitsyn's works in the original Russian are usually made with the following abbreviations, either in the Cyrillic or Latin alphabets:

OD	Odin den' Ivana Denisoviča
SK	"Slučaj na stancii Krečetovka"
MD	"Matrenin dvor"
PD	"Dlja pol'zy dela" ("For the Good of the Cause)
Krox.	Kroxotnye rasskazy (Prose poems, etudes)
ZK	"Zaxar Kalitá"
KP	V kruge pervom (First Circle)
RK	Rakovyj korpus (Cancer Ward)
Pr. kist'	"Pravaja kist'" ("Right Hand")
Sveča	Sveča na vetru (Candle in the Wind)
Pasx. kr. xod.	"Pasxal'nyj krestnyj xod" ("Easter Procession")
Olen'	Olen' i šalašovka (The Love Girl and the Innocent)
Avg. čet.	Avgust četyrnadcatogo (August 1914)

For all languages except Russian, months are identified by the first three letters of their English names, without periods: Jan, Feb, Mar, Apr, etc. In the Russian part of the bibliography, months are often identified by the Roman numerals I through XII. Volume numbers of English-language periodicals are usually given in Arabic numerals, followed by the issue number in small Roman numerals: 20, iv. This information is followed by the date, usually given within parentheses; page numbers appear last. Usage varies somewhat from this pattern for periodicals in other languages. The initial letters of the main words in the titles of periodicals are usually all capitalized, consistent with current usage in most international bibliographies. Abbreviations of periodical titles are frequently used; these are indicated in introductory notes to various sections of the bibliography. Such abbreviations are consistent only for a given section (or language). In other words, two or more magazines published in different languages may have the same abbreviation--but these abbreviations would never appear in the same section. MLA abbreviations are used for all periodicals that appear in the MLA master list; however, most of the periodicals cited are not on this list; hence, many abbreviations are used which are unrelated to MLA usage.

This bibliography could have been far more complete than it is. However, the point of diminishing returns had already long been reached by the middle of March when typing of the final manuscript commenced. One important requirement of an international bibliography of an active contemporary writer is that it be as current as possible. The publication of such a document about Solzhenitsyn needs no lengthy justification. Solzhenitsyn is a powerful and distinctive writer of compelling honesty and courage. Virtually everything he does and says seems to be of interest to everyone on the planet--though not necessarily always for the best reasons. Having by now read a great many of the published articles about this author, I would say that Solzhenitsyn is too much revered as a symbol and paragon by people who are disinclined to emulate him. Those in the West who admire him especially for political or moral reasons would do better to resist their own evil governments than to content themselves with writing smugly sympathetic articles about Solzhenitsyn's martyrdom in the Soviet Union. The bibliography which follows records faithfully--and exhaustively--what has been written about Solzhenitsyn. Hopefully, it will discourage repetition, yet still be of use to serious scholars and critics.

May 1973

Outline of Contents

(1) Russian

I. By Solzhenitsyn: First publication and reprints

1. Fiction, articles and selected letters

All but a few works by S. have appeared in the various editions of his writings published by Possev Verlag, Frankfurt a/M [Russian spelling: Posev]. The first of these appeared in 1966 (with a second printing in 1968)--one volume titled Sočinenija and containing Odin den', the first four stories and the first 15 prose poems. In 1968 a two-volume edition of Rakovyj korpus was published. In 1969-70 appeared the collected works in six volumes: Собрание сочинений в шести томах

т.1. Один день Ивана Денисовича. Повесть.--Рассказы.
     --Биографическая справка. 1970. 308 с.
т.2. Раковый корпус. Повесть. Часть 1, 2. 1969. 600 с.
т.3. В круге первом. Роман. Гл. 1-Гл. 47. 1969. 408 с.
т.4. В круге первом. Роман. Гл.48-Гл.87. 1970. 409-
     807 с.
т.5. Пьесы.--Рассказы.--Статьи. 1969. 270 с.
т.6. "Дело Солженицына".--О творчестве А. Солжени-
     цына.--Библиография произведений А. Солженицы-
     на. 1970. 400 с.

Vol. 1 contains only the first four stories in addition to Odin den'; vol. 5 contains the first 15 prose poems as well as the later stories. A second edition of the six-volume collected works is being released in 1973, the first five volumes bearing the date 1972, the sixth volume being dated 1973. The contents of the first five volumes are the same, except that errors have been corrected and the two later prose poems [see 5b below] have been added. Vol. 6 contains much new material. (For contents of both editions of vol. 6, see 428 & 429.) Avgust četyrnadcatogo is not included. These editions all were edited by A. N. Artemova; they appear (or will appear) in pocket-size format, soft-cover, as well as in standard hard-cover. They are referred to below as Posev, 1966; Posev, 1968; Posev, 1969 (or 1970); and Posev, 1972. (Note: Posev Verlag also publishes a journal, titled Posev, in which many of S.'s works first appeared.)

1 "Один день Ивана Денисовича," Новый Мир, № 11 (ноябрь 1962), 9-74. [Вступление А. Твардовского, "Вместо предисловия," с. 8-9; this introduction appears in most of the editions below.]
Reprintings:
Роман Газета (Москва), № 1 [277] (янв. 1963), 1-47.
Москва: Изд. "Советский писатель", 1963. 143 с.
Единение (Melbourne), No. 11-33 (1963).
London: Flegon Press, 1963. 67 pp.; 1966. 135 pp.
pp. 1-67 in: Избранное. Chicago: Russian Language Specialties, 1965. (With SK & MD)
Frankfurt a/M: Posev, 1966; 1970, v. 1, pp. 5-133; 1972, v. 1.

3

2 "Случай на станции Кречетовка," <u>Новый Мир</u>, № 1 (янв. 1963), 9-42.
Reprintings:
pp. 1-34 in: <u>Два рассказа</u>. London: Flegon Press, 1963. (Reissued 1965 under title <u>Матренин двор</u>.)
pp. 68-101 in: <u>Избранное</u>. Chicago: Russian Language Specialities, 1965. (With <u>OD</u> & <u>MD</u>)
Frankfurt: Posev, 1966; 1970, v. 1, pp. 135-93; 1972, v. 1.

3 "Матренин двор," <u>Новый Мир</u>, 1 (1963), 42-63.
Reprintings:
pp. 34-55 in: <u>Два рассказа</u>. London: Flegon Press, 1963. (Reissued 1965 under title <u>Матренин двор</u>.)
pp. 101-22 in: <u>Избранное</u>. Chicago: Russ. Lang. Spec., 1965.
Frankfurt: Posev, 1966; 1970, v. 1, 195-231; 1972, v. 1.

4 "Для пользы дела," <u>Новый Мир</u>, 7 (июль 1963), 42-63.
Reprintings:
Посев (1963), № 37, с. 5-8; № 38, с. 6-8; № 39, с. 5-6.
Chicago: Russian Language Specialties, 1963. 32 pp.
Frankfurt: Posev, 1966; 1970, v. 1, 233-89; 1972, v. 1.

5a "Этюды и крохотные рассказы," <u>Грани</u> (Франкфурт), № 56 (октябрь 1964), с. I-XI. Содержание, 15 крох. рассказов: Дыхание, Озеро Сегден [см. 313], Прах поэта, Утенок, Отражение в воде, Город на небе, Костер и муравьи, Приступая ко дню, Гроза в горах, Вязовое бревно, Шарик, На родине Есенина, Колхозный рюкзак, Мы-то не умрем [см. 313], Путешествуя вдоль Оки [см. 244].
Other editions:
Frankfurt: Posev, 1966; 1969, v. 5, 221-232; 1972, v. 5.
Paris: Librairie des Cinq continents, 1970. 32 pp. (Title: <u>Крохотные рассказы</u>)
Reprintings of individual stories:
<u>Вестник Русского Студенческого Христианского Движения</u> (Париж), 75/76 (1964/1965), 85. ("Путешествуя вдоль Оки")
Посев, 4 (22 янв. 1965), 6-7. ("Озеро Сегден", "Прах поэта", "Путешествуя вдоль Оки")
<u>Six Etudes</u>. Northfield, Minnesota: College City Press, 1971. 16 pp. ("Дыхание", "Утенок", "Отражение в воде", "Костер и муравьи", "Гроза в горах", "Путешествуя вдоль Оки"; and the same in English in translation of J. Walker [see 519].)
Эпоха (Adelaide), фев. 1972. ("Дыхание", "Озеро Сегден", "Прах поэта")
5б Two more recent prose poems:
"Старое ведро" и "Способ двигаться": <u>Грани</u>, 80 (сентябрь 1971), 8-9.
Переизд.: Посев, 1972, т. 5.

6 "Не обычай дегтем щи белить, на то сметана," <u>Ли-</u>

тературная Газета (Москва), 131 [3900] (4 ноября 1965), 3. (Brief article or letter in reply to the following article: В. В. Виноградов, "Заметки о стилистике современной советской литературы," Лит. Газ., 124 [19 окт. 1965].) Переизд.: Посев, 1969, т. 5, 261-67; 1972, т. 5.

7 "Захар Калита́," Новый Мир, 1 (1966), 69-76. Переизд.: Посев, 1966; 1970, т. 1, 291-304; 1972, т.1.

8 "Молитва," Вестник РСХД, 81 (1966), 22; Русская Мысль, 2809 (24 сент. 1970), 1. [самизд., см. 239]

9 В круге перв.ом. Beograd: Marija Čudina, Leonid Šejka & Slobodan Mašić, 1968. 640 pp. (Photocopy of typescript, printed by Posev; published later than Rakovyj korpus [which was finished in the summer of 1967] but written much earlier [1955-64].)
Other editions:
Frankfurt a/M: S. Fischer Verlag, 1968. 551 pp. (Orig. title of V pervom krugu changed to V kruge pervom in second edition released in 1969 but still dated 1968.)
New York: Harper & Row, 1968. 515 pp. (Hard & soft cover)
London: Flegon, 1968. 644 pp. (Title: V pervom krugu)
Paris: YMCA Press, 1969. 666 pp.
Frankfurt: Posev, 1969, v. 4, 408 pp. & 1970, v. 5., pp. 409-807; 1972, v. 4 & 5.

10 Раковый корпус. Milano: Il Saggiatore di Alberto Mondadori Editore, 1968. v. 1, 320 pp; v. 2, ?. (Excerpts earlier in Грани, 67 [март 1968], 5-39.)
Other editions:
Frankfurt: Posev, 1968, 2 vols., 317 & 255 pp.; 1969, v. 2, 600pp.
London: Bodley Head, 1968. 2 vols., 328 & 282 pp. (Photocopy of typescript)
Paris: YMCA Press, 1968. 446 pp.
London: Flegon Press, 1968. 425 pp.

11 "Правая кисть," Грани, 69 (ноябрь 1968), с. I-X; Вестник РСХД, 89/90 (1968), 80-89; Новый Журнал (Нью Йорк), 93 (дек. 1968), 25-35; Посев, 1969, т. 5, 209-20; 1972, т. 5.

12 "Свеча на ветру (Свет, который в тебе)," Студент: Журнал Авангарда Советской Литературы (Лондон), № 11-12 (дек. 1968), 1-80 с.; Грани, 71 (май 1969), 15-77; Посев, 1969, т. 5, 125-205; 1972, т. 5.

13 Олень и шалашовка. London: Flegon Press, 1968, 95 pp. Reprinted: Грани, 73 (окт. 1969), 3-95; Посев, 1969, т. 5, 7-124; 1972, т. 5.

14 "Пасхальный крестный ход," Посев, 2 (фев. 1969), 45-47; Русская Мысль (20 марта 1969); Грани, 71 (май 1969), 3-6; Вестник РСХД, 91/92 (1969), 71-74; Родной Терек, 2 (март-апрель 1970); Единение (26 апр. 1970), 8; Посев, 1969, т. 5, 233-37; 1972, т. 5. [самизд., см. 245]

15 "Читают 'Ивана Денисовича' (обзор писем)," Новый Журнал, 94 (март 1969), 146-60; Посев, 5 (май 1969), 36-42; Посев, 1969, т. 5, 241-60; 1972, т. 5. [самизд., см. 246]

16 "Ответ трем студентам (Рязань, октябрь 1967)," Новый Журнал, 94 (март 1969), 145-46; Русская Мысль (17 апр. 1969); Посев, 1969, т. 5, 269-70; 1972, т. 5. [самизд., см. 264]

17 "Вот как мы живем," Посев, 7 (июль 1970), 11. (Под загл., "Духовное убийство: выступление А. С-на") Переизд.: 464, с. 99-100. [самизд., см. 300]

18 "Автобиография," Грани, 80 (сент. 1971). Also in Le prix Nobel en 1970. Stockholm: Nobel Foundation, 1971; & in Le prix Nobel en 1971. Stockholm: Nobel Foundation, 1972 [see 23 below]; & in Posev, v. 6, 1973. [samizd., see 307]

19 Узел I. Август четырнадцатого (10-21 августа ст. ст.). Paris: YMCA Press, 1971. 573 pp.; "Послесловие к русскому зарубежному изданию 1971 г.," с. 572-73 (подпись: Май 1971 г. Солженицын) [посл. переизд.: Посев, 7 (июль 1971), 2; самизд., см. 308]. (Гл. 10 романа переизд.: Новое Русское Слово, 22346 [19 авг. 1971], 4)
Above edition reprinted illegally: London: Flegon Press, 1971. 573 pp.; and legally: New York: Association Press, 1972. 573 pp. [Note: Proposed second volume of trilogy will have probable title: Узел II. Октябрь шестнадцатого (16-20 октября ст. ст.)]

20 "Поминальное слово," Посев, 1 (янв. 1972), 64; Русская Мысль, 2878 (20 янв. 1972), 3 (под загл.: "К девятому дню: слово С-на памяти Твардовского"). [самизд., см. 312]

21 "Всероссийскому Патриарху Пимену: Великопостное письмо," Русская Мысль, 2888 (30 марта 1972), 3 (Крестопоклонная неделя); Зарубежье, № 1[33] (март. 1972), 1-2; Посев, 5 (май 1972), 8-9; Вестник РСХД, 103 (1-й трим. 1972), 145-49. [самизд., см. 315; ответ С. Желудкова, см. 316 и 490]

22 "Ответ о. Сергию Желудкову," Посев, 9 (сент. 1972), 11 (под. загл.: "Письмо С-на"); Вестник РСХД, 103 (1-й трим. 1972), 159. [самизд., см. 317]

23 "Нобелевская лекция 1970 года по литературе," pp. 129-40 in Les prix Nobel en 1971. Stockholm: Nobel Foundation [Imprimerie Royale P. A. Norstedt & Söner; also Amsterdam, London, New York: Elsevier Pub. Co.], 1972 (with "Autobiography", also in English and Swedish). Other appearances of Russian text: Грани, 85 (1972), 156-75; Новое Русское Слово, 22723-5 (30-31 авг., 1 сент. 1972), три ч., все на с. 2 (под загл. "Нобелевская речь С-на"); Русская Мысль, 2911 (7 сент. 1972), 3-4; reprinted as book: Frankfurt a/M: Posev, 1972. 21 pp; Paris: YMCA Press, 1972. 30 pp.; also pp. 37-69 in Nobel Lecture. New York: Farrar, Straus & Giroux, 1972.

Unpublished manuscripts

24 "Пир победителя". Play in verse, written 1950-53; mentioned by S. in letter of 16 May 1967 (see 30 & 250). [Note: A selection of passages from the play was published in a German translation by René Drommert: "Preussische Nächte," <u>Die Zeit</u>, 47 (9 Dec 1969), 10 (see 1954); publication of further passages in <u>Die Zeit</u> was halted by S.'s lawyer, Fritz Heeb; Burg & Feifer note (see 571, pp. 301-02) that the passages seem to be a compilation (perhaps by the KGB, which had seized the ms. from S. in 1965) rather than a reproduction of any one section of the play.]

25 "Знают истину танки". Screenplay written 1959; mentioned by S. in letter of 16 May 1967 (see 30 & 250).

[Note: A manuscript titled "Arxipelag gulag" has been attributed to S. (See "Russia: Four New Works," <u>Time</u>, 93 [21 Mar 1969], 28.) · However, S. wrote nothing by this title; probably there is no such manuscript by any author; the <u>Time</u> story was doubtless based on information that S. had begun work on <u>August 1914</u>.]

2. Open letters, interviews, correspondence, announcements, miscellaneous

Many of these items, related to the "Solzhenitsyn affair", have been widely reprinted; information given here probably not complete. Certain interviews are listed here (see 26, 29, 42, 51) because they include direct quotation of S.; other interviews of S. may be reported in Per Hegge's book (see 2295), which I have not seen; for an interview of friends and colleagues of S. in Berlik, Kazakhstan, see 191. Transcripts of various writers' meetings are listed because they include statements by S. (see 27, 28, 32, 40). Entries are listed in chronological order according to date of composition or utterance, rather than to date of first publication.

26 Буханов, В. "У С. в Рязани," Литературная Россия (25 I 1963), 8; Коммунист Таджикистана (30 I 1963); Советская Киргизия, 30 (31 I 1963).

27 "Стенограмма расширенного заседания Бюро творческого объединения прозы Московской писательской организации СП РСФСР, 16 ноября 1966," Посев, 1973, т. 6 (см. 429). [Самизд., см. 247]

28 "Обсуждение первой части повести 'Раковый корпус' на заседание секции прозы Московской организации, 17 ноября 1966," Новый Журнал, 93 (дек. 1968), 223-249; Посев, 1970, т. 6, 154-87 (см. 428). [Самизд., см. 248]

29 Личко, Павел. "Один день у Ал. Ис. С-на," Новое Русское Слово (21 V 1967). Интервью, март 1967; отрывки в переводе словацкого (см. 1604).

30 "Письмо IV съезду писателей СССР, 16 мая 1967," Вестник РСХД, № 2 [84] (1967); Посев (16 VI 1967); Новое Русское Слово (18 VI 1967); Русская Мысль (22 VI 1967); Грани, 66 (1967), 162-67; Посев, 1970, т. 6, 7-13 (см. 428); 1973, т. 6 (см. 429). [Самизд., см. 250]

31 "Письмо в Секретариат правления СП СССР, 12 сентября 1967 г.," Новый Журнал, 93 (дек. 1968), 221-222; Посев, 1970, т. 6, 31-32 (см. 428); 1973, т. 6 (см. 429). [Самизд., см. 261]

32 "Запись заседания Секретариата Союза писателей СССР, 22 сентября 1967 г.," Новый Журнал, 93 (дек. 1968), 250-68 (под загл. "Изложения заседания . . ."); Посев, 1970, т. 6, 33-57 (см. 428); 1973, т. 6 (см. 429). [Самизд., см. 262]

33 "Письмо Секретариату СП СССР, 1 декабря 1967 г.," Посев, 1970, т. 6, 62-63 (см. 428); 1973, т. 6 (см. 429). [Самизд., см. 266]

34 "Письмо членам Союза писателей СССР, 16 апреля 1968 г.," Новый Журнал, 93 (дек. 1968), 220-21; Посев, 1970, т. 6, 97-98 (см. 428); 1973, т. 6 (см. 429). [Самизд., см. 271]

35 "Письмо в Секретариат СП СССР, 18 апреля 1968 г. [копии в Новый Мир, Литературную Газету, членам союза]," Посев, 1970, т. 6, 99-100 (см. 428); 1973, т. 6 (см. 429). [Самизд., см. 272]

36 "Письмо в редакцию [21 апреля 1968 г.]," Литературная Газета, 26 (26 VI 1968), 5. Переизд.: Посев, 1970, т. 6, 101 (см. 428); 1973, т. 6 (см. 429). (S. also sent copy to L'Unita, where it was published in Italian translation 4 Jun 1968.) [Самизд., см. 273]

37 "Письмо в редакцию 'Литературной Газеты', 12 декабря 1968 г.," Новый Журнал, 98 (март 1970), 283; Посев, 1970, т. 6, 188 (см. 428); 1973, т. 6 (см. 429). (Не издано в ЛГ) [Самизд., см. 284]

38 Письмо Министру связи СССР, 22 февраля 1969, изд. стр. 80 в: Жорес Медведев. Тайна переписки охраняется законом, 1970 (см. 447). [О том, что заказное письмо от 9 фев. 1969 г. Союзу чехословацких писателей еще не доставлено. Ответ: 7 июля 1969 от Б. Ястребова, начальник Международного почтамта (изд. с. 81 в Медведеве).]

39 "Письмо А. С-на парижскому издателю [Juliard, 18 июня 1969]," Русская Мысль, 2820 (10 XII 1970), 10. (Facsimile of holograph; see also entry 1918, p. 416 b.)

40 "Запись заседания Рязанской писательской организации, 4 ноября 1969 г.," Посев, 1970, т. 6, 135-146 (см. 428); 1973, т. 6 (см. 429). [Самизд., см. 287]

41 "Открытое письмо Секретариату СП РСФСР, 12 ноября 1969 г.," Посев, 4 (апрель 1970), 26-27; переизд.: Посев, 1970, т. 6, 148-49 (см. 428); 1973, т. 6 (см. 429). [Самизд., см. 289] (Note: S. also made a public statement this date; noted in New York Times (see 1095.)

42 "Телефонный разговор с Хегге [8 октября 1970 г.]," Посев, 1973, т. 6 (см. 429). (Per Hegge; concerning Nobel Prize: preliminary acceptance statement.)

43 "Телеграмма постоянному секретарю Шведской Академии, [11] октября 1970 г.," Посев, 1973, т. 6 (см. 429). (To Karl Ragnar Gierow; date given in Posev as 9 Oct.;

Labedz [1285, p. 214] gives date as 11 Oct.; an article in the
New York Times [see 1135] says that the telegram was received on
11 Oct.)

44 "Письмо Королевской Шведской Академии, 27 ноября 1970 г.," Вестник РСХД, 98, IV (1970), 88; Посев, 1973, т. 6 (см. 429). [Самизд., см. 306]

45 "Телеграмма к Нобелевскому торжеству, [9] декабря 1970 г.," Вестник РСХД, 98, IV (1970), 89; Посев, 1973, т. 6 (см. 429). (Posev has the date incorrectly as 10 Dec.)

46 "Открытое письмо министру госбезопасности СССР Андропову [13 августа 1971]," Русская Мысль, 2857 (26 VIII 1971), 2; Посев, 9 (сент. 1971), 6. (Копия Косыгину с неск. словами: "Председателю Советы Министров СССР А. Н. Косыгину, 13 августа 1971 г.") [S. received a telephone call in reply from a colonel in the KGB about a week later (noted in New York Times; see 1195).] (Самизд., см. 309)

47 Письмо Ф. Хеебу [Fritz Heeb], 3 сентября 1971 г. См. самиздат, 310.

48 Письмо П. Хегге [Per Hegge], 18 сентября 1971 г. Отрывки: Посев, 1973, т. 6 (см. 429). (По-швед., см. 2383а; самизд., см. 311)

49 Письмо Ф. Хеебу [Fritz Heeb], 12 ноября 1971 г. См. самиздат, 310.

50 "Письмо К. Р. Гирову, 4 декабря 1971 г.," Посев, 1973, т. 6 (см. 429). [K. R. Gierow]

50а Заявление, 13 января 1972 г. Ответ на обвинения Литературной Газеты (см. 232); отрывок в: "Новые выпады против С.," Русская Мысль, 2878 (20 I 1972), 2. [Full text is in German: Die Zeit, 21 Jan 1972. Also about this time S. requested via a letter sent by his lawyer, Fritz Heeb, that Macmillan (London) not publish biography in preparation by Burg & Feifer (see 571); text of this letter appears in L'Aurore, early Jan. Russian back translations of both letters appear in: "Подкоп А. И. С-на," Русская Мысль, 2881 (10 II 1972), 3.]

51 "Выдержки из интервью А. С-на иностранным корреспондентам, 30 марта 1972 г.," Вестник РСХД, 103 (1-й трим. 1972); Посев, 1973, т. 6 (см. 429). [Самизд., см. 315а] (Interview with H. Smith & R. Kaiser; in English at 563, Russian back translation from Eng. at 486.)

52 "Телеграмма Гирову [7 апреля 1972]," Посев, 1973, т. 6 (см. 429). [K. R. Gierow]

53 Заявление, 8 апреля 1972 г.: Русская Мысль, 2891 (20 IV 1972), 2 (под загл. "С. заявляет"); Посев, 1973, т. 6 (см. 429).

53а Заявление [около 18 декабря 1972]. [Statement accepting offer of "loan" from A. Maltz (see article in New York Times at 1273b); do not know if full statement quoted anywhere in Russian (but see article in Russian at 499).]

About Solzhenitsyn: 1. Reviews, criticism and polemical articles published in the USSR.

A number of these articles have been published in translation (usually brief excerpts only), chiefly in Current Digest of the Soviet Press (see 1526-1559), in L. Labedz's Solzhenitsyn: A Documentary Record (see 1285) and in Nivat & Aucouturier's Soljénitsyne (see 1918). Notes indicating entry numbers of translations are preceded by such abbreviations as:англ.:[English]; Фр.:[French]; нем.:[German]. Many of the articles published after 1966 contain only very brief references to S., often without naming him. Abbreviations: ВЛ: Вопросы Литературы; ЛГ: Литературная Газета; ЛР: Литературная Россия; НМ: Новый Мир; Сов.: Советская.

1962

54 Твардовский, А. "Вместо предисловия," НМ, № 11, 8-9. (Вступление к ОД; многие переизд. и переводы.)

55 Симонов, К. "О прошлом во имя будущего," Известия (18 XI) [моск. веч. вып. (17 XI)]. (Англ.: 1285, с. 17-18; 1527; Фр.: 1918, с. 122-23)

56 Бакланов, Г. "Чтоб это никогда не повторилось," ЛГ (22 XI), 3. (Англ.: 1526; Фр.: 1918, с. 125-27)

57 Ермилов, В. "Во имя правды, во имя жизни," Правда (23 XI). (Англ.: 1285, 18-19; Фр.: 1918, 123-5)

58 Дымшиц, А. "Жив человек," Литература и Жизнь (28 XI). (Фр.: 1918, с. 127-8)

59 Косолапов, П. "Имя новое в нашей литературе," Сов. Россия, 279 (28 XI), 3. (Англ.: 1285, с. 5; 1331; Фр.: 1918, с. 104)

60 Кашницкий, И. [Рец., ОД] Сов. Литва (30 XI).

61 Кашкадамов, И. "Учитель с улицы Революции," Учительская Газета (1 XII). (Биог.)

62 Скульский, Г. "Вся правда," Сов. Эстония (1 XII).

63 Бройдо, Е. "Такому больше не бывать," Полярная Правда (2 XII). (Фр.: 1918, с. 128-9)

64 Кружков, Н. "Так было, так не будет," Огонек, № 49, 28-29. (Фр.: 1918, с. 128)

65 Чичеров, И. "Во имя будущего," Московская Правда (8 XII). (Фр.: 1918, с. 129-30)

66 Мазуревская, А. "Суровая правда," Тувинская Правда (12 XII).

67 Литвинов, В. "Да будет полной правда," Труд (12 XII).

68 Афонин, Л. "Чтоб вдаль глядеть наверняка...," Орловская Правда (14 XII).

69 Зорин, Н. "Правда горькая, но необходимая," Кузнецкий Рабочий (15 XII). (Фр.: 1918, с. 129)

70 Каган, Б. "Да будет полной правда," Кировский Рабочий (16 XII). (Фр.: 1918, с. 129)

71 Теракопян, Л. "Время, события, люди," Гудок (16 XII).

72 Астафьев, А. "Солнцу не прикажешь," Ульяновская Правда (18 XII). (Фр.: 1918, с. 129)

73 "Творить для народа, во имя коммунизма: речь секретаря ЦК КПСС Л. Ф. Ильичева," Правда (22 XII),

2-3; Известия, 303 (23 XII), 3-4. (Англ.: 1528)

74 Ермилов, В. "Бесславный полет 'Славик Ревью'," Известия (25 XII), 4 [моск. веч. вып. (24 XII)]. (On article in Slavic Review [Sep 1962] by H. McLean, R. Mathewson & G. Struve; brief mention of S.; English trans.: 1529.)

75 Ильичев, В. "Большая правда," Уральская Рабочий (26 XII).

76 Нольман, М. "Счет тяжких дней," Северная Правда (29 XII). (Фр.: 1918, с. 129)

1963

77 Кузнецов, М. "Человечность!" В Мире Книг, № 1, 22-27. (Фр.: 1682)

78 Чапчахов, Ф. "Номера и люди," Дон, № 1, 155-9. (Фр.: 1918, с. 133-5)

79 Друце, Ион. "О мужестве и достоинстве человека," Дружба Народов, № 1, 272-4. (Фр.: 1918, 135-7)

80 Кузнецов, Ф. "День, равный жизни," Знамя, № 1, 217-21. (Фр.: 1918, с. 137 [отрывок])

81 "Творить для народа--высшая цель художника," Коммунист, № 1, 86-94 (см. 93). (Фр.: 1918, с. 135)

82 Бровман, Г. "Традиции и новаторство в литературе наших дней," Москва, № 1, 195-205.

83 Самарин, Ф. "Так не будет!" Пензенская Правда (5 I).

84 "Силы творческой молодежи--на службу великим идеалам: Речь секретаря ЦК КПСС И. Ф. Ильичева," ЛГ, 5 (10 I), 1, 2, 3; Сов. Культура (10 I), 1-3. (Англ.: 1285, с. 19-20; 1530)

85 Фоменко, Л. "Большие ожидания: заметки о художественной прозе 1962 г.," ЛР (11 I), 6-7 (с примеч. ред.). (Фр.: 1918, с. 130-1)

86 Ломидзе, Г. "Несколько мыслей," ЛР (18 I), 6. (Фр.: 1918, с. 131)

87 Минаев, Г. "В редакцию 'Л. Г.'," ЛГ, 10 (22 I), 3 [письмо]. (Англ.: 1285, с. 20; фр.: 1681; 1918, с. 132-3)

88 Буханов, В. "У С-на в Рязани," ЛР (25 I), 8; Коммунист Таджикистана (30 I); Сов. Киргизия, 30 (31 I). (Англ.: 503; 1285, с. 5-9; 1303; фр.: 1685; 1918, с. 104-9; нем.: 1967)

89 Ермилов, В. "Необходимость спора," Известия, 25 (30 I), 3, 4 (см. 3) [ответ на 85]. (Фр.: 1918, 131)

90 Эльяшевич, Аркадий. "Вечная молодость реализма," ЛГ (12 II). (Англ.: 1285, с. 20)

91 Варламов, Л. "Люди большой совести," Пензенская Правда (15 II).

92 Новиков, В. "Сила правды," Калининская Правда (27 II).

93 Губко, Н. "Человек побеждает," Звезда, № 3, 213-15. (Фр.: 1918, 137-8)

94 Бушин, В. "Насущный хлеб правды," Нева, № 3, 180-85.

95 Кожевников, В. "Товарищи по борьбе," ЛГ (2 III).

(Рец.: МД)

96 Трофимов, И. "День, который не повторится," Тамбовская Правда (3 III). (ОД)

97 "Высокая идейность и художественное мастерство—великая сила советской литературы и искусства: речь товарища Н. С. Хрушева," ЛГ, 31 (12 III), 1-4 [речь 8-го марта]. (Англ.: 1285, с. 41)

98 Лагунов, К. "Вехи в пути," Тюменская Правда (17 III).

99 "Собрание актива писателей столицы," ЛГ, 34 (19 III), 1. (Англ.: 1285, с. 41-2)

100 Бабаевский, С. "Партия и литература," Сов. Кубань (19 III).

101 Павлов, С. "Творчество молодых—служению великим идеалам!" Комсомольская Правда, 69 (22 III), 2. (Фр.: 1918, с. 141)

102 Чалмаев, В. "'Я есть народ...'," ЛГ, 37 (26 III), 2.

103 Полторацкий, В. "Матренин двор и его окрестности," Известия (30 III), 3 [моск. веч. вып. (29 III)]. (Англ.: 1531; Фр.: 1918, с. 142-3)

104 Пусть звезды станут ближе. М: "Знание", 1963. (См. с. 14-17; Фр.: 1918, с. 139-40)

105 Дымшиц, А. "Рассказы о рассказах, заметки о повестях," Огонек, № 13, 30-31. [СК и МД] (Фр.: 1918, с. 143-44)

106 "За идейность и социалистический реализм," НМ, № 4, 3-10.

107 Сергованцев, Н. "Трагедия одиночества и 'сплошной быт'," Октябрь, № 4, 198-207. [СК, МД и рассказ А. Яшина, "Вологодская свадьба"] (Фр.: 1918, 144-7)

108 Мотяшов, И. "Время романтики и время анализа," Подъем, № 4, 126-33. [МД]

109 Соколов, М. "Партия учит требовательности," ЛГ (2 IV). (Англ.: 1285, с. 43)

110 Семенова, А. "Фальшивым голосом," Сов. Клайпеда (9 IV).

111 Колесов, В. "Действительно, вокруг да около," Сов. Россия (13 IV).

112 [От ред.] Дон, № 5, 161.

113 Букин, В. "Читая С-на...," Наука и Религия, № 5, 90-91. [ОД]

114 Бушин, В. "Добро, обернувшееся злом (Герой—жизнь—правда)," Подъем, № 5, 112-21. [ОД, СК, МД] (Фр.: 1918, с. 148-9)

115 Твардовский, А. "Литература социалистического реализма всегда шла рукой об руку с революцией," Правда (12 V), 4-5. (Interview of T. by H. Shapiro of United Press International; Engl. trans: 1285, pp. 43-4; 1532.)

116 Панков, В. "День бегущий, стремительный," Известия (19 V), 2.

117 Михайлов, М. "Создавайте произведения, достойные нашей эпохи! (Слово колхозников о долге писателя)," Волгоградская Правда (21 V).

118 Мотяшов, И. "Правда и 'правдочка'," ЛГ (4 VII).

119 Кедрина, З. "Человек--современник--гражданин," ВЛ, № 8, 27-50.

120 Твардовский А. "Убежденность художника: Из речи на сессии Совета Европейского сообщества писателей," ЛГ (10 VIII).

121 Барабаш, Ю. "Что есть справедливость?" ЛГ, 105 (31 VIII), 3. [ПД] (Англ.: 509, с. 97-106; 1285, с. 44-6; 1533; фр.: 1918, с. 150-51)

122 Чалмаев, В. "'Святые' и 'бесы'," Октябрь, № 10, 215-17. [ПД] (Англ.: 1278, с. 272-5; 1535)

123 "О рассказе А. С-на 'Для пользы дела'," НМ, № 10, 193-98:

Ямпольская, Е. и И. Окунева и М. Гольдберг. "Удача автора". (Англ.: 509, с. 117-19; 1285, с. 49-50; 1537; фр.: 1918, с. 153)

Резников, Л. "Открытое письмо Ю. Барабашу" [ответ на 121]. (Англ.: 509, с. 119-28; 1285, с. 50-51; 1537; фр.: 1918, с. 153-4)

Шейнис, В. и Р. Цимеринов. "Так надо?". (Англ.: 509, с. 128-30; 1537; фр.: 1918, с. 154)

124 Атаджанян, И. "Письмо в ред.," ЛГ (1 X).

125 Гудзенко, А. "Мы оставались людьми...," Казахстанская Правда (6 X), 4. [Письмо журналисту О. Мацкевичу, с заметкой Мацкевича] (Англ.: 1534)

126 Синельников, М. "Правда--без 'приправ'," ЛГ, 121 (8 X), 3-4. (Фр.: 1918, с. 151)

127 Гранин, Д. "Прав ли критик?" ЛГ, 124 (15 X), 3. [ПД; ответ на 121] (Англ.: 509, с. 106-14; 1285, с. 46-7; 1535; фр.: 1918, с. 151)

128 Селиверстов, Н. "Сегодняшнее--как позавчерашнее," ЛГ, 126 (19 X), 3 [с примеч. ред., зам. о письме Я. Дунаевского]. (Ответ на 127) [Англ.: 509, с. 114-116; 1285, с. 48-9; 1535; фр.: (примеч. ред.) 1918, 152]

129 Пузанова, Н. "'За' и 'против'--почему?" ЛГ, 126 (19 X), 4 [письмо в ред.]. (Фр.: 1918, с. 152-3)

130 Овчаренко, А. "Жизнеутверждающая сила социалистического реализма," Дружба Народов, № 11, 234-50. (Фр.: 1918, с. 158-61 [отрывок])

131 Перцовский, В. "Сила добра," ВЛ, № 11, 21-44. (С. 36 по-фр.: 1918, с. 147-8)

132 Мотылева, Т. "В спорах о романе," НМ, № 11, 225.

133 Кочетов, В. "Не так все просто," Октябрь, №11, 217-221 [см. 217].

134 "Пафос утверждения, острота споров," ЛГ, 148 (12 XII), 1. [ПД] (Англ.: 509, с. 130-32; 1285, с. 51-52; 1537; фр.: 1918, с. 154-5)

135 Макаров, А. "Читая письма," ЛГ, 149 (14 XII). [Обзор писем читателей о сов. лит.; фр.: 1918, 157-8]

136 ЛГ, 154 (26 XII), 1 [ПД]:

"В редакцию 'Л. Г.'" [От ред. НМ: обзор 56 писем за С-на, 1 против, от: Ю. Сулин, Ф. Селиванов, В. Нехорошев, Х. Молчан, Н. Марченко и др.] (Англ.: 509, с. 132-4; 1285, с. 52-3; 1537; фр.: 1918, с.

155-56)
"От редакции [ЛГ]". (Англ.: 1537; фр.: 1918, 156-7)
137 Иванов, В. "Не приукрашен ли герой?" Известия, 306 (29 XII), 4 [моск. веч. вып. (28 XII)]. (ОД; письмо в ред.; англ.: 1536; фр.: 1918, с. 164-6)
138 "В комитете по Ленинским премиям в области литературы и искусства при Совете Министров СССР," ЛГ, 155 (28 XII), 1. (Англ.: 1285, с. 53-4)
139 Артамонов, С. "О повести С-на," Ученые Записки Литературного института им.Горького, вып. 2, 51-61.
140 Кожинов, В. Происхождение романа. М: "Сов. Писатель", 1963. 401 с. [Корот. зам. о С.]

1964

141 "Солженицын, Ал. Ис.," Энциклопедический Словарь. М: Изд. "Сов. Энц.", 1964. т. 2, с. 416.
142 Дремов, А. "Идеальные схемы и псевдоидеализация (Действительность--идеал--идеализация)," Октябрь, № 1, 204-207. [МД]
143 Бровман, Г. "Правда исторического оптимизма," Москва, № 1, 186-195. [ПД]
144 Сурганов, В. "А надо помнить...," Москва, № 1, 196-205. (Фр.: 1918, с. 161-3)
145 Лакшин, В. "Иван Денисович, его друзья и недруги," НМ, № 1, 223-45. Переизд.: Посев, 1970, т. 6, 243-86 (см. 428); 1973, т. 6 (см. 429). (Англ.: 1278, с. 275-88; 1540; фр.: 1918, с. 174-9; нем.: 2118)
146 ЛР (1 I) [МД] (Англ.: 1538) :
Жуховицкий, Л. "'Автор хотел сказать...' (Ищу со-
    автора)," с. 17-18.
Бровман, Г. "Обязательно быть соавтором?", с. 19.
147 Панков, В. "Исторический пароль," Огонек, №2, 24-25. [ПД]
148 Бушин, В. "Снова и снова: жизнь!" ЛР (10 I), 18-19. [МД] (Англ.: 1538)
149 "Наше мнение," ЛГ (11 I), 3:
Лезинский, М. [Письмо об ОД; англ.: 1538; фр.:
    1918, 166-7)
Молчанюк, Н. [Письмо об ОД; англ.: 1538; фр.: 1918,
    с. 167)
150 Паллон, В. "Здравствуйте, кавторанг," Известия (15 I), 4 [моск. веч. вып. (14 I)]. (Интервью с Б. Бурковским, прототип Буйновского [ОД]; англ.: 1315; 1536, фр.: 1918, 167-9)
151 "Рассказ кавторанга Бурковского," Известия (17 I).
152 Панков, В. "Носители света," ЛГ, 8 (18 I). (Фр.: 1918, с. 169-70)
153 Ставицкий, А. "За малым--многое," ЛГ, 10 (23 I). [ОД] (Фр.: 1918, с. 170-71)
154 Маршак, С. "Правдивая повесть," Правда (30 I) [моск. веч. вып.], 4. [ОД] (Англ.: 1538; фр.: 1918, с. 171-3)
155 Труфанова, В. "Политик, гражданин, художник,"

14

ЛР (31 I), 18. [МД] (Англ.: 1539)

156 Газизов, Р. "Глубина и свежесть критической мысли," ЛР (31 I), 18. [МД] (Англ.: 1539)

157 Скуйбин, В. "Глубинное постижение жизни," Искусство Кино, № 2. (Фр.: 1918, с. 182)

158 Бровман, Г. "Диалог о герое," ЛР (7 II), 6-7.

159 "Взыскательность," ЛГ (8 II), 3-4. (Англ.: 1540; фр.: 1918, с. 173-4)

160 Митин, Г. "Издержки спора," ЛР (14 II), 14-15. [МД]

161 "От Комитета по Ленинским премиям в области литературы и искусства при Совете министров СССР," Правда (19 II).

162 "Общий труд критики," ЛГ, 22 (20 II), 1-2. [Ответ на 145] (Англ.: 1540; фр.: 1918, с. 179-82)

163 Ерёмин, Д. и В. Сурганов. "Ответственность," ЛР (6 III), 2-3, 10 (с примеч. ред.). [ОД]

164 ЛР (27 III), 11 [ОД]:
Губко, Н. "Живые традиции".
Сергеев, Н. "Преддверье...".
Савин, С. "Односторонность". (Фр.: 1918, с. 182-3)

165 Лапшин, М. "Достойный вклад в советскую литературу," Политическое Самообразование, № 4, 54-60. [ОД]

166 Буковский, К. "Экономическая реплика литераторам," ЛГ (2 IV). [ОД]

167 Полторацкий, В. "В поисках 'пружины'," ЛГ (9 IV).

168 "Высокая взыскательность," Правда (11 IV), 4. (Англ.: 1285, с. 54; 1541; фр.: 1918, с. 183-5)

169 Греков, Л. "Достойна!" За Медицинские Кадры (14 IV). (Фр.: 1918, с. 185-6)

170 "Добрая строгость," Труд (19 IV). (Фр.: 1918, 185)

171 "Искусство героической эпохи," Коммунист, № 10, 33.

172 Крячко, Л. "Позиция творца и бесплодие мешанина," Октябрь, № 5, 207-19. [ПД]

173 Серебровская, Е. "Опекунша из ФРГ," ЛР (8 V), 18-19. [СК и МД]

174 Барабаш, Ю. "'Руководители', 'руководимые' и хозяева жизни," ЛГ (12 V). [ОД; ответ на 145] (Фр.: 1918, с. 186-90)

175 ЛГ (4 VI):
Лакшин, В. "В редакцию 'Л. г.'". [Ответ на 174] (Фр.: 1918, с. 190-191)
"От редакции (спор идет)". (Фр.: 1918, 191-2)

176 Первенцев, А. "Высокая миссия литературы," Сов. Кубань (7 VI).

177 ВЛ, № 7:
Стариков, Д. "Реальная нравственность," 26-31.
Сарнов, Б. "Это было невозможно 10 лет назад," 31-6.
Коган, А. "Герой и время," 36-42.

178 Баранов, В. "За жанровую определенность," ЛР (3 VII).

179 Иванов, В. "Не простое это слово," Известия (20 VIII).

180 Карякин, Ю. "Эпизод из современной борьбы идей,"

Проблемы Мира и Социализма, № 9, 79; переизд.: НМ, № 9, 231-39. [К полемике об ОД] (Англ.: 1319; Фр.: 1717; 1918, с. 193-201; польск.: 2317)

181 Волгин, Н. "Всегда в строю солдаты революции," Красноярский Рабочий (27 IX). (Фр.: 1918, с. 192-3)

182 Твардовский, А. "'Новый мир' в 1965-ом году," ЛГ (27 X), 1. (Англ.: 1542)

183 Золотусский, И. "Подводя итоги," Сибирские Огни, № 11, 163.

184 Власенко, А. "Труд--поэзия!" Октябрь, № 12, 193-203. [ОД]

185 "Высокий долг писателя," Приокская Правда (17 XII).

1965

186 Барабаш, Ю. "За" и "против": Полемические заметки. М: "Правда", 1965. 48 с. (С. 34 по-фр.: 1918, 202-03)

187 Винокур, Т. "О языке и стиле повести А. И. Солженицына Один день Ивана Денисовича," Вопросы Культуры Речи (1965), 16-32. (Нем.: 2118)

188 Бровман, Г. "Нравственная требовательность и историзм," Октябрь, № 1, 193-202. (С. 200 по-фр.: 1918, с. 201)

189 Бровман, Г. "Образ современника," Наш Современник, № 1, 111.

190 НМ, № 1:
Твардовский, А. "По случаю юбилея," 3-18. (Англ.: 1285, с. 54-55; 1544; фр.: 1918, с. 201 [от с. 10])
Дементьев, А. и Н. Дикушин. "Пройденный путь (К 40-летию журнала 'Новый мир')," 236-54. (Англ.: 1545)

191 Кунгурцев, Ю. "Солженицын в Казахстане," Ленинская Смена (Казахстан) (10 I). [Интервью: Ф. Черноусова, З. Сырымбетов, Е. Шмидт, Т. Меиркулов, У. Баяубаев и К. Мельничук.] (Фр.: 1918, с. 110-13)

192 Егорычев, Н. "Воспитание молодежи--дело партийное," Коммунист, № 3, 15-28. (С. 15 по-фр.: 1918, с. 201-02)

193 "Второй съезд писателей РСФСР," ЛГ, 28 (5 III), 3:
"На земле кубанской". [Речь В. Лапина; о МД]
" Высокий долг художника". [Речь Н. Егорычева]
(Англ.: 1543)

194 Вучетич, Е. "Внесем ясность: некоторые мысли по поводу одного юбилейного выступления," Известия, 88 (15 IV), 3. [Ответ на 190] (Англ.: 1546; фр.: 1918, с. 202)

195 "От редакции," НМ, № 9, 283-88. (Англ.: 1547)

196 "Выступление первого секретаря ЦК ВЛКСМ тов. С. П. Павлова," Комсомольская Правда (29 XII). (Фр.: 1918, с. 202)

1966

197 Макаров, А. "Через пять лет: Статья вторая," Знамя, № 3, 224-243. [О В. Семине; кр. зам. о С.] (Фр.: 1918, с. 203-04)

198 [Речь И. И. Бодюла], Правда (3 IV), 3-4.
(Англ.: 1548)

199 Алексеев, М. "Этапы большого пути," ЛР (22 IV),
7-9, 14-15. (Фр.: 1918, 204)

200 "'Писать глубоко, правдиво...' (читатели о литературе)," ВЛ, № 5, 44-69. (Фр.: 1918, с. 210)

201 Кожевников, С. "За Давыдовых и Корчагиных наших дней," ЛР, 19 (6 V), 8, 9, 10. (Фр.:1918, 204-5)

202 Лакшин, В. "Писатель, читатель, критик: статья вторая," НМ, № 8, 216-256 [см. 219-231; о МД].
(Англ.: 1549; фр.: 1918, с. 205-08)

203 Можнягун, С. "'Литература факта' и натурализм,"
Октябрь, № 7, 205-07. (С. 207 по-фр.: 1918, с. 203)

204 Абалкин, Н. "На добрую память," Знамя, № 10,
241.

205 Григорьев, Б. "В плену предвзятости," ЛГ, 125
(22 X). [Ответ на 202] (Фр.: 1918, с. 209-10)

206 Иванов, В. "Реализм сегодня," ЛГ (29 X),1 и
(10 XI), 3. [Ответ на 202] (Англ.: 1549)

207 "Идейная борьба: Ответственность писателя,"
ЛГ, 26 (26 VI), 5 [с письмом С. от 21 IV (см. 36)].
(Англ.: 1284, с. 391-8; 1285, с. 163-72; 1550; фр.:
1918, с. 300-06) Переизд.: Посев, 1970, т. 6, 104-
115 (см. 428); 1973, т. 6 (см. 429).

208 Микулина, Е. "Жизнь как она есть," Октябрь, №
11, 149-67. [Карикатура С-на] (Фр.: 1918, 211-12)

209 "Жизнь и позиция газеты: обзор печати," Правда,
330 (25 XI), 3. (Англ.: 1551)

210 Панков, В. Воспитание гражданина: советская
литература, годы шестидесятые, изд. 2, переп. и доп.
М: "Художественная литература", 1969. 376 с. (Information [corrected] from Radosh & Tikos [see 674], p. 3; book
was searched, nothing found; probably only a brief ref. to S.)

211 Елкин, А. "Закат вифлеемской звезды," Москва,
№ 2, 204.

212 Гребенщиков, А. "Пока не поздно," Октябрь, №
3, 200-202. [О черновиках статей к Больш. сов. энц.
о С. и др.] (Англ.: 1371)

213 Дроздов, И. "Закат бездуховного слова," Журна-
лист, № 3, 53.

214 Федосеев, В. "О чем шумит югославская пресса,"
Сов. Россия (5 IV).

215 Метченко, А. "'Актуальные ретроспективы' или
реакционные мифы," Октябрь, № 5, 191.

216 "В Союзе писателей РСФСР," ЛГ (12 XI); переизд.: 449; 428, с. 147; 429. (Англ.: 1285, с. 192)

217 "В Союзе писателей РСФСР," ЛР, 46 (14 XI), 10;
переизд.: 449. (Англ.: 1552)

218 "От секретариата правления Союза писателей
РСФСР," ЛГ, 48 (26 XI), 3; переизд.: 449. (Англ.:
1553; фр.: 1918, с. 320-21)

219 "Речь М. А. Шолохова," Известия (28 XI), 4.

220 "От секретариата правления Союза писателей РСФСР," ЛГ (29 XI); переизд.: 449. (Нем.: 2065)

221 "В секретариате правления Московской писательской организации," ЛГ (3 XII); переизд.: 431, с. 156-7.

221а "Идеи Ленина--источник вдохновения," Правда (11 XII), 2. [Речь С. Михайлова] (Отрывки по-англ.: 1105)

1970

222 Грибачев, Н. "Слезы на экспорт: Открытое письмо Генеральному секретарю европейского сообщества писателей," ЛГ, 8 (18 II), 15. [Concerning protest against persecution of S. by Giancarlo Vigorelli, Gen. Sec. of Eur. Writers' Community.] (Отрывок по-словен.: 2455, с. 327-330)

223 "Недостойная игра: по поводу присуждения А. С-ну Нобелевской премии," Правда (10 X), 6; Известия (10 X), 5. (Англ.: 1285, с. 215; 1554)

224 "К вопросу о приоритете," ЛГ, 42 (14 X), 9; переизд.: 429. (Англ.: 1285, с. 216)

225 "Слово писателя--на службу современности," Сов. Россия, 240 (14 X), 2. (Англ.: 1285, с. 215-16; 1554)

226 "Где ищет писательский талант и славу Новелевский комитет?" Комсомольская Правда (17 X), 3; переизд.: 429. (Англ.: 1285, с. 217-18; 1554)

227 Кожанов, Н. и Г. Кондратенко. "Могучее средство воспитания: с пленума МГК КПСС," Правда (13 XI), 2. (Англ.: 1555)

227а Пилотович, С. [Речь 17-го ноября], Сов. Белоруссия (18 XI). (Отрывки по-англ.: 1148)

228 "А судьи кто?" ЛГ (16 XII).

229 Александров, И. "Нищета анти-коммунизма," Правда (17 XII), 4. (Англ.: 1165 [отрывки]; 1285, с. 228-9; 1556)

230 Синельников, М. "По компасу коммунистической партийности," Красная Звезда, 300 (26 XII), 2-3. (Англ.: 1557)

1971

231 Рид, Дин. "Открытое письмо А. С-ну," ЛГ (27 I), 3.*

231а "Доклад Г. М. Маркова," Правда, 181 (30 VI), 3. (Отрывки по-англ.: 1185)

231б Маркин, Е. [Два стих.] НМ, № 10: "Белый бакен," 96-98; "Невесомость," 98. [Скрытая защита С.? см. 1208)   *[See 2224 for Italian tr. of 231]

1972

232 "Журнал 'Штерн' о семье Солженицыных," ЛГ, 2 (12 I), 13 [с примеч. ред.]. (Перевод 2094; по-англ.: 1558)

233 ЛГ, 8 (23 II), 13:
"Когда историю ставят в угол". (Перевод 2407; по-англ.: 1559)
"В кривом зеркале". (Перев. 2095; по-англ.: 1559)

234 "'Август четырнадцатого' Ал. С-на или правда о книге и мифе," Труд, 83 (7 IV), 3; ЛР, 15 (7 IV), 10-11. (Перев. 2322; по-англ.: 1513)

235 "Из редакционной почты," ЛГ, 15 (12 IV), 13: Прокша, Л. "По какой России плачет С.?" Мамедов, Д. "Истоки озлобления". Мкртич, М. "Достойная отповедь". "Строки из писем": Н. Жарканбаев; И. Савченко, И. Даньков, Ж. Бешук, Н. Коновалова и Г. Мазур; Г. Ордян; А. Михалевич; С. Розенфельд и Л. Оляндер; Г. Рыкунов; А. Якшин.

236 ЛГ, 16 (19 IV), 13: Письмо с подписями: М. Танк, М. Лыньков, И. Шамякин, И. Мележ, А. Кулаковский. Феррари, Э. "Кто заказывает музыку?" (Перев. 2235)

237 Пресса о Солженицыне. М: Изд. агентства печати "Новости", 1972. 107 с. (500 экз.; также по-англ. и по-фр.; свед. от Артемовой [см. 429])

Forthcoming: probably there will be articles about S. in Vol. 7 of Краткая Литературная Энциклопедия and in the appropriate volume of Большая Советская Энциклопедия.
See also: 1136, 1138, 1227, 1273b, 1274a, 1316, 1429, 1500, 1593, 1876, 2060 & 2455; also 572a.

2. Samizdat documents

The following list of documents which have circulated in the USSR in samizdat includes most of the main items relating to S. All but a few have been published in the West, as indicated by cross references (the exceptions: 249a, 270, 277, 288, 296a, 304, 310, 314, 316a). Entries are chronological according to (probable) date of composition. An important source of information: "A Serial Register of the Arkhiv Samizdata" (current list for June 15, 1972, containing 1126 entries), compiled by Albert Boiter (assisted by Raja Tkac & William Murray) and published by the Information Division of the Radio Liberty Committee. The Register lists the samizdat documents more or less in the order that they were first received in the West, assigning to each a number. Copies of the documents may be obtained by applying to any one of the following institutions, each of which has a master copy of all the documents in Radio Liberty's Samizdat Archive: Slavic and East European Division, The Library of Congress, Washington, D. C.; Slavonic Section, Bodleian Library, Oxford, England; Center for Slavic and East European Studies, Ohio State University, Columbus, Ohio; Center for International Studies, Massachusetts Institute of Technology, Cambridge, Mass.; Oost-Europa Instituut, University of Amsterdam, Amsterdam, Netherlands; The Alexander Herzen Foundation, Amsterdam, Netherlands; Hoover Institution, Stanford, California. Not all of the items in the list below are mentioned in the Register; for those that are, I have indicated the register number within square brackets at the end of the entry: e. g., [AS 413]. A. Artemova also gives information about samizdat documents in her bibliography (see 429); she mentions two manuscript collections (see 284a & 299)

but does not indicate a location for them. Another list of these
items is to appear in the forthcoming book by Dunlop, Haugh and
Klimoff (see 574). For further information on books containing
samizdat documents, see 428-31, selected entries between 1275 &
1292, esp. 1285, and the index following 1292.

238 Документ о реабилитации А. С-на, 6 фев. 1956.
2 с. [АС 139] Изд.: 428, с. 151-2; англ.: 1285, с.
3-5; словен.: 2455.
239 С. "Молитва," 1962. 1 с. [АС 413] Изд.: см. 8;
англ.: см. 532.
239а Благов, Д. [псевд.]. "Ал. С. и духовная миссия писателя," осень 1963. 63 с. [АС 545] Изд.:
334; 428, с. 287-355; 429.
240 Читатель. "Об историчности повести А. С-на
'Один день Ивана Денисовича'," 1964[?]. [См. 284а,
с. 81-92]
241 Захарова, А. Письмо главному редактору "Изве-
стий", 1964[?]. [См. 284а, с. 96-105]
242 Григорьев, А. Письмо в Комитет по Ленинским
премиям в области литературы и искусства, 1964[?].
[См. 284а, с. 160-64]
243 Библиографическая записка к В круге первом,
1964[?]. 2 с. [АС 457]
244 С. "Путешествуя вдоль Оки," 1964. 1 с. [АС
721] Изд.: 5а.
245 С. "Пасхальный крестный ход," 10 апр. 1966.
4 с. [АС 544] Изд.: 14; англ.: 512.
246 С. "Читают 'Ивана Денисовича' (обзор писем),"
1966. 15 с. [АС 135] Изд.: 15; англ.: 528; фр.:
1918, с. 212-23.
247 Стенограмма расширенного заседания Бюро творческого объединения прозы Московской писательской
организации СП РСФСР, 16 ноября 1966. [См. 284а, с.
210-254] Изд.: 27; фр.: 1918, с. 225-59.
248 Обсуждение первой части повести "Раковый корпус" на заседании секции прозы Московской писательской организации, 17 ноября 1966. 14 с. [АС 237]
Изд.: 28; англ.: 545.
249 Библиографическая записка к Раковому корпусу,
1967[?]. 2 с. [АС 458]
249а Запись заседания Секретариата Союза писателей
СССР, 15 марта 1967 [А. Твардовский, А. Чаковский и
др. о НМ и С.]. В самизд. период. изд. Политический
Дневник [дата?] (см. 1194).
250 Открытое письмо С-на IV съезду писателей СССР,
16 мая 1967. 6 с. [АС 170] Изд.: 30; англ.: 547;
фр.: 1918, 259-63.
251 Антонов, С. Письмо в Президиум IV съезда писателей, май 1967; Телеграмма В. Войновича, В. Кор-
нилова и Ф. Светова в Президиум IV съезда писателей, май 1967. 2 с. [АС 185] Изд.: 428, с. 396-7,
391; англ.: 1285, 92-94, 90; фр.: 1918, 269-70, 264.
252 Катаев, В. Телеграмма в Президиум IV Всесоюз-
ного съезда советкских писателей, май 1967. 1 с.

[АС 177] Изд.: 428, с. 391; 429; англ.: 1285, с. 89; фр.: 1918, с. 264.

253 Антокольский, П. Письмо секретарю ЦК КПСС Демичеву, май 1967. 2 с. [АС 172] Изд.: 428, с. 14-15; англ.: 527, с. 542-3; 1284, с. 251; 1285, с. 96-7; 1331; фр.: 1918, с. 268-9.

254 Соснора, В. Письмо в Секретариат Правления СП СССР, май 1967. [в 284a и 299] Изд.: 429; фр.: 1918, с. 270-1.

255 Письмо 80 членов Союза писателей в Президиум IV съезда писателей, май 1967. 2 с. [АС 171] Изд.: 428, с. 389-90; 429; англ.: 1285, с. 88-89; фр.: 1918, с. 263.

256 Дар, Д. Письмо в Призидиум IV съезда писателей, 20 мая 1967. 2 с. [АС 184] Изд.: 428, с. 392-93; 429; англ.: 1285, с. 90-91; фр.: 1918, с. 264-5.

257 Конецкий, В. Письмо в Президиум IV съезда писателей, 20 мая 1967. 2 с. [АС 183] Изд.: 428, с. 394-5; 429; англ.: 1285, с. 91-92; фр.: 1918, 265-6.

258 Владимов, Г. Письмо в Президиум IV съезда писателей, 26 мая 1967. 4 с. [АС 173] Изд.: 428, с. 16-20; 429; англ.: 1285, с. 94-6; фр.: 1918, 266-8.

259 Каверин, В. "Речь не произнесенная на IV съезде писателей,"[май-июнь 1967]. [См. 284a, с. 199-208] Изд.: 476.

260 Костерин, А. Письмо М. А. Шолохову, июль 1967. 8 с. [АС 33] Изд.: 428, с. 21-30; 429; англ.: 1285, с. 98-101.

261 Письмо А. С-на в Секретариат Правления СП СССР, 12 сент. 1967. 2 с. [АС 174] Изд.: 31; англ.: 548.

262 Запись заседания Секретариата Союза писателей СССР, 22 сент. 1967. 22 с. [АС 175] Изд.: 32; англ: 549; фр.: 1918, с. 272-86. (Сделано С-ным; см. 284a, с. 270-87)

263 Из выступления редактора "Правды" М. В. Зимянина [и П. Н. Федосеева] в Доме печати в Ленинграде, 5 окт. 1967. 4 с. [АС 176] Изд.: 428, с. 58-60; 429; англ.: 1284, с. 269-71; 1285, с. 126-7; 1331, с. 128-9; фр.: 1918, с. 287-8.

264 С. "Ответ трем студентам," окт. 1967. 1 с. [АС 89] Изд.: 16; англ.: 528.

265 Воронков, Н. [для Секретариата СП СССР]. Письмо А. С-ну, 25 ноября 1967. 1 с. [АС 178] Изд.: 428, с. 61; 429; англ.: 1285, с. 127; 1331, с. 129-30; фр.: 1918, с. 286.

266 Письмо А. С-на Секретариату СП СССР, 1 дек. 1967. 2 с. [АС 179] Изд.: 428, с. 62-63; 429; англ.: 1284, с. 271-2; 1285, с. 128-9; 1331, с. 130; фр.: 1918, с. 287-8.

267 Твардовский, А. Письмо К. Федину, 7-15 янв. 1968. 18 с. [АС 41] Изд.: 428, с. 64-79; 429; англ.: 1284, с. 272-9; фр.: 1842; 1918, с. 289-96; нем.: 2037. Also in Eng. at 1285, pp. 129-40 and at 1348.

268 Свирский, Г. Запись выступления на собрании

Московского отделения Союза писателей, 16 янв. 1968.
15 с. [АС 26] Изд.: 428, с. 80-93; 429; англ.: 1284,
с. 283-90.

269 Каверин, В. Письмо К. Федину, 25 янв. 1968.
2 с. [АС 32] Изд.: 428, с. 94-6; 429; англ.: 1284,
с. 279-81; 1285, с. 141-3; фр.: 1918, с. 297-8.

270 Желудков, С. Открытое письмо А. С-ну, 21 марта 1968. 21 с. [АС 888]

271 Письмо А. С-на членам Союза писателей СССР, 16
апр. 1968. 2 с. [АС 180] Изд.: 34; англ.: 551; фр.:
1918, с. 298-9.

272 Письмо А. С-на в Секретариат СП СССР, 18 апр.
1968. 2 с. [АС 181] Изд.: 35; англ.: 552; фр.: 1918,
с. 299-300.

273 Письмо А. С-на в редакцию "Литературной газеты", 21 апр. 1968. 2 с. [АС 182] Изд.: 36; англ.:
553; фр.: 1918, с. 300; ит.: 2159.

275[sic]Турчин, В. Письмо А. Чаковскому, 28 июня.
4 с. [АС 125] Изд.: 428, с. 116-21; 429; англ.:
1285, с. 176-9. (Ответ на 207)

276 Штейн, Ю. Письмо А. Чаковскому (ответ на 207).
[в 299] Изд.: 429.

277 Кизиева, Л. Письмо С-ну, [июнь?] 1968. [См.
284а, с. 305-06]

278 Чуковская Л. "Ответственность писателя и безответственность 'Литературной газеты'," 27 июня--4
июля 1968. 12 с. [АС 117] (Ответ на 207; см. 284а,
с. 307-16) Изд.: 428, с. 122-34; 429; 440; англ.:
1285, с. 172-6; фр.: 1918, с. 306-12.

279 "Хроника Текущих Событий," № 2 (30 июня 1968).
26 с. [АС 61 т. X] (Includes note on Victor Louis and KGB;
Eng. tr. at 1285, p. 151 [excerpt] and 1290, pp. 336-8.)

280 Попов, Б. "Черная поподёлка 'идейной борьбы',"
[июнь-июль?] 1968. [См. 284а, с. 317-19] Изд.: 429.

281 Чистяков, инж. Письмо Чаковскому, [июнь-июль?]
1968. [См. 284а, с. 320-21] Изд.: 429.

282 Лукшин, Д. "Писателю С-ну," [лето?] 1968.
[См. 284а, с. 322-4] Изд.: 429.

283 Российский, И. "В защиту справедливости," [лето?] 1968. [См. 284а, с. 324-6] Изд.: 429.

284 Письмо А. С-на в редакцию "Литературной газеты", 12 дек. 1968. 1 с. [АС 199] Изд.: 37; англ.:
554.

284а Самарин, А. (составитель). Слово пробивает
себе дорогу, 1969. 338 с. (Сборник статей и документов об А. С.) [Свед. от Артемовой (429); содержания: см. 240-42, 247, 254, 259, 262, 277-8, 280-83]

285 Желудков, С. [Мысли об интеллектуальной свободе: ответ акад. А. Д. Сахарову], 12 марта 1969. 6
с. [АС 331] Изд. в итал. переводе: 2193.

286 "Хроника Текущих Событий," № 7 (30 апр. 1969).
33 с. [АС 196] (В этом №, записка о 275) По-англ.:
1290, с. 338-9.

286а "Хроника Текущих Событий," № 10 (31 окт. 1969).
47 с. [АС 275 т. X] (В этом №--записка о В. Селине и

Рак. корп.) Изд. по-англ.: 1290, с. 339.

287 Запись заседания Рязанской писательской организации, 4 ноября 1969. 11 с. [АС 276] Изд.: 40; англ.: 555; фр.: 1918, с. 313-19.

288 Антипов, А. "Ему не место в наших рядах," [ноябрь?] 1969. [Свед. от Артемовой [429])

289 Открытое письмо А. С-на Секретариату СП РСФСР, 12 ноября 1969. 2 с. [АС 277] Изд.: 41; англ.: 556; фр.: 1918, с. 319-20. (Тоже в 297)

290 Копелев, Л. Письмо в Правление СП СССР, [ноябрь?], 1969. Изд.: 429.

291 Чуковская, Л. Телеграмма в Президиум СП СССР, [ноябрь?], 1969. Изд.: 429.

292 Литвинова, Т. Письмо Секретариату Правления СП СССР, [ноябрь?], 1969. Изд.: 429.

293 Медведев, Ж. Открытое письмо Союзу советских писателей, 21 ноября 1969 [тоже в 297]. Изд.: 429; 449, с. 28-9; англ.: 1285, с. 206-07; 1290, с. 340.

294 В Союз советских писателей: протест 39-ти, 9 дек. 1969. 2 с. [АС 289] Изд.: 429; 431, с. 158; 449, с. 28; англ.: 1285, с. 204-05.

295 Открытое письмо членам СП СССР: протест 14-ти, 19 дек. 1969. Изд.: 429; 449, с. 28.

296 Дополнительные материалы по поводу исключения А. С-на из Союза писателей, [ноябрь-дек.?], 1969. [Тоже в 298?] Изд.: 429; 450.

296а "Политический Дневник", дек. 1969. [This issue includes results of poll of readers conducted by LG in 1968, never published; 10,000 readers indicated their favorite journals were NM, Junost', fav. writers, Simonov, M. Bulgakov & S.; poet, Evtušenko. (Source: 1194)]

297 "Хроника Текущих Событий," № 11 (31 дек. 1969). 57 с. [This issue includes 289; 293; note on woman named Arcimoviča punished for possessing copy of Rak. korp.; excerpt from H. Böll (see 2039); and other material, probably 288, 290-92, 294-95. Published in English at 1290, pp. 339-349.] [АС 333]

298 "Хроника Текущих Событий," № 12 (28 фев. 1970). 35 с. [АС 366 т. X] (Includes paper on S.'s expulsion from Writers' Union [possibly 296?]; quotes articles by Pierre Emmanuel and Gabriel Laub [see 2048]; excerpts in English at 1285, pp. 200-03.)

299 Его послал Бог гнева и печали, 1970. 364 с. (Сборник документов по "делу А. С-на") [Включает 254, 276, большинство содерж. 284а, м. б. 297; свед. от Артемовой (см. 429).

300 С. "Вот как мы живем," 15 июня 1970. 2 с. [АС 386] (Тоже в: "Хроника Текущих Событий," № 14, 30 июня 1970, 39 с. [АС 407, т. X]) Защита Ж. Медведева. Изд.: 17; англ.: 531.

301 Вольпин-Есенин, А. "Вечную руку Петру Григорьевичу Григоренко! (Открытое письмо А. С-ну)," 20 июля 1970. Изд.: 451.

302 Письмо заключенных Мордовских политических лагерей [Ю. Галансков и др.], окт. 1970. Изд.: 429; англ.: 1285, с. 218.

303 Заявление 37-ых советских интеллигентов [В. Гершуни, П. Якир, З. Григоренко и др.], 10 окт. 1970. 2 с. [АС 516] Изд. по-англ.: 1285, с. 214-15.

304 "Две тысячи рабочих слов" (Москва), 19 окт. 1970. (Анон. памфлет в форме открытого письма в агентство печати "Новости" о статье в Ком. Пр. [см. 226]; свед. от Артемовой [см. 429].)

305 Ростропович, М. "Открытое письмо главным редакторам газет 'Правда', 'Известия', 'Литературная газета' и 'Советская культура'," 31 окт. 1970. 3 с. [АС 447] Изд.: 429; 461; англ.: 1285, с. 220-23; 1146; нем.: 2077.

306 С. Письмо Королевской Шведской Академии, 27 ноября 1970. 2 с. [АС 480] Изд.: 44; англ.: 559.

307 С. "Автобиография," весна 1971. 3 с. [АС 665] Изд.: 18; англ.: 534.

308 С. "Послесловие" к заграничному русскому изданию Августа четырнадцатого, май 1971. 1 с. [АС 670] Изд.: 19; англ.: 533.

309 С. "Открытое письмо министру госбезопасности СССР Андропову," 13 авг. 1971. 2 с. [АС 683] Изд.: 46; англ.: 561.

310 С. Два письма Ф. Хеебу, 3 сент и 12 ноября 1971. 3 с. [АС 1046]

311 С. Письмо П. Хегге, 18 сент. 1971. 2 с. [АС 1045] Изд.: 48,

312 С. "Поминальное слово [А. Твардовскому]," 21 дек. 1971. 1 с. [АС 1040] Изд.: 20; англ.: 535.

313 Eesti demokrat, No. 1 (5) 1972. (Estonian samizdat; listed by Artemova [see 429]; contains Estonian translations of "Ozero Segden" and "My to ne umrem" [see 5a].)

314 "Вече", № 4 (31 янв. 1972) [свед. от Артемовой (см. 429)]: В. Алексеев, "Наедение с Россией"; "Показательный дуэт" [о статье в ЛГ (см. 232)]; А. Скуратов, "Писатель С. и профессор Серебряков".

315 С. "Великопостное письмо Патриарху Пимену," [21 марта] 1972. 3 с. [АС 315] Изд.: 21; англ.: 536; нем.: 2119.

315а Выдержки из интервью А. С-на иностранным корреспондентам, 30 марта 1972. Изд.: 51; англ.: 563.

316 Желудков, С. Письмо С-ну [ответ на 315], апр. 1972. 3 с. [АС 1107] Изд.: 490; 497, с. 156-8; нем.: 2119.

316а "Травля А. С-на," Обозрение, № 3 (апрель 1972). [Свед. от Артемовой (см. 429)]

317 С. Ответ С. Желудкову [см. 316], [май?] 1972. Изд.: 22; нем.: 2119.

317а Карелин, Ф. "По поводу письма о. Сергия Желудкова А. С-ну: отзыв читателя," [лето] 1972. Изд.: 497, с. 160-172; нем.: 2119.

318 Телегин, С. "Как быть?" [лето] 1972. [Тема: Творение настоящей русской культуры путем "несотрудничества" с угнетателями.] Изд.: 497.

318а Сборник рецензий об Авг. чет. [12 псевд., 2 Ж. Медведева]. 1972. 120 с. Изд.: 323.

See also: 447; 464; 1226; 1918, pp. 370-81; 2119 [Ešliman & Ja-
kunin]; & 2205; also 572a.

3. Literary criticism and reviews published in the Russian language abroad

i. Books

319 Плетнев, Р. А. И. Солженицын. Мюнхен: Изд.
автора, 1970. 152 с. (Библиография, с. 145-46)
Рецензии: см. 371 и 642, с. 253-60.
320 Гуль, Роман. Читая "Август 1914-го" А. И. Солженицына. Нью-Йорк: Раусен, 1972. (Раньше: 398)
321 Ржевский, Л. Творец и подвиг. Франкфурт: Посев, 1972. 168 с.
322 Гуль, Р. К вопросу об "Автокефалии": Письмо А.
И. Солженицына Патриарху Пимену. Нью-Йорк: Изд. автора, 1972. 31 с.
323 "Август Четырнадцатого" Солженицына читают на
родине: сборник статей-рецензий. Paris: YMCA Press,
1973. (Reprinted from samizdat [see 318a]; 12 pseudonymous essays, 2 by Ž. Medvedev; excerpts in English at 1271.)
323a Белинков, А. Судьба и книги Солженицына.
1973 или 1974. (См. 577)

See also 429-431; for books on S. in other languages, see indexes
following entries 577 & 1292.

ii. Periodicals

Included here are a few articles published in books and an-
nuals. Many of the authors listed have published articles in
English, French, German and other languages. (See name index.)
About 35 of the entries were copied from bibliography of A.
Artemova (see 429). Abbreviations used: Воз.: Возрождение;
ВРСХД: Вестник Русского Студенческого Христианского
Движения; НЖ: Новый Журнал; НРС: Новое Русское Сло-
во; РЛДж: Russian Language Journal; РМ: Русская Мысль;
ССЛ: Studies in Slavic Linguistics and Poetics in Honor of
Boris O. Unbegaun. New York: New York University Press, 1968.

1962

324 Гушин, К. "Событие, о котором заговорила вся
страна," Посев, 50 (14 XII), 3.
325 Гаранин, Е. "'Повесть, после которому писать
по старому нельзя...'," Посев, 51-52 (23 XII), 9-10.

1963

326 Горбов, Я. [Рец.: ОД], Воз., 133 (янв.), 144-8.
327 Гуль, Р. "А. С., соцреализм и школа Ремизова,"
НЖ, 71 (март), 58-74.
328 Первушин, Н. "Повесть С-на и русская классиче-
ская литература," A Guide to Teachers of the Russian Language (San Francisco), XVII, No. 65, 20-29.
329 Тарасова, Н. "По гоголевским заветам: О новом
рассказе А. С-на," Посев, 39 (27 IX), 7-8.

330 Завалишин, В. "Повесть о 'мертвых домах' и советском крестьянстве," Грани, 54 (ноябрь), 133-50.

1964

331 Таубер, Е. "'Матренин двор' А. С-на и 'Живые мощи' И. Тургенева," Грани, 55 (июнь), 229-32.

1965-66

332 Михайлов, М. "Мертвый дом Достоевского и С-на (К феноменологии рабства)," Посев, 49 (3 XII), 8; 50 (10 XII), 8; 51 (17 XII), 7; 52 (24 XII), 8-9; 1 (1 I), 4-5; 2 (7 I), 6-7; 3 (14 I), 5. Переизд.: с. 137-82 в: М. Михайлов. Лето Московское, пер. Я. Трушнович. Франкфурт: Посев, 1967. (Перев. 2430)

1966-67

333 Первушин, Н. "Мастеровщина или литература," НРС (30 X 1966).
334 Благов, Д. [псевд.]. "А. С. и духовная миссия писателя," Грани, 64 (1967), 116-49; 65 (1967), 100-28. Переизд.: 428, с. 287-355; 429. [Самизд., см. 239a]
335 Морозов, И. "Ал. Ис. С.," ВРСХД, 84 (1967),1-4.

1968

336 Ржевский, Л. "Образ рассказчика в повести С-на Один день Ивана Денисовича," с. 165-178 в ССЛ, 1968. Переизд.: 362.
337 Оболенский, С. "Дела и люди," Воз., 199 (июль), 150-58.
338 Донатов, Л. "Великий летописец," Посев, 8 (август), 50-55.
339 Домогацкий, Б. "Удивительная, потрясающая книга," Единение (23 VIII), 9-10.
340 Адамович, Г. "'Раковый корпус': повесть Ал. С-на," НРС (25 VIII).
341 ВРСХД, 89/90:
Вейдле, В. "Два слова о 'Рак. корп.' А. С-на," 94.
В. И. "'Раковый корпус' А. И. С-на," 105.
342 Татищев, Н. "Под небом страха," РМ (21 XI), 6.
343 Белинков, А. "А. С. и больные 'Рак. корпуса'," НЖ, 93 (дек.), 209-20. (Часть записи засед. пис., 17 XI 1966; см. самизд., 247; по-англ.: 1372)
344 Померанцев, К. "Мысли о С.," РМ (12 XII).

1969

345 Келер, Л. "'Рак. корп.' С-на: высокое мастерство и предельная искренность," Воз., 205 (янв.), 57-69.
346 Константинов, Д. "Религиозные идеи 'Рак. корпуса'," НРС (7 II), 3.
347 Ростов, В. "'Рак. корп.'," НЖ, 94 (март),91-100.
348 Русская Мысль (20 III), прил. стр. I и II:
Адамович, Г. "Солженицын," I.

26

Померанцев, К. "С. и его мир," I.
Марголин, Ю. "Читая С-на," II.
Шаховская, З. "Мужество души," II.
349 Вейдле, В. "О С-не," ВРСХД, № 91/92, 43-50.
350 Келер, Л. "Торжество духа (О романе А. С-на 'В круге первом')," Воз., 209 (май), 71-86.
351 Морт, В. "'В круге первом' А. С-на," Единение (9 V).
352 Ржевский, Л. "Мастерство С-на," Наша Страна (Буенос Айрес) (27 V), 4.
353 Новый Журнал, 95 (июнь):
Померанцев, К. "Добро и зло у С-на," 149-58.
Шиляев, Е. "'Лагерный язык' по произведениям А. И. С-на," 232-47.
354 Первушин, Н. "О литературном мастерстве С-на," НРС (15 VI), 5.
355 ВРСХД, № 94:
Зайцев, Б. "Письмо С-ну," 97-98.
Плетнев, Р. "А. С.--великий писатель земли СССР," 102-112. (Глава книги; см. 319)
356 Ржевский, Л. "Творческое слово у С-на," НЖ, 96 (сент.), 76-90. Переизд.: 362.
357 Залуцкая, М. "Матрена и ее двор," НРС (28 IX),5.
358 Гребенщиков, В. "'Матренин двор' Ал. С-на," РЛДж, XXIII, 86 (окт.), 3-11.
359 А. О. "Еще о 'Круге первом': По поводу исключения А. И. С-на из Союза писателей," РМ (20 XI), 3.
360 Гребенщиков, В. "Матрена, Фаддей и другие," НРС (30 XI).
361 Перов, Р. "Круги Ада," НРС (14 XII).

1970

362 Ржевский, Л. Прочтенье творческого слова: Литературоведческие проблемы и анализы. Нью-Йорк: Н-И. Унив. Пресс, 1970. 275 с. Содерж.: с. 219-35, см. 336; с. 237-52, см. 356.
363 Тарасова, Н. "Вхождение С-на в советскую литературу и дискуссии о нем," с. 197-242 в: т. 6, Посев, 1970 (см. 428; тоже в 429). [Раньше, по-нем.: 1977]
364 Торн, Л. "Библиография произведений А. С-на," 182-93 в: Дело С-на, 1970 (см. 430).
365 Залуцкая, М. "Герой-борец А. С-на: 'В круге первом'," НРС (27 I), 2.
366 Ильина, Т. "Об одном женском образе у С-на," РЛДж, 87 (фев.), 3-6. [Агиня в КП]
367 Коряков, М. "Символ России," НРС (26 IV), 5.
368 Рафальский, С. "Записки читателя," НРС, 21754 (4 I), 5. [Не в хронолог. порядке]
369 Можайская, О. "Английский писатель о 'Рак. корп.' С-на," НРС (24 V), 5. [См. 609]
370 Можайская, О. "Мысли английской писательницы о 'Рак. корп.' С-на," Воз., 222 (июнь), 136-8. [См. 610]
371 Дынник, А. "Вечное и временное в творчестве

С-на," НРС, 21957 (26 VII), 5. Рец.: 319.

372 Струве, Н. "А. С.--Нобелевский лауреат," ВРСХД, № 97, 2-3.

373 Ильина, Т. "От детского лепета," РЛДж, № 89, 33-35.

374 Журба, А. "Читая С-на," НРС (14 IX), 5. [Could not find this; listed by both Havrlant (642) and Walker (694).]

375 Гребенщиков, В. "С., человек и писатель, лауреат Нобелевской премии по литературе за 1970-ый год," РЛДж, 89 (окт.), 3-7.

376 Донатов, Л. "Все правильно--Солженицын!" Посев, 11 (ноябрь), 57-60.

377 Залуцкая, М. "Художественная правда А. С-на," НРС, 22055 (1 XI), 2, 5.

378 Шмеман, А. "О Солженицыне," ВРСХД, 98, IV, 72-87.

379 Райс, Э. "Ал. С.," Воз., 227 (дек.), 92-94.

380 Бергер, Я. "Бунин и С.," НРС, 22090 (6 XII), 5.

1971

381 Левицкий, С. "Этика С-на," НЖ, 102 (март), 111-123.

382 А. Ф. "Свеча на ветру," Единение (28 V), 4.

383 Адамович, Г. "'Август Четырнадцатого': Роман А. С-на," РМ, 2848 (24 VI), 1.

384 Шаховская, З. "Просветленная мудрость," РМ, 2848 (24 VI), 1. [Рец.: Авг. чет.]

385 Шмеман, А. "Зрачая любовь," ВРСХД, № 100, 141-52. (По-нем.: 2118; по-евр.: 2142) [Об Авг. чет.]

386 Оболенский, С. "'Ткань истории' у С-на," Воз., 234 (июль), 151-59. [Об Авг. чет.]

387 Франк, В. "С. и Толстой," Посев, 7 (июль), 54-6.

388 Адамович, Г. "Новый роман С-на," НРС, 22300 (4 VII), 5.

389 Седых, А. "Плач по России: 'Авг. чет.' Ал. С.," НРС (11 VII), 2.

390 Рутыч, Н. "Исторические взгляды С-на," Посев, 8 (авг.), 57-59.

391 Ульянов, Н. "Загадка С-на," НРС, 22328 (1 VIII), 2. [См. полемику: 393, 405]

392 Киселев, А. "Обновляющаяся Россия," НРС (8 VIII), 2.

393 Поспеловский, Д. "Загадка Н. И. Ульянова," НРС, 22342 (15 VIII), 2. [См. 391]

394 Битенбиндер, А. "Вторжение в Пруссию," НРС (16 VIII), 4. [Письмо в ред.]

395 Слоним, М. "О языке С-на," НРС, 22349 (22 VIII), 5. [См. ответ, 407]

396 Каннак, Е. "Книга о С-не," РМ, 2857 (26 VIII), 8. Рец.: 1918.

397 НРС (29 VIII):
Крузенштерн-Петерец, Ю. "Пленный талант," 2 и 7.
Коряков, М. "Листки из блокнота: Красносотенцы и черносотенцы (Об 'Авг. чет.')," 3.

398 Гуль, Р. "Читая 'Август Четырнадцатого' (О

C-не)," <u>НЖ</u>, 104 (сент.), 55-82. Переизд.: 320. (Полемика, <u>см.</u> 414, 422)

399 Кремнев, Н. [Рец.: <u>Авг. чет.</u>] Часовой, 543
(сент.).

400 Сокольский, А. "Волнующие темы романа С-на 'В
круге первом'," <u>НРС</u>, 22363 (5 IX), 2.

401 Струве, Г. "Кое-что о новом романе С-на," <u>НРС</u>,
22370 (12 IX), 2; ч. 2: 22377 (19 IX). 2.

402 НРС (15 IX):
Нефедов, Н. "Ошибки С-на," 4. [Письмо; об Авг. ч.]
Тарсаидзе, А. "'Август четырнадцатого'."

403 Борман, А. "Читая 'Авг. чет.'," <u>РМ</u>, 2860 (16
IX), 8.

404 Сергеев, А. "Неправильности г-жи Крузенштерн-
Петерец," <u>НРС</u> (17 IX), 4. (См. 397)

405 "Ответ Н. И. Ульянова," <u>НРС</u>, 22384 (26 IX), 2.
(См. 391, 393)

406 Струве, Г. "Об одном источнике 'Авг. чет.':
С. и ген. Франсуа," <u>НРС</u>, 22391 (3 X), 2 и 4.

407 Андреев, Г. "С. и мокроступы," <u>НРС</u>, 22405 (17
X), 5. (Ссылает на 395)

408 Битенбиндер, А. "С. на военном поприще," <u>НРС</u>
(18 X), 2.

409 Константинов, Д. "Духовные основы 'Авг. чет.',"
<u>НРС</u>, 22419 (31 X), 2.

410 <u>РМ</u>, 2869 (18 XI), 7:
Воробьев, А. "'Авг. чет.' с военной точки зрения."
Плетнев, Р. "'Авг. чет.'."

411 Пашин, Н. "Язык и структура 'Авг. чет.'," <u>НРС</u>,
(21 XI), 2.

412 Прянишников, Б. "С., Верховский и другие," <u>НРС</u>,
22444 (25 XI), 4.

413 Неймирок, А. "'Россию жалко...' (О романе А. И.
С-на 'Авг. чет.')," Грани, 82 (дек.), 173-82.

414 "Письмо Н. Е. Андреева Р. Б. Гулю об 'Авг.
1914-го'," <u>НЖ</u>, 105 (дек.), 301-02. (См. 398)

415 Афонский, Г. "Духовная природа человека в ро-
манах С-на," <u>НРС</u> (5 XII), 2.

416 Карпович, В. "Читая 'Авг. Чет.'," <u>НРС</u>, 22475
(26 XII), 5.

1972

417 Криворотов, В. "С. и возрожденческая идея,"
Часовой, 547 (янв.).

418 Залуцкая, М. "Некоторые этические проблемы в
творчестве С-на," НРС (9 I), 2 и 7.

419 Дубинин, М. "А. С. и Л. Толстой," <u>РМ</u>, 2883
(24 II), 6.

420 Залуцкая, М. "С. и Достоевский," <u>НРС</u> (23 IV),2.

421 Первушин, Н. "Запад и творчество С-на," РМ,
2894 (11 V), 5. (Полемика с Г. Гибианом [см. 704])

422 В. О. Часовой, 552 (июнь). [Отзыв о 398]

423 Рутыч, Н. "Страх перед Воротынцевым: По поводу критики романа С-на 'Авг. чет.'," Посев, 6
(июнь), 46-49.

424 Крыжицкий, С. НЖ, № 107, 285-6. Рец.: 569.

425 Оболенский, А. "Алеша Достоевского и Солженицына," РМ, 2911 (7 IX), 6-7.

426 Клейман, Л. "Заметки о 'Раковом корпусе' А.
С-на," Грани, № 83, 79-112.

427 Карпович, В. "Некоторые черты языка С-на," с.
36-44 в: 687 (дек.).

427a Полторацкий, Н. Русская литература в эмиграции: сборник статей. Pittsburgh: Department of Slavic Languages and Literatures, Faculty of Arts and Sciences, University
of Pittsburgh, 1972. 409 pp. Contains several brief references
to Solzhenitsyn:

  с.12 в: Вейдле, В. "Традиционное и новое в русской
  литературе двадцатого века," 7-14.

  с. 19, 35 в: Андреев, Н. "Об особенностях и основ-
  ных этапах развития русской литературы за рубежом
  (опыт постановки темы)," 15-38.

  с. 44 в: Фостер, Л. "Статистический обзор русской
  зарубежной литературы," 39-44.

  с. 105, ред. сноска к: "И. А. и В. Н. Бунины в ка-
  нун эмиграции: Из дневника В. Н. Буниной" (Публи-
  кация Л. Ф. Зурова), 105-106.

  с. 264, 269 в: Плетнев, Р. "Русское литературове-
  дение в эмиграции," 255-70.

  с. 327, 331 в: Гуль, Р. "'Новый журнал'," 321-32.

See also: 473; 495; 709 (Pervushin); & 1918, pp. 365-9 & 400-411.

4. Biography, news items, "the Solzhenitsyn affair": Russian
  language abroad

(i) Books

  Most of the articles, letters and documents published in the
books listed below are listed elsewhere in this bibliography;
such items are referred to by entry number only (in the descrip-
tions of contents). Of the four books listed, I have seen only
428 and 431; but I was sent a description of the contents of 429
(without indication of page numbers). The contents of 430 probably duplicates closely that of 431. Most of the items in 431
are not cross-indexed. Contents for 428 and 429 are listed in
approximate page order only; for page numbers of items in 428,
see entries cited. For books in other languages dealing with
the Solzhenitsyn affair, see 1285 and the brief index following
entry 1292.

428 "Дело Солженицына".--О творчестве Солженицына,
т. 6. (в: Александр Солженицын. Собрание сочинений в
шести томах, ред. А. Артемова) Франкфурт а/М: Посев,
1970. 400 с. Именной указатель, с. 357-65. "Библиография произведений А. Солженицына," А. Артемова
(сост.), с. 369-385.

  содержание: 238, 30, 248, 251-53, 255-58, 260, 31-
32, 262-63, 265, 33, 267-69, 34-36, 207, 275, 278,
37, 287, 216, 41; переводы: 1860, 1104, 1394; 363,
145, 334; не изд. раньше: "Сообщение редакции журнала 'Грани' (30 IV 1968), с. 102-03 [англ.: 1285, с.150].

429 "Дело Солженицына".--Нобелевская премия.--О творчестве А. Солженицына, т. 6 (в: Александр Солженицын. Собрание сочинений в шести томах, 2-ое изд., ред. А. Артемова) Франкфурт а/М: Посев, 1973. примерно 650 с. "Библиография" [произведения и критика], А. Артемова, (сост.).

Содержание: Same as in 428 except does not have 248; has the following in addition: 247, 254, 259, 276, 280-83, 220, 290-96; Нобелевская премия по литературе за 1970 год: Ал. С. (Обоснование) [англ.: 1285, с. 211]; 42; Телеграмма постоянного секретаря Шведской Академии С-ну (8 окт. 1970); 43, 302, 223-24; Письмо постоянного сек. Швед. Акад. в "Лит. газ."; 226, 305; Иностранные отклики на присуждение С-ну Ноб. прем.; 44; Вручение Нобелевских премий 1970 г.; "Александр Солженицын": вступительная речь К. Р. Гирова на Ноб. торжестве 1970 г. [англ.: 1285, с. 225-7]; 45; переводы: 2398, 1197, 1198; 48, 50-53, 18, 23; Краткий библиографический указатель к разделам "Дело С-на" и "Нобелевская примия".

430 Дело Солженицына. Лондон, Онт.: Изд. "Союз Борьбы за Освобождение Нардов России", 1970. "Библиография произведений А. С-на," Л. Торн (сост.), с. 182-93.

Рец.: В. Завалишин. НЖ, 102 (1971), 297-8.

431 Дело Солженицына, т. 1, 2-ое изд. Paris: Editions de la Seine, [1971]. 174 с. [т. 2??] "Библиография произведений А. С-на," с. 161-74.

Содержание: 248, 30, 253, 258, 31, 262, 263, 265, 33, 267, 269, 34, 36, 278, 275, 287, 216, 41, 221, 294.

(ii) Periodicals

A few articles in books are included. For abbreviations used, see p. 25, this bibliography.

1963-68

432 Борисов, К. "Журнал 'Наука и религия' и А. С.," Посев, 45 (8 XI 1963), 10-11. (См. 113)

433 Полынов, А. "Борьба вокруг С-на: Бурное столкновение лагерей на писательском собрании в Москве," Посев, 8 (21 II 1964), 1-2.

434 Полынов, А. "С-ну премию не дадут: Пошатнувшееся положение Твардовского?" Посев, 16 (17 IV 1964), 3.

435 Сергеев, Л. "Друзья и недруги С-на: Статья критика В. Лакшина в 'Новом мире' и бои 'лагерей'," Посев, 10 (16 III 1964), 7-9. (См. 145)

436 "О России, для России, из России," Посев, 4 (22 I 1965), 6. (Об 'Этюдах' С. в Гранях [см. 5а])

437 Михайлов, М. "Лакшин и С.," в: Лето московское 1964, пер. Я. Трушнович. Франкфурт а/М: Посев, 1967. (Перев. 2433; англ.: 1279) [В русск. изд. тоже 332]

438 Личко, П. "Один день у Ал. Ис. С-на," НРС (21

V 1967). (Отрывки: перев. 1604)

439 [Протокол 22 сент. 1967] Посев, 8 (авг. 1968). (Отрывки [см. 262]; перев. с сербохорв. и ит. перев.)

440 Чуковская, Л. "Оветственность писателя и без-ответственность 'Лит. газ.'," НЖ, 93 (дек. 1968), 114-24. [Самизд., см. 278]

441 "Дело С-на," НЖ, 93 (дек. 1968), 209-68. (Содержание: 343, 28, 37, 32, 34)

1969

442 "А. И. Солженицын в жизни: рассказ очевидца," Воз., 205 (янв.), 70.

443 Горбов, Я. "'Русская мысль' о С-не," Воз., 208 (апр.), 147-8.

444 "Солженицын," По советскому союзу, 318 (28 XI), 1-2. (Еженед. обзор, составлено Ком. "Радио Свобода")

445 Натова, Н. "С.--почтенный член Американской академии и Национального института искусств и литературы," НЖ, 97 (дек.), 280-82.

446 Оболенский, С. "'Исключенный' С.," Воз., 216 (дек.), 147-49.

1970

447 Медведев, Ж. [I] Международное сотрудничество ученых и национальные границы и [II] Тайна переписки охранется законом. London: Macmillan; New York: St. Martin's Press, 1970. [I] 270 pp.; [II] 164 pp. [Engl. tr., see 1288] (См. I, с. 30-38, о Н. Решетовской, перв. жена С.; отрывки по-англ., из с. 31-33, см. 1285, с. 80-81. См. II, с. 80, письмо С-на [см. 38].)

448 "Солженицын," НРС (15 II).

449 "Исключение А. И. С-на из Союза писателей," Посев, 4 (апр.), 26-30. (Содерж.: 216-218, 293-295)

450 "Дополнительные материалы по поводу исключения А. И. С-на из союза советских писателей," Посев, 6 (июнь), 13-14. [Самизд., см. 296]

451 Вольпин-Есенин, А. "Вечную руку Петру Григорьевичу Григоренко!" РМ, 2809 (24 IX), 4. [Самизд., 301]

452 В. "На хребте славы," Воз., 225 (окт.), 5-6.

453 Посев, 10 (окт.): "С. и Нобелевская премия," 1; "А. С.--лауреат Нобелевской премии," 2.

454 Адамович, Г. "С.--Нобелевский лауреат," РМ, 2811 (8 X), 1. [См. другие статьи, с. 1 и 2]

455 "А. С-ну присуждена Нобелевская премия," НРС, 22032 (9 X), 1.

456 Завалишин, В. "Литература, страдания, совесть: о нобелевском лауреате А. С-не," НРС, 22041 (18 X), 5.

457 Посев, 11 (ноябрь): "С.: Торжество правды и честности," 18-19; "'Совесть России и человека': иностранная пресса о С-не," 19-23.

459[sic] Самарин, В. "Литературные заметки: 'Дело С-на'," НРС (1 XI), 5.

460 Самарин, В. "Литературные заметки: ПЕН-Клуб, С. и коммунисты," НРС, 22069 (15 XI), 5.

461 "Открытое письмо М. Ростроповича . . .," ВРСХД,

98, IV, 90-92; Посев, 12 (дек.), 2. [Самизд.,305]
462 РМ, 2820 (10 XII), 7: "Статья Михайлы Михайлова" [перев. 1139]; "Награда по заслугам" [перев. 1420 (Т. Фооте)]
463 РМ, 2820 (10 XII):
Померанцев, К. "Свидетельство С-на," 7.
Гаев, А. "Ал. С.--лауреат Нобелевской премии," 8.
Ельцов, И. "Время, пресса и С.: Время лучший судья," 8.
Л. В. "Чем люди живы? Вашингтонский симпозиум, посвященный С-ну," 10. (См. 703)

1971

464 Медведев, Ж. и Р. Медведев. Кто сумасшедший? Лондон: Макмиллан, 1971. 163 с. [По-англ.: 1289] См. с. 99-100, письмо С. [см. 16].
465 Астрау, И. "Слово о С-не," Воз., 228 (янв.), 129-30. [Буенос Айрес; перев. с испанского]
466 Милованов, А. и Г. Рар и Н. Широкова. "Солженицынские дни," Посев, 1 (янв.), 16-21.
467 "Симпозиум о С-не," Посев, 3 (март), 12-13. (См. 703)
468 "Кто цензурирует С-на?" Посев, 4 (апр.), 9.
469 РМ, 2840 (29 IV), 2: "Новый роман С-на"; "А. И. С. и советские издательства".
470 Завалишин, В. "'Один день Ивана Денисовича' на экране," НРС (28 V), 3.
471 Посев, 7 (июль): "'Россию жалко': Почему 'Авг. чет.' не опубликован в России," 2; "Послесловие С-на к русскому изданию 1971 г.," 3 [см. 19].
472 "Новый роман С-на выйдет по-английски," НРС, 22303 (7 VII), 1.
473 Орехов, В. [Краткий разбор военных действий армии ген. Самсонова в восточной Пруссии, описанных в "Авг. чет."] Часовой, 542 (авг.).
474 Коряков, М. "Листки из блокнота: Просьба С-на," НРС (26 VIII), 3.
475 "С.: Шведская демонстрация," Посев, 10 (окт.), 6. (Содерж.: переводы 1197 и 1198; переизд.: 429)
476 Каверин, В. "Насущные вопросы литературв: Речь, не произнесенная на IV съезде писателей," Посев, 10 (окт.), 59-63. [Самиод, см. 259]
477 "Арагон о С-не," РМ, 2863 (7 X), 8. (См. 1926)
478 Коряков, М. "Листки из блокнота: Новое об Ал. С-не," НРС (17 X), 3.
479 Рар, Г. "Удар по С-ну," Посев, 11 (ноябрь), 51-54.
479a Сорокина, Т. "Симпозиум об А. И. С-не," НРС (1 XI), 3. (См. 703)
480 РМ, 2869 (18 XI):
Померанцев, К. "Чем нам дорог С.," 1.
Малевский-Малевич, С. "О слове, С-не и Русском Мире," 3.
Шаховская, З. "О правде и свободе С-на," 7.
Ошаров, М. "Один год Ал. С-на: 8 окт. 1970 г.- 8

33

окт. 1971 г.," РМ, 2869 (18 XI), 8. [Включено письмо Ростроповича, см. 305]

481 Т. Р. "'С. обвиняет'," РМ, 2870 (25 XI), 2. Рец.: 1919.

482 "С.: Авторские права: Английский суд запрещает пиратское издание," Посев, 12 (дек.), 28.

1972

482а "'Плач по Твардовскому'," РМ, 2877 (13 I), 2. [Перев. с англ.; русский текст, см. 20]

482б "Новые выпады против С-на," РМ, 2878 (20 I), 2. [Включен отрывок заявления С. (см. 50а)]

483 "Союз 'Штерна' с литературной госбезопасностью," Посев, 2 (фев.), 10-13. (См. 232)

484 Вронская, Ж. "О фильме 'Один день Ивана Денисовича'," РМ, 2880 (3 II), 9.

485 "Подкоп под А. И. С-на," РМ, 2881 (10 II), 3. (См. 50а)

486 "Интервью С-на," РМ, 2889 (6 IV), 1-2; 2890 (13 IV), 2. (Перевод 1485; см. 50)

487 "С. заявляет," РМ, 2891 (20 IV), 2. (См. 52)

488 Архиепископ Иоанн С.-Ф. "Письмо С-на Патриарху," РМ, 2892 (27 IV), 5. [Переведено, в 2119?]

489 Посев, 5 (май): "Власть и С.," 1; "'Сила правоты'," 2-5; "'Нагнетают кампанию клеветы'," 6-7; С. "Великопостное письмо," 8-9 [см. 21]; "'Ущелье между блокнотом агитатора и угольным кодексом'," 10-12.

490 Желудков, С. "'Воскресное письмо' С-ну," РМ, 2900 (22 VI), 5 (с предисловием Арх. Иоанна С.-Ф.). [Самизд., см. 316] (По-нем.: 2119)

491 Бывш. студент Ростовского университета. "Еще немного о С-не и его персонажах," РМ, 2897 (1 VII), 5.

492 Туркина, В. "Чужие руки," Посев, 8 (авг.), 16-17; НРС (22 VII); РМ, 2906 (3 VIII), 5. (Протест против книги Бурга и Файфера [см. 571]; по-енгл.: 1264)

493 "Генерал Самсонов," НРС, 22713 (20 VIII), 7. (Глава книги Г. Гребенщикова)

494 Л. Т. "Новая форма в русской литературе: вермонтский симпозиум, посвященный С-ну," РМ, 2909 (24 VIII), 8. (См. 709)

494а "С.: Ответ священнику Сергию Желудкову," Посев, 9 (сент.), 11. (Заметки о 315, 316, 317, 317а; включено письмо С-на Желудкову [см. 317])

495 РМ, 2917 (19 X), 5: "О премии мира С-ну" [см. 2408]; "Милован Джилас об 'Авг. чет.' Ал. С-на" [перев. 1014 Е. Жиглевич].

496 "По поводу биография С-на в Англии," РМ, 2918 (26 X), 4. (Письма Дж. Файфера и Д. Панина [о 571])

497 ВРСХД, 103 (1-й триместр): содержание: 315, 315а, 316, 317, 317а, 318 и заметки о "Великопостном письме" С-на: А. Шмеман, "Пророчество," 150-51; Иоанн Мейендорф, [без. загл., перев. с англ., Orthodox Church (Apr. 1972)], 151-53; Арх. Иоанн [Шаховской] С.-Ф. [без загл.], 153-56. (Часть перев. на нем.: 2119)

498 "По поводу выхода биографии С-на в Англии,"

PM, 2921 (16 XI 1972), 4. (Письмо Д. Бурга: ответ
Д. Панину [см. 496])
499 С. М. "Американский автор дарит свои гонорары
С-ну," PM, 2929 (11 I 1973), 8. [А. Малтз]

See also 363.

(2) English (United States, Canada, Great Britain, India, Aus-
      tralia, New Zealand)

I. By Solzhenitsyn: Translations. 1. Fiction, articles, selec-
    ted letters

    All editions of a given translation are included in the same
entry. Entries are in approximate chronological order according
to date of first publication, but an effort is made to group different translations of the same work near each other. All of
Solzhenitsyn's more important works [entries 1-23] have been or
are being translated into English except one of the later prose
poems ("Sposob dvigat'sja" [see 5b]) and his open letter to Fr.
S. Želudkov [see 22].

    500 One Day in the Life of Ivan Denisovich, tr. Max Hayward &
Ronald Hingley. New York: Praeger, 1963. 210 pp. Bantam, 1963 &
1968. 203 pp. "Introduction," by Hayward and L. Labedz, pp. v-
vii in 1963 ed'ns., pp. xiii-xv in 1968 ed'n. (1968 ed'n. also
has S's letter of 16 May 1967 [see 547], pp. v-x.) Other editions: Toronto: Burns & MacEachern; London: Pall Mall; London:
Fontana Modern Books, all 1963; another 1963 ed'n. has same title
and translator with subtitle: Adapted as a Play by Robert Brome
(Chicago: Dramatic Publishing Co., 1963. 36 pp.). Condensation
of trans. appeared earlier in Saturday Evening Post, 236 (9 Feb
1963), 35-47[+]; a few excerpts were pub. in Saturday Review, 46
(9 Feb 1963), 28 & 40.

    501 One Day in the Life of Ivan Denisovich, tr. Ralph Parker.
New York: Dutton, 1963. 160 pp. "Introduction, by M. Kalb, pp.
5-11; "Foreword,"by A. Tvardovsky, pp. 13-15. Also: Signet (New
American Library), 1963: "Introd.," pp. v-vii; "Foreword," pp.
x-xiv; text, pp. 17-158. Other editions: Toronto: Doubleday,
1963; London: Golancz, 1963 & 1970; all 192 pp. Earlier appearances: serialized in Moscow News, 50-52 (15, 22 29 Dec 1962) &
1-6 (5, 12, 19, 26 Jan & 2, 9 Feb 1963); also in Soviet Literature (Moscow), 2 (1963), 6-95 (with foreword by A. Tvardovsky,
pp. 4-5: "By Way of Introduction") [but the two texts are not
identical (see final pages)]. Also excerpts in Saturday Review,
46 (9 Feb 1963), 28 & 40.

    502 One Day in the Life of Ivan Denisovich, tr. Bela von Block.
New York: Lancer Books, 1963. Introductory essay by Jacques Katel.

    503 One Day in the Life of Ivan Denisovich, tr. Thomas P. Whit-
ney. New York: Crest (Fawcett Pub. Co.), 1963. Introductory
essay by Whitney; tr. of article by V. Buxanov in appendix [see 88].

504 <u>One Day</u> <u>in the Life of Ivan Denisovich</u>, tr. Gillon Aitken. London:Bodley Head; New York: Farrar, Straus & Giroux, 1971. rev. ed. 174 pp. (Appeared first in: London: Sphere Books, 1970. 157 pp.--same title, but screen play by R. Harwood included.) Aitken's trans. also in: <u>The Making of One Day in the Life of Ivan Denisovich</u>. New York: Ballantine, 1971. vi, 271 pp., with introduction and screenplay by R. Harwood. The screenplay appears separately in: <u>Solzhenitsyn's "One Day in the Life of Ivan Denisovich": A Screenplay by Ronald Harwood from the Translation by Gillon Aitken</u>. London: Sphere Books, 1971. 95 pp.

505 "<u>We Never Make Mistakes</u>": <u>Two Short Novels</u>, tr. Paul W. Blackstock. Columbia, S. C.: U. of South Carolina Press, 1963. xix, 100 pp. Contents: "An Incident at Krechetovka Station," pp. 1-60 and "Matryona's House," pp. 61-100, with "Translator's Preface," pp. vii-viii and "Introduction,", pp. ix-xviii.
  Revised ed. of above pub. 1971, with "Afterword" by Blackstock, pp. 103-110. Other ed'ns.: New York: W. W. Norton (paper), 1971 & London: Sphere Books, 1972, both 138 pp.

506 "Matryona's Home," tr. Harry T. Willets. <u>Encounter</u>, 20 (May 1963), 28-45. Repr. in: <u>Halfway to the Moon</u>: <u>New Writings from Russia</u>, ed. P. Blake & M. Hayward. New York: Holt, Rinehart & Winston; London: Weidenfeld & Nicholson, 1964, pp. 51-91. (Also in 508)

507 "Incident at Krechetovka Station," tr. Andrew R. McAndrew, in <u>Great Russian Short Novels</u>. New York: Bantam, 1969.

508 <u>Fifty Years of Russian Prose</u>: <u>From Pasternak to Solzhenitsyn</u>, ed. K. Pomorska. Cambridge: Massachusetts Institute of Technology Press, 1971. 2 vols. Vol. 2 includes:
  "Incident at Krechetovka Station," tr. Helen Colaclideo, pp. 42-91.
  "Matryona's Home," tr. H. T. Willets, pp. 92-144.

509 <u>For the Good of the Cause</u>, tr. David Floyd & Max Hayward. New York: Praeger, 1964. xvii, 134 pp. 2nd. pr., 1970, hrd. & soft cover. Other editions with same pagination: Toronto: Burns & MacEachern; London/Dunmow: Pall Mall Press; Delhi, India: National Academy, 1964. (Also: London: Sphere Books, 1971. 142 pp.)
  With "Introduction" by Floyd, pp. vii-xvii and Appendix, pp. 97-134 containing translations of following Soviet articles: 121, 123, 127, 128, 134, 136.

510 "Zakhar the Pouch," in <u>For Freedom</u>: <u>Theirs and Ours</u>, ed. R. G. Davis-Poynter. New York: Stein & day, 1969. (Neither translator nor author named; see another trans. at 520, pp. 133-50.)

511 "The Right Hand," <u>Atlantic</u>, 223, v (May 1969), 45-49 [tr. not named]; <u>Sunday Telegraph</u> (London), 29 Dec 1968 [tr. not named]; <u>Atlas</u>, 17, v (May 1969), 30-34 [tr. from Czech (see 1573); tr. not named]. (For another trans., see 520, pp. 151-56)

512 "Easter Procession," tr. Manya Harari. <u>Time</u>, 93 (21 Mar 1969), 28-9; (4 Apr 1969), 13 [last 3 paragr. on p. 13: unintentionally omitted from initial publication]. Another tr. pub. in <u>Observer</u> (6 Apr 1969). (See also 520, pp. 125-32) [Samizd., 246]

Prose poems

513 "Prose Poems," New Leader, 48, ii (18 Jan 1965), 5-7 [tr. not named]. Contents: "Breathing," 5; "Lake Segden," 5-6; "A Poet's Dust," 6-7; "Traveling Along the River Oka," 7.

514 "Breathing," Encounter, 24, iii (Mar 1965), 3-9: all the prose poems are included, tr. H. T. Willets. Contents appear in same order as in first Russian publication (see 5a): "Breathing," 3; "Lake Segden," 3-4; "Poet's Ashes," 4-5; "The Duckling," 5; "Reflections in Water," 5; "The City on the Neva," 5-6; "The Ants and the Fire," 6; "Starting the Day," 6; "A Storm in the Mountains," 6; "Elm Log," 6-7; "Sharik," 7; "Yesenin's Birthplace," 7; "The Kolkhoz Rucksack," 7-8; "We Shall Live Forever," 8; "Along the Oka," 8-9.

515 "City on the Neva," tr. M. Glenny. New York Times (10 Dec 1970), 47. (Repr.: 517 & 520, pp. 252-3)

516 "Three Prose Poems," Christian Science Monitor (6 Jan 1971), 8, tr. John M. Gogol: "A Duckling", "An Elm Log", "Reflections in the Water".

517 "Solzhenitsyn," Vogue, 157 (15 Feb 1971), 90-93; three prose poems, tr. M. Glenny: "City on the Neva," 91; "Lake Segden," 92; "Ashes of a Poet," 93. (Repr.: 520, pp. 252-3, 244-5, 248-9)

518 "Elm Log" & "A Storm in the Mountains," tr. M. Glenny. Mademoiselle, 73 (Jun 1971), 74. (Repr.: 520, pp. 250, 261-2)

519 Six Etudes, tr. James G. Walker; ed. Dale R. Eskra; ill. Judith Grosfield. Northfield, Minn.: College City Press, 1971. 15 pp. [unnumbered]. 2 ed'ns. Russian and English: "Dyxanie," [1]; "Breath," [2]; "Šarik," [4]; "Sharik," [5]; "Otraženie v vode," [6]; "Reflections in the Water," [7]; "Koster i murav'i," [8]; "Bonfire and Ants," [9]; "Utenok," [13]; "The Duckling," [12]; "Groza v gorax," [14]; "Storm in the Mountains," [15].

520 Stories and Prose Poems, tr. Michael Glenny. New York: Farrar, Straus & Giroux, 1971. 267 pp. London: Bodley Head, 1971. 242 pp. Harmondsworth: Penguin, 1973. 205 pp. Contents same as German edition, Im Interesse der Sache [see 1956], except that One Day not included (pages apply to American ed'n):
"Matryona's House," 3-52.
"For the Good of the Cause," 53-124.
"The Easter Procession," 125-132.
"Zakhar -the-Pouch," 133-150.
"The Right Hand," 151-166.
"An Incident at Krechetovka Station," 167-240.
Prose Poems, 243-67; not in same order as in 5a; contains trans. of "Staroe vedro" [see 5b], pp. 255-6 (below), but not of "Sposob dvigat'sja" [5b]. Contents: "Freedom to Breathe," 243; "Lake Segden," 244-5 [earlier in 517]; "The Duckling," 246-7; "The Ashes of a Poet," 248-9 [earlier in 517]; "The Elm Log," 250 [also 518]; "Reflection," 251; "The City on the Neva," 252-3 [also 515 & 517]; "The Puppy," 254 [tr. of "Sarik"]; "The Old Bucket," 255-6 [see 5b, "Staroe vedro"]; "In Yesenin Country," 257-8; "The Kolkhoz Rucksack," 259; "The

Bonfire and the Ants," 260; "A Storm in the Mountains," 261-2
[also 518]; "A Journey along the Oka," 263-4; "At the Start
of the Day," 265; "We Will Never Die," 266-7.

521 The First Circle, tr. Thomas P. Whitney. New York: Harper
& Row, 1968. 580 pp. with "Introduction" by tr., pp. ix-x. Also:
New York: Ballantine, 1969. 674 pp. & New York: Bantam, 1969.
   Excerpt appeared earlier: "Liars," Saturday Evening Post, 241
(21 Sep 1968), 32-4.

522 The First Circle, tr. Michael Guybon. London: Collins &
Harvill, 1969. 581 pp. London: Fontana Modern Books, 1970. 700pp.

523 "News from the Cancer Ward: Extracts from Solzhenitsyn's
Unpublished Novel," Times Literary Supplement (London), 11 Apr
1968, 375-6 [tr. not named].

524 "Atlas Translation from 'The Cancer Ward'," Atlas, 16, i
(Jul 1968), 58-59. [Brief excerpt; tr. not named]

525 The Cancer Ward, tr. Rebecca Frank. New York: Dial 1968;
Dell, 1968, 1973; all 616 pp. "Publisher's Foreword," v-ix;
"Translator's Note," x-xi.

526 "Can There Be Socialism Then?" Times (London), 22 Feb 1969,
19. [Excerpt from Cancer Ward; have not seen this; probably tr.
of Bethell & Burg, see below.]

527 Cancer Ward, tr. Nicholas Bethell & David Burg. London:
Bodley Head, 2 vols., 1968 & 1969. 338 pp. & 279 pp.; one-vol.
ed'n., 1970. 619 pp. Harmondsworth: Penguin, 1971. 570 pp.
New York: Farrar, Straus & Giroux, 1969. xiv, 560 pp.; Bantam,
1969. Additional material in New York ed'n. (have not seen
others): "Afterword," by Vladimir Petrov, pp. 539-541, with front
and back material tr. by him from samizdat documents: 250, pp.
vii-xii; 261, xiii-xiv; 253, pp. 542-3; 262, pp. 543-59; 272, pp.
559-60; 273, p. 560.

528 "Letter to three students," Survey, 73 (Autumn 1969), 194;
Dissent, 17, vi (Nov-Dec 1970), 558; also in Labedz (1285), 125-
126 [tr. not named]. (Samizdat, 264)

529 "How People Read 'Ivan Denisovich' (A Survey of Letters),"
Survey, 74/75 (Winter-Spring 1970), 207-220; also in Labedz (1285),
21-37 [tr. not named]. (Samizd., 246)

530 The Love-Girl and the Innocent, tr. Nicholas Bethell & David Burg. London: Bodley Head, 1969; New York: Farrar, Straus &
Giroux, 1969; both 131 pp. New York: Bantam, 1971. 133 pp. &
Harmondsworth: Penguin, 1971. 140 pp. [Note: Title of play as
first performed in English in 1970 was "A Play by Alexander Solzhenitsyn"; see note at 696 and brief index to play reviews,
etc., following entry 865.]

531 "This Is How We Live," New York Times (17 Jun 1970), 6;
repr.: New York Times Magazine (7 Nov 1971), 116 [tr. not named];
another version in Labedz (1285), 207-08. Also in translation
of Ellen de Kadt at 1289, pp. 135-136. [Protest of detention of
Ž. Medvedev; 15 Jun 1970; see samizd., 300.]

532 [Prayer], Catholic Worker, 37, vii (Sep 1971), 8 [untitled; tr. not named; first line: "How easy it is for me to live with you, O Lord!"]; Vogue, 158 (Dec 1971), 87 [untitled; tr. not named; first line: "How simple for me to live with you, O Lord!]; Modern Age, 17, i (Winter 1973), 51 [untitled; first line: "How easy it is to live with You, O Lord."; quoted in article by Edward E. Ericson, prob. in his trans. (see 689)]. (Samizd., 239)

533 "An Author's Appeal," New York Times (16 Jun 1971), 45 [translation of "Posleslovie" in Avg. čet., May 1971, tr. not named]; another version in Canadian Slavonic Papers, 13, ii/iii (Summer-Fall 1971), 261-2 ("A Soviet Author's Appeal for Information" [tr. not named]). [Samizd., 308]

534 [Autobiographical statement for Nobel Prize Committee], New York Times (4 Jul 1971), IV, 11 (under title "Solzhenitsyn's Life"), repr. of official text published in Russian, Swedish & English in: Les prix Nobel en 1970 (later included with speech in Les prix Nobel en 1971, same publisher [see 538 for full description]); also in Vogue, 160 (15 Sep 1972), 98 & 124 (under title "Solzhenitsyn, the Man, His Fate, and His Country" [tr. not named]). [Samizd., 307]

535 "Lament for Tvardovsky," New York Times (12 Feb 1972), 29 [tr. not named]; a trans. had appeared in International Herald-Tribune (Paris) early in January; a later version: "In Memoriam: Alexander Tvardovsky," New York Review of Books, 19, v (5 Oct 1972), 14 [tr. not named]. (Samizd., 312)

536 A Lenten Letter to Pimen, Patriarch of All Russia, tr. Keith Armes; ed. Theofanis G. Stavrou. Minneapolis, Minn.: Burgess Pub. Co., 1972. 12 pp. "Foreword" by Stavrou (9 Apr 1972), pp. 1-3; "Commentary" by Wassilij Alexeev, pp. 9-12. Review of book: Library Journal, 97 (15 Aug 1972), 2622 (R. Neiswender). Excerpts of "Letter" appeared earlier in "Church Accused by S.," New York Times (23 Mar 1972), 7; another version, full text: "Solzhenitsyn: Lenten Letter," National Review, 24 (28 Apr 1972), 445-47 [tr. not named]. (Samizd., 315)

537 August 1914, tr. Michael Glenny. London: Bodley Head, 1972. 645 pp.; New York: Farrar, Straus & Giroux, 1972. 622 pp. (Has brief "Foreword" signed "A. S."--condensed version of Russian "Posleslovie"; for full Engl. version of orig. afterword, see 534.) Pre-publication excerpts: "The Artillery Barage," Life, 72 (23 Jun 1972), 42-44B; "Soldier's Death: from S.'s Aug. 1914," Time, 97 (28 Jun 1971), 34; "Al. S.: Aug. 1914 [Chap. 63]," Harper's Magazine, 245 (Aug 1972), 53-68; "August 1914 [excerpts]," Vogue, 160 (15 Sep 1972), 98-9.

538 [The Nobel Lecture on Literature for 1970] in: Les prix Nobel en 1971. Stockholm: Nobel Foundation, 1972 [Stockholm: Imprimerie Royale P. A. Norstedt & Söner; avail. in USA from Elsevier Pub. Co. (Amsterdam, London, New York)]; in Engl. & Swedish, pp. 141-6; Russian, pp. 129-40 (with Autobiography) [have not seen this]. Excerpts from this text [tr. not named]: "Excerpts from Nobel Lecture by S.," New York Times (25 Aug 1972), 2; "Truth and the World's Values," Wall Street Journal (6 Sep 1972), 14.

539 "One Word of Truth...": The Nobel Speech on Literature, 1970.
London: Bodley Head, 1972. 27 pp. [tr., members of BBC Russian
Service]. (Review: see 572, TLS) Appeared earlier with some
omissions: "Al. S.'s Nobel Prize Speech," Listener, 88, No. 2268
(14 Sep 1972), 335-8.

540 The Nobel Lecture on Literature, tr. Thomas P. Whitney. New
York: Harper & Row, 1972. 38 pp. Repr. of: "Art--for Man's Sake,"
New York Times (30 Sep 1972), 31; (7 Oct 1972), 33. [Rev.: 1525b]

541 Nobel Lecture, tr. F. D. Reeve. New York: Farrar, Straus
& Giroux (Noonday Press), 1972. 71 pp. (Also, Toronto: Doubleday
Canada, 1972) Engl. text, pp. 3-34; Russian, pp. 37-69 ("Nobelev-
skaja lekcija"); biog. note, p. 71.*

542 A Candle in the Wind, tr. Keith Armes & Arthur G. Hudgins.
Minneapolis: U. of Minnesota Press, 1973. [Tr. of 11]

543 "It Is Not the Custom to Lighten Cabbage Soup with Tar--
For that We Have Sour Cream" [trans. of entry 6 by D. Fiene, to
appear in forthcoming issue of Russian Literature Triquarterly,
prob. No. 8 (1974)]. (Have seen no other trans. of this except
for version in Slovene by Klopčič [see 2455, pp. 272-6].)

2. Open letters, interviews, correspondence, announcements, mis-
    cellaneous

    Listed in chronological order according to date of composition
or utterance. Five items in this category have not yet been translated into English, as far as I know: see entries 27, 39, 47, 49, 50a,
& 53a. Exact titles of the items as published are not always
listed in full; for most, name of translator was not given.

544 Bukhanov, V. "Visiting S. in Ryazan," Moscow News (16 Feb
1963); also in Crest ed'n. of One Day (see 503), and pp. 5-9 in
Labedz (see 1285). [Tr. of 88]
545 "Moscow Writers on Cancer Ward [17 Nov 1966]," pp. 60-80
in Labedz (1285); statements by S., pp. 61, 77-79. (Samizd.,
248; see also 1372)
546 [Ličko, P.] "One Day with S.--An Interview," Survey, 64
(Jul 1967), 181-5; repr. pp. 10-15 in Labedz (1285). [Tr. of 1604]
547 "Open Letter to the Fourth Congress of Soviet Writers [16
May 1967]," New York Times (5 Jun 1967) 36 & (6 Jun 1967), 4;
Sunday Times (London), 4 Jun 1967 [excerpts]; Survey, 64 (Jul
1967), 177-81; Overland, 37 (1967), 14-16; Time, 92 (27 Sep 1968),
25 [excerpts in "Writer's Pen Should Not Be Stopped"]; pp. v-x
in 1968 ed'n. of One Day [see 500]; pp. vii-xii in Cancer Ward
[see 527]; pp. 245-50 in Brumberg (1284); pp. 80-87 in Labedz
(1285). [Samizd., 250]
548 "Letter to the Writers' Union [12 Sep 1967]," Problems of
Communism, 17, v (Sep-Oct 1968); pp. xiii-xiv in Cancer Ward
(see 527); pp. 252-3 in Brumberg (1284); pp. 101-03 in Labedz
(1285). [Samizd., 261]
549 "Session of the Soviet Writers' Secretariat [22 Sep 1967],"
Problems of Communism, 17, v (Sep-Oct 1968); pp. 543-59 in Cancer Ward (see 527); pp. 253-69 in Brumberg (1284); pp. 103-24 in
Labedz (1285). [Samizdat, 262]   (Has statements by S.)

---
* Another tr. of Nobel lecture appears in 1973 ed'n. of Labedz
  (see 1285).

550 "Letter to Secretariat of Writers' Union [1 Dec 1967]," Survey, 67 (Apr 1968), 130; Brumberg (1284), pp. 271-2; Labedz (1285), 128-9. [Samizd., 266]

551 "Letter to Members of the Writers' Union [16 Apr 1968]," Brumberg (1284), 283; Labedz (1285), 143-4. [Samizd., 271]

552 "Letter to Newspapers and Writers [18 Apr 1968]," Problems of Communism, 17, v (Sep-Oct 1968); Brumberg (1284), 282; Labedz (1285), 147-8. [Samizd., 272]

553 "Letter to Literaturnaya Gazeta [21 Apr 1968]," Survey, 68 (Jul 1968), 185-6 [back trans. of letter as pub. in L'Unita (4 Jun 1968)]; p. 560 in Cancer Ward (see 527) [trans. of letter as pub. in LG (see 207)]; Brumberg (1284), 281 [both versions]; Labedz (1285), 148-50 [both versions]. (Samizd., 273)

554 Letter to Literaturnaya Gazeta (copy to Novy Mir) [12 Dec 1968], p. 179 in Labedz (1285) under title "S. expresses gratitude for congratulations". [Samizd., 284]

554a Letter to the Ministry of Communications of the USSR [22 Feb 1969], pp. 379-80 in The Medvedev Papers by Zhores Medvedev, 1971 [see 1288; tr. of Russ. 447]. (With reply by B. Yastrebov, 7 Jun 1969 [p. 380])

555 "Meeting of Ryazan Writers [4 Nov 1969]," Labedz (1285), 180-191 (transcript; has statements by S.). [Samizd., 287]

556 "Letter to Writers' Union [12 Nov 1969]," New York Times (15 Nov 1969), 11; Survey, 73 (Autumn 1969), 194-6; Dissent, 17, vi (Nov-Dec 1970), 558-9; Labedz (1285), 193-5. [Samizd., 289] (Note: S. also made a public statement this date; see 1095.)

557 "Acceptance of Nobel Prize [Statement dictated to Per Hegge in telephone conversation of 8 Oct 1970]," Labedz (1285), 211; quoted in New York Times (9 Oct 1970), 16 [see 1127] and prob. also in Atlas, 19 (Dec 1970), 31-32 [see 1432].

558 Telegram to Dr. Karl Ragnar Gierow, Permanent Secretary of the Swedish Academy [11 Oct 1970], New York Times (12 Oct 1970), 5 ("Cablegram from S."); Labedz (1285), 214.

559 Open Letter to Swedish Academy [27 Nov 1970], New York Times (1 Dec 1970), 10 ("Novelist's Letter on Nobel Prize"); Labedz (1285), 223-24 [L. has date mistakenly as 1 Dec.]. (Samizdat, 306)

560 Telegram to K. Gierow [9 Dec 1970], Labedz (1285), 225.

561 Open Letter to Yu. V. Andropov, head of KGB [13 Aug 1971], quoted almost in full in New York Times (15 Aug 1971), 1 & 24 [see 1192]. (Samizdat, 309)

561a Letter to Per Hegge, 18 Sep 1971. One sentence quoted in New York Times (22 Oct 1971), 34 [see 1204], where it is implied that the letter appeared in the Swedish press [see 2383a].

562 Letter to K. R. Gierow, 4 Dec 1971: "Text of S. Letter to Swedish Academy," New York Times (24 Dec 1971), 2.

563 "Excerpts from the Transcript of the Conversation with S. in Moscow [interview with H. Smith & R. Kaiser, 30 Mar 1972]," tr. Theodore Shabad. New York Times (3 Apr 1972), 10. Other articles in NYT on Apr. 3, one by H. Smith, see 1232 & 1233; article in Washington Post Apr. 3 by R. Kaiser, repr. in Manchester Guardian Apr. 3, 4 & 5, see 1484. Excerpts of interview also in "What S. Had to Say," Newsweek, 79 (17 Apr 1972), 49 and "S. Speaks Out," Time, 99 (17 Apr 1972), 46. [Samizd., 315a]

564 Telegram to K. R. Gierow, 7 Apr 1972; quoted, evidently in full, in New York Times (8 Apr 1972), 7, under heading "'It's a Shame'". Also quoted in "S. Speaks Out," Time, 99 (17 Apr 1972), 46.

565 Declaration made available to Swedish correspondents, 8 Apr 1972. Excerpts in: "S. Hints Hope Gone on Nobel," New York Times (9 Apr 1972), 5; "S. Rules Out Nobel Award in Private," New York Times (10 Apr 1972), 22; "Soviet Union: The Unsilenced Voice," Newsweek, 79 (17 Apr 1972), 50.

II. About Solzhenitsyn: 1. Books

566 Saunders, G. Rebels and Bureaucrats: Soviet Conflicts as Seen in Solzhenitsyn's "Cancer Ward". New York: Merit Pub., 1969. 59 pp. (Repr. of 612)

567 Lukács, G. Solzhenitsyn, tr. W. Graf. Cambridge, Mass.: MIT Press, 1971. (Tr. of 2052) Contents: "S.: One Day in the Life of Ivan Denisovich [1964]," 7-32 [also in Engl. at 581]; & "S.'s Novels [1969]," 33-88.

568 Reviews of Lukács:
East Europe, 4 (1971), 31-2. (G. Steiner: "George Lukács & S.").
Encounter, 36 (Mar 1971), 47-51. (M. Esslin: "S. and Lukács").
Library Journal, 96 (1 Nov 1971), 3614. (R. Neiswender)
New Statesman, 81 (26 Feb 1971), 273. (I. Mészáros)
Russian Review, 31, iii (Jul 1972), 316-17. (P. Blake)
Saturday Review, 54 (4 Dec 1971), 60. (M. Friedberg)
Times (London) Literary Supplement (4 Jun 1970), 604. ("For S.": rev. of Ger. ed'n.)
___ (18 Jun 1970), 662. (M. Eve: "Lukács on S."; challenges above review, with reply by reviewer.)
___ (23 Jul 1971), 868. (Rev. of trans.)
Virginia Quarterly Review, 48 (Winter 1972), p. xiv.
See also review-article at 642, pp. 253-60.

569 Rothberg, A. Aleksandr Solzhenitsyn: The Major Novels. Ithaca, N. Y.: Cornell University Press, 1971. 215 pp. "Bibliography," pp. 203-210. (Parts pub. earlier; see 631 & 635)
569a Reviews of Rothberg:
Choice, 8 (Feb 1972), 1591.
Economist, 241 (11 Dec 1971), 64.
Library Journal, 96 (15 Nov 1971), 3761. (R. Neiswender)
Modern Language Journal, 56, viii (Dec 1972), 533. (A. Obolensky).
New Republic, 166 (19 Feb 1972), 29.
Russian Review, 31, iv (Oct 1972), 431-32. (H. Muchnic)
Saturday Review, 54 (4 Dec 1971), 59-60. (M. Friedberg)
See also 424.

570 Björkegren, H. Aleksandr Solzhenitsyn: A Biography, tr. K. Eneberg. New York: Third Press [Jos. Okpaku Pub. Co.], 1972. 186 pp. "Bibliography," pp. 181-82. (Tr. of 2397)

571 Burg, D. & G. Feifer. Solzhenitsyn: A Biography. London: Hodder & Stoughton; New York: Stein & Day, 1972. 371 pp.
572 Reviews of Burg & Feifer:
Esquire, 78 (Dec 1972), 24 & 28. (M. Muggeridge)
Library Journal, 97 (15 Aug 1972), 2573. (S. Haffner)
NYRB, 20, viii (17 May 1973), 32-34. (Zh. Medvedev: "Getting S. Straight" [tr. P. Reddaway])

Times (London), 2 Nov 1972. (M. Glenny)
Times (London) **Literary Supplement** (10 Nov 1972), 1369. ("Searching for the Real S.")[Also reviews Nobel Speech (see 539)]
Also see 946.

572a Medvedev, Zh. **Ten Years After "One Day in the Life of Ivan Denisovich".** London: Macmillan, 1973. 240 pp. (Circulated in **samizdat** before tr. into Engl.)

Forthcoming

573 Scammell, M. **Solzhenitsyn.** London: Pall Mall; New York: Praeger, 1973?. [Book has been advertised by dealers as having 224 pp., with bibl. & index, though ms. is not yet completed; subtitle: **A Biography**; or possibly: **A Biographical and Critical Study.**]

574 Dunlop, J. & R. Haugh & A. Klimoff, eds. **Aleksandr Solzhenitsyn: Critical Essays and Biographical Materials.** Belmont, Mass.: Nordland Pub. Co., 1973. With bibliography on S. from **samizdat** movement. Contents include previously published essays (some revised, some in translation) and many new articles, by the following (and others): T. Bird, H. Böll, T. Bradley, E. Brown, M. Djilas, V. Erlich, J. Dunlop, D. Fanger, K. Feuer, X. Gasiorowska, I. Howe, R. Lamont, V. Liapunov, M. McCarthy, H. Muchnic, M. Nicholson, N. Pashin, A. Schmemann [2 articles], V. Seduro, G. Struve, N. Struve, B. Unbegaun & G. Žekulin.

575 Tikos, L. **Solzhenitsyn: A Man Against His Time.** New York: Frederick Ungar & Co. Probably late 1973.

576 Blake, P. [**Solzhenitsyn**]. New York: Harcourt, Brace, Jovanovich. Probably early 1974. Title not certain.

577 Belinkov, A. [& N. Belinkov(a)]. **The Destiny and Work of Solzhenitsyn.** Garden City, N. Y.: Doubleday. Probably early 1974. Tentative title of book begun by Arkadij V. Belinkov, now being completed by his widow, Natalija A. Belinkova; probably will be published first in Russian (see 323a).

See also the following books on S. in languages other than English (most of them tending to emphasize literary evaluation): Demets (1646), Chaix-Ruy (1870), Nivat & Aucouturier (1918), Lukács (2052, plus translations), Ingold & Markstein (2118), Ingold & Rakusa (2119), Grazzini (2233), Uchimura (2255), Hegge (2295, plus trans.), Björkegren (2397, plus trans.), Pletnev (319), Gul' (320, 322), Rževskij (321) & 323. Non-English books containing long sections or chapters devoted to literary evaluation of S. include: Drozda (1585), Fischer (1979), Bieneck (2096), Risalti (2232) & Lombardo-Radice (2234). For books dealing primarily with the "Solzhenitsyn affair" see Labedz (1285) and others briefly indexed following entry 1292.

2. Critical essays, chapters and important references in books, annuals and Festschriften.

578 Brown, E. **Russian Literature Since the Revolution.** New York: Collier, 1963. See pp. 290-91. (Rev. ed'n., 1969, see 588)
579 **Essays and Reviews from the Times Literary Supplement, 1963**, v. 2. Oxford U. Press, 1964. Contains following on **One Day**: "A Cold Spring: A Soviet Land Mark," 25-28 & "A Cold Spring: Follow Up," 28-30. [Have not seen this; could not find such titles in **TLS** in 1963; for those I did find, see 751, 1296, -98, 1300.]

580 Alexandrova, V. A History of Soviet Literature, 1917-1964: From Gorky to Solzhenitsyn, tr. M. Ginsburg. Garden City, N. Y.: Anchor Books, 1964. 464 pp. (See pp. 413, 420, 423, 426, 438)

581 Lukács, G. "Solzhenitsyn and the New Realism," tr. M. Brown, pp. 197-215 in Socialist Register, ed. R. Miliband & J. Saville. London: Merlin Press, 1965. (Tr. of 1971; also in Eng. at 567)

582 Slonim, M. Soviet Russian Literature: Writers and Problems, 1917-1967. London/New York: Oxford U. Press; New York: Galaxy Book, 1967. 373 pp. (See pp. 333-36, 346, 348)

583 Bradley, T. "Alexander Isaevich Solzhenitsyn," pp. 329-339 in Soviet Leaders, ed. G. Simmons. New York: T. Y. Crowell, 1967. 405 pp. (Bibliography, pp. 338-39; see also pp. 5, 7, 10, 270, 342, 346)

584 Rossbacher, P. "Solzhenitsyn's 'Matrena's Home'," pp. 156-62 in Proceedings, Pacific Northwest Conference on Foreign Languages, ed. R. Baldner. Victoria, B. C.: U. of Victoria, 1967 [Eighteenth Annual Meeting, 17-18 Mar 1967, vol. XVIII]. (Also at 607)

585 Gasiorowska, X. Women in Soviet Fiction, 1917-1964. Madison/Milwaukee/London: U. of Wisconsin Press, 1968. (See pp. 69, 72, 227)

586 Mihajlov, M. "Dostoevsky's and Solzhenitsyn's House of the Dead," in his Russian Themes, tr. Marija Mihajlov[a]. New York: Farrar, Straus, 1968 (pp. 78-118). (Repr. of 601; tr. of 2430)

587 Fischer, E. "End Game [Beckett] and Ivan Denisovich," pp. 7-34 in his Art Against Ideology, tr. A. Bostock. London: Allen Lane The Penguin Press, 1969. 227 pp. (Tr. of 1979)

588 Brown, E. "Solzhenitsyn's Letter and His Forbidden Works," pp. 301-07 in his Russian Literature Since the Revolution, rev. ed. New York: Collier, 1969. (See also pp. 290-91, 298-300, 312. First ed'n., 1963, see 578)

589 Herling-Grudziński, G. "Yegor and Ivan Denisovich," tr. [from Polish] R. Strom, pp. 192-97 in Kultura Essays, ed. L. Tyrmand. New York: Macmillan (Free Press in Cooperation with the State Univ. of New York at Albany), 1970. [Have not seen original.]

590 Posell, E. "Alexander Isayevich Solzhenitsyn," pp. 218-235 in her Russian Authors. Boston: Houghton Mifflin, 1970. 253 pp.

591 Field, A., comp. The Complection of Russian Literature: A Cento. New York: Atheneum, 1971. (Brief note, pp. 297-8)

592 Pomorska, K., ed. Fifty Years of Russian Prose: From Pasternak to Solzhenitsyn, 2 vols. Cambridge, Mass.: MIT Press, 1971. (Brief biog. note, v. 2, p. 354; see also entry 508)

593 Muchnic, Helen. "Aleksandr Solzhenitsyn," pp. 400-450 in her Russian Writers: Notes and Essays. New York: Random House, 1971. 462 pp. (Part pub. earlier; see 622)

594 Galler, M. & H. Marquess, comps. Soviet Prison Camp Speech, a Survivor's Glossary: Supplemented by Terms from the Works of A. I. Solženicyn. Madison, Wisc.: U. of Wisconsin Press, 1972. 216 pp.

595 Clive, G. "Solzhenitsyn and the Inconsequence of Politics," pp. 128-156 in his The Broken Icon. New York: Macmillan, 1972.

596 Brown, E. "Solzhenitsyn's Cast of Characters," in his Major Soviet Writers: Modern Essays in Criticism. New York/London: Oxford U. Press, 1973. (Repr. of 640)

596a Billington, J. The Icon and the Axe: An Interpretive History of Russian Culture. New York: Alfred A. Knopf, 1966. 786 pp. (See pp. 568, 581-82, 587) [Out of chronological order.]

See also entries 1275-92 (relating to the "Solzhenitsyn affair"); for introductions, forewords and afterwords in books, see 500-505, 509, 521, 525, 527, 536 & 1285 (Salisbury).

3. Important critical articles in journals and magazines

Bibliographical sources consulted include MLA International Bibliography for 1971, but not for 1972. Listed are several articles on the original Russian edition of August 1914, 1971-72, which could be classified as reviews. (For book reviews of English translations of S.'s works, see entries 710-1019.) Abbreviations used: AUMLA= Journal of the Australasian Universities Language & Literature Association; BISUSSR: Bulletin of the Institute for the Study of the USSR; ES1: Études Slaves et Est-Européennes (Canada); NZSJ: New Zealand Slavonic Journal; RusR: Russian Review; SlavR: Slavic Review.

1963-66

597 Rubin, B. "The Shock of Recognition," Survey, 47 (Apr 1963), 160-171 [see pp. 162-69].
597a Zavalishin, V. "S., Dostoevsky and Leshenkov-Klychkov," BISUSSR, 10, xi (Nov 1963), 40-48.
598 Zisserman, N. "The Righteous Ones: A Study in Figural Interpretation," Landfall, 18, i (Mar 1964), 140-51.
599 Žekulin, G. "S.'s Four Stories," Soviet Studies, 16, i (Jul 1964), 45-62.
600 SlavR, 23, iii (Sep 1964):
Erlich, V. "Post Stalin Trends in Russian Literature," 405-19 [see 409-11].
Gibian, G. "Themes in Recent Soviet Russian Literature," 420-431 [reply to Erlich; refers to S. p. 421].
Hayward, M. "S.'s Place in Contemporary Soviet Literature," 432-36.
Erlich, V. "Reply," 437-40 [on S., pp. 438-40].
601 Mihajlov, M. "Dostoevsky's and S.'s House of the Dead," BISUSSR, 12, viii (Aug 1965) 3-18; x (Oct 1965), 13-25. (Repr.: 586; tr. of 2430)
602 Pervushin, N. "The Soviet Writer S., His Critics and the Classical Russian Literature," ES1, 10, fasc. i-ii (1965/1966), 3-19.
603 Varnai, P. "The Hungarian Solzhenitsyn," Canadian Slavonic Papers, 8 (1966), 260-66. [Compares József Lengyel & S.]

1967

604 Žekulin, G. "Aspects of Peasant Life as Portrayed in Contemporary Soviet Literature," Canadian Slavic Studies, 1 (Winter), 552-65.
605 Sikdar, A. "Two Inmates of the Dead House," Quest (Bombay), 53, pp. 47-52.
606 Koehler, L. "Al. S. and Russian Literary Tradition," RusR, 26 (Apr), 176-84.
607 Rossbacher, P. "S.'s 'Matrena's Home'," ES1, 12, fasc. ii-iii (Summer-Fall), 114-21. (Also at 584)

1968

608 Todd, A. "The Spiritual in Recent Soviet Literature," Survey, 66 (Jan), 92-107. [Refers to MD.]

609 Weissbort, D. "S.'s 'Cancer Ward'," Survey, 68 (Jul), 179-85.

610 Harari, M. "'The Cancer Ward', Part II," Survey, 69 (Oct), 145-49. [See also obit. note "Manya Harari," by L(eopold) L(abedz), Survey, 73 (Autumn 1969), 197-99.] (See 369 & 370)

1969

611 Koehler, L. "Eternal Themes in S.'s The Cancer Ward," RusR, 28 (Jan), 53-65.

612 Saunders, G. "Rebels and Bureaucrats: Soviet Conflicts in S.'s Cancer Ward," Intercontinental Press (10 Feb-24 Mar). [Repr.: 566]

613 Foreman, D. "Candle in the Wind: A Play by S.," NZSJ, No. 3 (Winter [June]), 50-53.

614 Esam, I. "The Imagery of S.," NZSJ, No. 3 (Winter), 83-99.

615 Rogers, T. "The Ironic Mode in Recent Soviet Russian Prose," SEEJ, 13, iii (Fall), 295-308 [see 299, 301-302].

616 Christesen, N. "Al. S.'s Dialogue with Tolstoy," Meanjin Quarterly (Melbourne), 28, iii, 351-58.

617 Wrassky, H. "Some Examples of Recent Soviet Short Stories: Their Significance and Common Characteristics," NZSJ, No. 4 (Summer [Dec]), 41-53.

1970

618 Humphries, G. "Al. S.," Journal of Russian Studies, 19, pp. 17-23.

619 Mark[stein], E. "The Difficulty of Writing About Soviet Literature," tr. G. Skelton, Mosaic, 3, ii (Winter), 27-39. [Written in Vienna, Dec. 1969; do not know if Ger. text was pub.; for French trans., see 1918, pp. 389-99.]

620 Kenedy, R. "The First Circle," Art International & Lugano Review, 14 (20 Feb), 21-27.

621 Webb, K. "Al. I. S.: A Study in the Attainment of Self-Knowledge and Freedom Through Imprisonment," Hollins Symposium (Virginia), 6, i (Spring), 71-80.

622 Muchnic, H. "S.'s The First Circle," RusR, 29, ii (Apr), 154-66. [Later expanded, repr.: 593]

623 Bethell, N. "S. Can Still Write--He Just Can't Publish," New York Times Magazine (12 Apr), 36-7, 42, 44, 46, 50, 52, 54, 56, 59.

624 Iswolsky, H. "The World of Al. S.," Catholic Worker, 36, v (Jun), 4-7. [On First Circle & Cancer Ward]

625 Brooks, M. "Revisionist Ideology of the Self," Literature and Ideology (Montreal), 7, pp. 15-24. [Also on Zamjatin]

626 Callaghan, M. "Solzhenitsyn," Tamarack Review, 55, pp. 71-6.

627 Blackburn, R. "The First Circle," New Left Review, 63 (Sep/Oct), 56-64.

628 Clardy, J. "Al. S. and the Impending Event: An Added Dimension to Solve an Old Problem," Cimmaron Review, 13 (Oct), 16-23.

1971

629 Atkinson, D. "S.'s Heroes as Russian Historical Types," RusR, 30 (Jan), 1-16.

630 Garrard, J. "The 'Inner Freedom' of Al. S.," Books Abroad,

45, i (Winter), 7-18.

631 Rothberg, A. "Al. S.: The Obsession of Morality," Interplay, 4, ii (Feb), 35-39. (Repr. with changes: 569)

632 Bourdeaux, M. "A. S.: Religious Writer," Christian Century, 88 (10 Feb), 202-03.

633 Kovaly, P. "Humanism and Antihumanism in the Life and Work of Al. S.," Humanist, 31 (Mar-Apr), 20-23.

634 Kovaly, P. "Problems of Humanism and Anti-Humanism in the Life and Works of Al. S.," Studies in Soviet Thought, 11, i (Apr), 1-18.

635 Rothberg, A. "One Day--Four Decades: S.'s Hold on Reality," Southwest Review, 56 (Spring), 109-25. [Repr.: 569, ch. 2]

636 Lindsay, J. "Al. S.," Anglo-Soviet Journal, 31, iii (May), 15-26.

637 Unbegaun, B. "The Language of Ultimate Clarity," Melbourne Slavonic Studies, No. 5-6, pp. 91-?.

638 Wrassky, H. "Two Articles in Retrospect," NZSJ, No. 7 (Winter [Jun]), 42-49. [On articles by A. Dubrovin & Ju. Šrejder, 1969; includes comments on S.]

639 Blake, P. "'My Hands Are Burning'," New York Times (11 Jul), IV, 3. [On Avg. čet.]

640 Brown, E. "Solženicyn's Cast of Characters," SEEJ, 15, ii (Summer), 153-66. (Repr.: 596)

641 Wilson, E. "Solzhenitsyn," New Yorker, 47 (14 Aug), 83-87.

642 Canadian Slavonic Papers, 13, ii-iii (Summer-Fall):

Melnikov, G. "A. I. S.: A Brief Biography," 125-29.

Obolensky, A. "S. in the Mainstream of Russian Literature," 131-39.

Pervushin, N. "Preliminary Remarks on the Literary Craft of S.," 140-46.

Grebenschikov, V. "Les cercles infernaux chez Soljénitsyne et Dante," 147-64. (See Engl. tr. at 687)

Rus, V. "One Day in the Life of Ivan Denisovich: A Point of View Analysis," 165-78.

Žekulin, G. "S.'s Play The Candle in the Wind," 179-92.

Student articles

Windle, K. "Symbolism and Analogy in S.'s Cancer Ward," 193-208.

Rea, N. "Nerzhin: A Sartrean Existential Man," 209-18.

Kisseleff, N. "Literary Allusions and Themes in The First Circle," 219-34.

Whitehorn, A. "What Men Live By: An Analysis of S.'s Writings," 235-42.

Havrlant, L., comp. "A Solzhenitsyn Selected Bibliography, December 1962-October 1970," 243-52.

e.e. [Review-article on Lukács (2052) and Pletnev (319)], 253-60.

[Solzhenitsyn] "A Soviet Author's Appeal for Information," 261-62. [See 533].

643 Day, D. "On Pilgrimage," Catholic Worker, 37, vii (Sep), 1, 7-8. ["Solzhenitsyn," p. 8; includes partial reply to Wilson (641)].

644 Des Pres, T. "Survivor: On the Ethos of Survival in Extremity," Encounter, 37, iii (Sep), 3-19.

645 Luplow, R. "Narrative Style and Structure in One Day in the Life of Ivan Denisovich," Russian Literature Triquarterly, No. 1 (Fall), 399-412.

646 Mayne, M. "Look at S.: One Day in the Life of Ivan Deniso-vich and The First Circle," English Journal, 60 (Fall), 205-07.

647 Iswolsky, H. "S.: August 1914," Catholic Worker, 37, viii (Oct-Nov), 5 & 7.

648 Christesen, N. "August 1914: Al. S., " AUMLA, No. 36 (Nov), 153-6.

649 Scammell, M. "Frontier Profile: Al. S.," Frontier, 14 (Nov), 226-230.

670[sic] Lawrence, J. "Al. S.: August 1914," Frontier, 14 (Nov), 243-46.

671 California Slavic Studies, VI [ed. R. Hughes, S. Karlinsky & V. Markov. Berkeley: U. of Cal. Press, 1971]:
Feuer, K. "Solženicyn and the Legacy of Tolstoy," 113-128.
Miłosz, C. "On Modern Russian Literature and the West," 171-75.

672 Fitzlyon, K. "Russian Knots," London Magazine, 11, v (Dec 1971/Jan 1972), 139-43. [On Avg. čet.]

1972

673 Atkinson, D. & N. Pashin. "'August 1914': Art and History," RusR, 31, i (Jan), 1-10.

674 Radosh, S. & L. Tikos. "Al. Is. S.: A Selected Bibliogra-phy," Bulletin of Bibliography and Magazine Notes, 29, i (Jan-Mar), 1-6.

675 Williams, R. "On S.," TriQuarterly, 23/24 (Winter/Spring), 318-334.

676 McCarthy, M. "A Guide to Exiles, Expatriates and Internal Émigrés," New York Review of Books, 18, iv (9 Mar), 4, 6-8. [See pp. 4 & 8]

677 Glenny, M. "A New Russian Epic: S.'s 'August 1914'," Sur-vey, 18, ii (Spring), 112-122.

678 Carlisle, O. "Russian Hero's Tale of War," Vogue, 159 (1 Apr), 36 & 58. [On Avg. čet.]

679 Deutscher, T. "S.: An Appraisal," Ramparts, 10, xi (May), 57-60.

680 Fanger, D. "S.: Art and Foreign Matter," Problems of Com-munism, 21, iii (May-Jun), 57-63.

681 Windle, K. "The Theme of Fate in S.'s August 1914," SlavR, 31, ii (Jun), 399-411.

682 Natov, N. [Review of Nivat & Aucouturier (see 1918)], SEEJ, 16, ii (Summer), 238-40.

683 Mark[stein], E. "S. in the Context of Soviet Literature," tr. K. Rees, Mosaic, 5, iv (Summer), 135-48. [Tr. from Ger., do not know if orig. ms. was pub.]

684 Glenny, M. "Al. S. and the Epic Tradition: Introducing 'Aug-ust 1914'," Harper's Magazine, 245 (Aug), 50-52.

685 Erlich, V. "S.'s New Novel," Dissent, 19, iv (Fall), 639-41. [On Avg. čet., not on trans.]

686 Porter, R. "Literature, Politics and the S. Affair," Modern Languages (London), 53, iv (Dec), 177-83.

687 Transactions of the Association of Russian-American Scholars in U.S.A. (Zapiski Akademičeskoj gruppy v S.S.A.) [ed. C. Belou-sow, New York, dated 1972 but released 1973], VI:
Grebenschikov, V. "The Infernal Circles of Dante and S.," 7-20 [tr. of 642, pp. 147-64].
Dunlop, J. "S.'s Sketches," 21-28.

Boldyreff, C. "S.: The Conscience of Russia," 29-35.
Carpovich, V. "Nekotorye čerty jazyka S-na," 36-44 [in Russian].

1973

688 Korg, J. "S.'s Metaphors," Centennial Review, 17, i (Winter), 70-91.

689 Ericson, E. "The Literature of Dissent in the Soviet Union," Modern Age, 17, i (Winter), 39-52. [See pp. 39, 47-51]

689a Vidal, G. New York Review of Books, 20, ix (31 May). [Article on top six best sellers, including August 1914.]

689b Lottridge, S. "S. and Leskov," Russian Literature Triquarterly, No. 6.

See also 586 (M. Esslin in Encounter), 1345, 1372, 1405, 1406, 1461, 1522, 2118 (Tikos & Nicholson). Also see section on book reviews of English translations, entries 710-1019, some of which are of article length--in particular 877, 904, 959, 961, 962, 991, 1014 & 1018. Forthcoming publications are to be expected, based on dissertations and papers listed in entries 690-709.

4. Dissertations and theses

690 Dovhiy, W. "Dostoevsky's House of the Dead and S.'s One Day in the Life of Ivan Denisovich: Studies in Extreme Reality," M. A. Thesis. U. of Toronto, 1965.

691 Perelmuter, J. "The Language of S.'s Odin den' Ivana Denisoviča," M. A. Thesis. McGill U., 1967.

692 Windle, K. "S., A Socialist Humanist," M. A. Thesis. McMaster U., 1969.

693 Rea, N. "S.'s First Circle: A Humanist View of Soviet Society," M. A. Thesis. U. of Toronto, 1970.

694 Walker, J. "S.'s Cancer Ward: An Introductory Study," Ph.D. diss. Indiana University, 1971. 187 pp. "Bibliography," pp. 181-187. (Advisor: W. Edgerton)

695 Moody, L. "Al. S.'s Prose: A Study of Phraseology and Characterization," Ph.D. diss. Ohio State U., 1971. 134 pp. "Bibliography," pp. 124-30. (Adv.: Hongor Oulanoff)

696 Mezz, J. "S. On Stage: A Critical Study of Olen' i Šalašovka (A Play by Aleksandr Solzhenitsyn) and Its World Premiere Production by the Minnesota Theatre Company, 1970," Ph.D. diss. U. of Minnesota, 1972. 315 pp. (Advisors: F. Whiting & T. Stavrou) [Note: The script for the play prod. (at the Tyrone Guthrie Theater) was adapted by P. Mayer & dir. by M. Langham; the bibliog. of this diss. includes materials related to prod. of play, script drafts, reviews of performance, personal interviews.]

698[sic] Porter, R. "Form and Content in Al. S.'s The First Circle and Cancer Ward," thesis for M. Phil. degree, Leeds U. Expected completion date: Spring 1973.

699 Hatfield, H. [The Peasant as a Literary Character in the Works of Al. S. (prob. title)], Ph.D. diss. U. of Colorado. Probable completion date: 1973.

700 Cohen, L. "Al. S.: Art and the Artist," Ph.D. diss. Northwestern U. In progress.

See also 707 (Webb) and French thesis at 1928a.

5. Symposia, unpublished papers

701 Rolland, P. "Al. Is. S.: An Attempt at Complete Bibliography, 1963-1965," unpub. paper, Dept. of Slav. Lang. & Lit., Ind. U., Jan 1968. 8 pp.

702 Sheldon, R. "Dissent with No Rhyme: The Etudes of Al. S.," unpub. article, Center for Advanced Study, U. of Ill., 1969. [Cited by Moody, p. 127 [see 695].]

703 Symposium on S., 13 Nov 1970, at Washington, D. C. Sponsored by George Washington U. & American U.: R. Lager, Chrmn.; F. Fadner, Introd. remarks; papers by: D. Grigorev, B. Filippov, S. Levitsky & V. Medish. [See articles on symp. at 463 & 467.]

704 Symposium on S., 19 Apr 1971, at State U. of N. Y., Albany:
G. Gibian, "Perspectives on S." [unpub.](Reply by Pervušin: 421)
A. Obolensky, "S. in the Main Stream of Russian Literature". [pub. at 642, pp. 131-39].
N. Pervushin, "The Literary Craft of S." [pub. in abbridged form at 642, pp. 140-46].

705 Symposium on S., 23 Oct 1971, conducted by the Russian-American Scholars in the U.S.A. and the Russian Institute of Fordham U., at Fordham. Papers were read by C. Boldyreff, J. Dunlop, D. Fanger & L. Rževskij; those by Boldyreff & Dunlop were later published (see 687).

706 Orth, S. "S.'s Portrait of the 'Establishment Writer': Galakhov in 'The First Circle'": paper read at Slavic I Section, 9 AM, 27 Apr 1972, 25th annual Kentucky Foreign Language Conf., U. of Ky., Lexington, 27-29 Apr.

707 NE Slavic Conf., 27-29 Apr 1972, U. of Vermont, Burlington; section on S.: G. Zekulin, Chrmn.; papers by: L. Tikos ("Lukács and S."); S. Lottridge ("S. and Leskov" [rev. for pub. (see 689b)]); M. Kantorczyk ("S. and Narodnichestvo"); N. Pervushin; & K. Webb ("S. and the Revival of the Humanistic and Artistic Values of the Nineteenth Century," 30 pp., based in part on unpublished senior thesis for Hollins College, Va., titled: "A Song in Chains: An Analysis of the Works of Al. I. S.," 125 pp. [see also 621].)

708 Rickwood, T. "Themes and Styles in S.'s August 1914"; paper delivered at Canadian Ass'n. of Slavists, Montreal, 2-4 Jun 1972.

709 Symposium on S., 30 Jun, 1-3 Jul 1972, at Norwich U., Vt.:
N. Belinkova, "The Role of the Biographical Factor in the Works of S.".
B. Filippov, "The Main Principles of Composition of S.'s Works".
N. Natov-Popliuyko, " The Sense of History in the Works of S.".
A. Obolensky, "Two Alëshas (Karamazov and the Baptist)"; rev. for pub'n. (in Russian [see 425]).
N. Pervushin, "S., His Readers and Critics"; to be pub. in 1973 in expanded form in Russian, prob. in Novyj Žurnal or Novoe Russkoe Slovo.
A. Popliuyko, "The Concept 'For the Good of the Cause' and S.'s Story".
L. Rzhevsky, "On S.'s Realism"; pub. in Russian, 321, pp. 141-63.
G. Zekulin, "Good and Evil in the Works of S." (Dobro i zlo u S.)

6. Book reviews

All are listed in alphabetical order according to title of reviewing periodical. Abbreviations used: CSM: Christian Science Monitor; HudR: Hudson Review; KR: Kenyon Review; LJ: Library Journal; ModA: Modern Age; NatO: National Observer; NatR: National Review; NL: New Leader; NR: New Republic; NS: New Statesman; NYHT: New York Herald Tribune; NYRB: New York Review of Books; NYT: New York Times; NYTBR: New York Times Book Review; PubW: Publishers' Weekly; RusR: Russian Review; SatR: Saturday Review; SEEJ: Slavic and East European Journal; SlavR: Slavic Review; SSF: Studies in Short Fiction; TLS: Times (London) Literary Supplement; VQR: Virginia Quarterly Review; YR: Yale Review.

(i) One Day in the Life of Ivan Denisovich

All of the reviews listed were published in 1963. All are about the Max Hayward–Ronald Hingley translation (500) or the Ralph Parker translation (501) or both of these translations. The following notations are used to indicate these distinctions (where known): [H] (Hayward–Hingley); [P] (Parker); [Both]. I have not seen all the reviews; standard reference works sometimes give only the first page on which multi-page reviews appear.

710 America, 108 (9 Mar): M. Koriakov, "Russia's Voice," 338-39; R. Gustafson, 342 [Both].
711 Atlantic, 211 (Apr), 144. (W. Barrett) [Both]
712 Best Sellers, 22 (1 Feb), 412. (R. Grady)
713 Books Abroad, 37, ii (Spring), 217. (R. Vlach) [Both]
714 Chicago Sunday Tribune Magazine of Books (27 Jan), 2. (E. Janeway) [Both]
715 Christian Century, 80 (13 Mar), 339. (M. Brown) [P]
716 CSM (24 Jan), 7. (E. Pisko)
717 Dissent, 10, ii (Spring), 187. (G. Siegel) [Both]
718 Extension, 58, ii (Aug), 30. (W. Smallwood) [P]
719 HudR, 15, i (Spring), 112. (S. Monas) "Both]
720 Guardian (31 Jan), 8. (V. Zorza: "Story of the Stalinist Terror")
721 KR, 25, ii (Spring), 356-60. (F. Reeve: "The House of the Living") [Both]
722 LJ, 88 (1 Feb), 576. (R. Neiswender) [Both]
723 Listener, 68 (31 Jan), 215. (L. Lerner) [P]
724 ModA, 7, iii (Summer), 333. (P. Mosely) [H]
725 Month, 29 (Mar), 176-7. (D. B. Wyndham Lewis)
726 Nation, 196 (2 Feb), 100-01. (E. Pawel: "The Triumph of Survival") [Both]
727 NL, 46 (4 Feb), 22. (J. Katel) [Both]
728 NR, 148 (11 May), 19-20. (I. Howe: "Predicaments of Soviet Writing") [Both]
729 NS, 65 (1 Feb), 158. (L. Schapiro) [Both]
730 NS, 65 (22 Mar), 424. (F. Kermode) [Both]
731 NYHTBooks (7 Apr), 10. (M. Fainsod: "Among Many Stalinist Days, One in Particular") [Both]
732 NYRB, 1, i (Sep), 4. (P. Rahv) [Both]
733 NYT (22 Jan), 7. (H. Salisbury)

734 NYTBR (7 Apr), 4-5, 34. (M. Slonim: "The Challenge Was the Need to Stay Alive") [Both]

735 New Yorker, 39 (27 Apr), 168-9. (A. West: "Ordeal by Fire") [P]

736 Newsweek, 61 (4 Feb), 81. [Both]

737 Partisan Review, 30 (Summer), 297-99. (A. Field: "A Soviet 'Eastern'") [Both]

738 Progressive, 27 (Jun), 44. (P. Carden: "Shaking the Ghost") [H]

739 Punch, 244 (6 Mar), 354. (J. Bowen) [P]

740 Reporter, 28 (28 Feb), 52-54. (W. H. Auden:"Beyond Politics") [Both]

741 RusR, 22, iii (Jul), 336-7. (D. Hull) [Both]

742 SatR, 46 (9 Feb), 27-29. (G. Reavey: "Now It Can Be Told in Moscow") [Both]

743 Show, 3, iv (Apr), 52. (R. Schickel) [Both]

744 SEEJ, 7, iii (Fall), 418-19. (T. Magner) [H]

745 SlavR, 22, ii (Jun), 375-77. (I. Shapiro) [Both]

746 Spectator (8 Feb), 171. (H. Willets) [Both]

747 Spectator (5 Apr), 441. (J. Griffiths) [Both]

748 Sunday Times (London), 27 Jan. (J. Bowen) [P]

749 Sunday Times (London), 3 Feb. (C. Connolly: "Hope and Happiness in Siberia")

750 Time, 81 (8 Feb), 90. [Both]

751 TLS, 3179 (1 Feb), 71. ("House of the Dead") [Both]

752 Times Weekly Review (London), 7 Feb., p. 13. [P]

753 VQR, 39 (Summer), p. xcii. [Both]

754 Wall Street Journal (21 Feb), 16. (W. Chamberlin: "Stalin's Death Camps as Seen from Inside")

755 Washington Post (27 Jan). (B. Morris: "What a Red Prisoner Lived For")

See also 597 and articles about or reviews of the movie based on the novel: 1090, 1110, 1178, 1475, 1459, 1460.

(ii) "We Never Make Mistakes" (reviews)

For information on translation, see 505. Abbreviations: see p. 51.

756 Book Week (3 Nov 1963), 20. (R. Maurer)

757 CSM (26 Dec 1963), 5. (E. Pisko)

758 East Europe, 13, iv (1964), 53. (S. M. M.)

759 LJ, 89 (1 Jan 1964), 136. (R. Neiswender)

760 Nation, 197 (9 Nov 1963), 301. (E. Pawel)

761 NYRB, 3 (24 Sep 1964), 13. (A. Alvarez: "Bread and Kvass") [Also reviews For the Good of the Cause (509)]

762 NYT (1 Aug 1963), 25. (H. Salisbury)

763 NYTBR (8 Dec 1963), 6 & 40. (P. Blake: "Wounds of Stalinism"; also see Blake's letter in NYTBR, 29 Dec 1963, p. 20, correcting error in review)

764 Newsweek, 62 (9 Dec 1963), 97B.

765 SatR, 46 (2 Nov 1963), 29. (M. Friedberg: "Crisis and Continuity")

766 SSF, 9, i (Winter 1972[sic]), 112-113. (V. Mihailovich)

767 Time, 82 (20 Dec 1963), 82.

768 TLS (21 May 1971), 581. ("Incidental"; brief note on new ed.)

(iii) For the Good of the Cause (reviews)

For information about translation, see 509. Abbreviations: see p. 51.

769 Best Sellers, 24 (1 Jul 1964), 139.
770 Book Week (5 Jul 1964), 6. (P. Viereck)
771 Chicago Sunday Tribune (21 Jun 1964), Books Today, p. 7. (W. Chamberlain)
772 Christian Century, 81 (24 Jun 1964), 832.
773 CSM (14 Jan 1971), 6. (M. Maddocks: "A Coded Search"; on second printing)
774 HudR, 17 (Winter 1964-65), 597. (S. Monas)
775 LJ, 89 (1 Oct 1964), 3776. (R. Neiswender)
776 Listener, 72 (22 Oct 1964), 637. (S. Wall)
777 NR, 163 (19 Dec 1970), 21. [On 2nd printing]
778 NS, 68 (23 Oct 1964), 615. (R. Taubman: "Raise High the Roofbeam")
779 NYTBR (12 Jul 1964), 26. (H. Salisbury: "The Bureaucrats Took Over")
780 New Yorker, 46 (17 Apr 1971), 147. [On 2nd printing]
781 Newsweek, 64 (13 Jul 1964), 87B.
782 SatR, 47 (27 Jun 1964), 30. (E. Janeway)
783 Time, 84 (3 Jul 1964), 90.
784 Times (London), 15 Oct 1964, p. 15. ("New Fiction")
785 TLS (22 Oct 1964), 964. ("Which Cause?")
786 TLS (14 May 1971), 555. ("On the Record" [on 2nd printing])
787 VQR, 40 (Autumn 1964), p. cxlix.

See also 761.

(iv) Reviews of The First Circle

All reviews are of the Whitney translation (521) unless otherwise indicated (with the notation: [Guybon]; see 522). Note that additional reviews of Circle are listed in the next section. Abbreviations: see p. 51.

788 America, 119 (5 Oct 1968), 295. (C. McNaspy)
789 Atlantic, 222 (19 Oct 1968), 143-4. (E. Weeks)
790 Best Sellers, 28 (1 Oct 1968), 253. (R. Grady)
791 Choice, 6 (Oct 1969), 1024.
792 CSM (23 Jan 1969), 11. (P. Wohl)
793 Commentary, 47 (May 1969), 81-84. (D. Jacobson: "The Example of S.")
794 Critic, 27 (Apr 1969), 77. (M. O'Malley)
795 Guardian, 99 (15 Nov 1968), 14. (R. Williams: "Work on the Human Voice")
796 Interplay, 2, ix (April 1969), 59-60. (A. Rothberg: "Squaring the Circle")
797 Kirkus, 36 (15 Aug 1968), 931.
798 Listener, 80 (14 Nov 1968), 647. (S. Hood: "The Fiftyeighters")
799 London Magazine, 8 (Jan 1969), 97-101. (K. Fitzlyon)

800 Nation, 207 (7 Oct 1968), 341-2. (D. Fanger: "Ring of Truth")

801 NatR, 20 (19 Nov 1968), 1172. (G. Davenport)

802 NR, 159 (19 Oct 1968), 32-4. (J. Laber: "Indictment of Soviet Terror")

803 NS, 76 (15 Nov 1968), 680. (D. Haworth)

804 NYHT (19 Sep 1968), 7. (G. Wolff: "From Dante's Inferno a Russian Voice Speaks")

805 NYT (11 Sep 1968), 45. (T. Lask: "The Bars Are Never Invisible")

806 NYTBR (15 Sep 1968), 1, 37-41. (H. Salisbury: "The World as a Prison"; see also unsigned summary review at NYTBR, 1 Dec 1968, p. 82)

807 Newsweek, 72 (30 Sep 1968), 108D. (P. Flynn: "Stalin's Victory")

808 Observer Review (10 Nov 1968). (E. Crankshaw: "A Masterpiece from Russia")

809 PubW, 194 (12 Aug 1968), 45.

810 Punch, 255 (20 Nov 1968), 746. (D. Williams)

811 RusR, 27 (Jul 1968), 379-81. (H. Muchnic)

812 SatR, 51 (14 Sep 1968), 36. (M. Friedberg: "The Party Imposes Its Will")

813 Sunday Telegraph (London), 10 Nov 1968. (N. Dennis)

814 Sunday Times (L), 10 Nov 1968. (J. Symons: "Russian Novel of Genius")

815 Tablet, 222 (21-28 Dec 1968), 1284. (V. Frank)

816 TLS (21 Nov 1969), 1301. ("Infernal Machinery" [Guybon])

817 Toronto Mail & Globe (4 Feb 1969). (S. Young: "Admiration for a Brilliant Russian Who Writes History as Literature")

818 VQR, 45 (Winter 1969), p. xv.

See also 620, 622, 627, 1623; articles on movie based on novel: 1210, 1410; and review of movie: 1522.

(v) Reviews of both First Circle and Cancer Ward

Reviews are of Whitney trans. of Circle unless otherwise indicated and of Bethell and Burg trans. of Cancer Ward unless otherwise indicated (with the notation: [Frank]; see 525). See next section for other reviews of Cancer Ward. Abbreviations: see p. 51.

819 American Scholar, 39 (Winter 1969-70), 166, 168, 170. (E. Rovit: "In the Center Ring")

820 Book World (6 Oct 1968), 6-7. (F. Reeve: "A Disease that Erodes What Is Human")

821 Chicago Literary Review, 3 (1969), 1. (R. O'Sullivan: "My Chains and I Grew Friends")

822 HudR, 22, i (Spring 1969), 148-54. (R. Garis: "Fiction Chronicle") [Frank]

823 NatO (30 Dec 1968). (B. Cook: "Two Novels by Mr. S. Prove Even Saints Can Be Dull")

824 NYRB, 11 (19 Dec 1968), 3. (V. Pritchett: "Hell on Earth")

825 SEEJ, 14, i (Spring 1970), 78-80. (P. Carden) [Frank]

826 SlavR, 28, ii (Jun 1969), 304-13. (D. Brown)

827 Spectator, 221 (15 Nov 1968), 698-99. (R. Hingley: "The Evil Men Do") [Part I only of Cancer Ward]

828 <u>YR</u>, 59 (Autumn 1969), 111. (M. Ellmann)

See also 624, 641 & 1345.

(vi) Reviews of <u>Cancer</u> <u>Ward</u>

Reviews are of Bethell and Burg trans. (527) unless otherwise indicated (with notation:[Frank]; see 525). Some of the reviews are of only the first or second part of the B. & B. trans. (so indicated). Abbreviations: see p. 51.

829 <u>Christian</u> <u>Century</u>, 86 (17 Sep 1969), 1200. (E. Snodgrass: "Politics versus Literature")
830 <u>Encounter</u>, 32 (Jan 1969), 83. (D. Rees) [Pt. I]
831 <u>Guardian</u>, 99 (26 Sep 1968), 15. (R. Williams: "How We See Suffering") [Pt. I]; 100 (6 Mar 1969). (R. Williams: "A Report on Suffering") [Pt. II]
832 <u>Journal</u> <u>of</u> <u>the</u> <u>American</u> <u>Medical</u> <u>Association</u>, 212 (6 Apr 1970), 96. (A. Brass: "A Latter-Day Tolstoi") [Frank]
833 <u>LJ</u>, 94 (15 Apr 1969), 1651. (R. Neiswender)
834 <u>Listener</u>, 80 (19 Sep 1968), 373. (S. Hood: "Last Days") [Pt. I]
835 <u>Listener</u>, 81 (6 Mar 1969), 320. (S. Hood: "Adversities") [Pt. II]
836 <u>London</u> <u>Daily</u> <u>Telegraph</u> (20 Sep 1968). (D. Floyd: "A Diseased Society")
837 <u>Nation</u>, 208 (6 Jan 1969), 20-21. (E. Capouya: "S.: Optimist and Realist") [Frank]
838 <u>Nation</u>, 208 (17 Mar 1969), 344. (E. Capouya: "A Note on 'Cancer Ward'")
839 <u>NS</u>, 76 (20 Sep 1968), 364. (J. Elliott: "Mirrors") [Pt.I]
840 <u>NS</u>, 77 (28 Feb 1969), 302. (J. Elliott: "In Sickness") [Pt. II]
841 <u>NYT</u> (28 Feb 1969), 37. (T. Lask: "As the Clock Nears Midnight") [Both translations]
842 <u>NYTBR</u> (27 Oct 1968), 2-3. (P. Blake: "A Diseased Body Politic")
843 <u>Newsweek</u>, 73 (17 Mar 1969), 58-9. (R. Littell)
844 <u>Observer</u> <u>Review</u> (9 Mar 1969). (E. Crankshaw)
845 <u>PubW</u>, 194 (7 Oct 1968), 48.
846 <u>SatR</u>, 51 (9 Nov 1968), 42-4. (M. Friedberg: "Gallery of Comrades Embattled Abed") [Pt. I]
847 <u>SatR</u>, 52 (15 Mar 1969), 36. (M. Friedberg: "Gallery of Comrades Revisited") [Pt. II]
848 <u>Spectator</u>, 222 (7 Mar 1969), 311-12. (R. Hingley: "Killing Kanker") [Pt. II]
849 <u>Sunday</u> <u>Telegraph</u> (London), 29 Sep 1968. (S. Constant: "Great Russian Realist")
850 <u>Sunday</u> <u>Times</u> (L), 22 Sep 1968. (E. Morgan: "Patients in a Sick Society")
851 <u>Tablet</u>, 222 (23 Nov 1968), 1160. (V. Baiocchi)
852 <u>Time</u>, 92 (8 Nov 1968), 121. ("Remission from Fear") [Frank]
853 <u>Times</u> (L), 8 Mar 1969, <u>Saturday</u> <u>Review</u>, p. 20. (I. McDonald: "Russia: Novelist and Allegory")
854 <u>TLS</u> (19 Sep 1968), 1041. ("Mortal Coils") [Pt. I]
855 <u>TLS</u> (13 Mar 1969), 263. ("More Mortal Coils") [Pt. II]

See also 609, 610, 611.

(vii) Reviews of The Love Girl and the Innocent

For information about trans. see 530. Abbreviations: see p. 51.

856 Book World (12 Jul 1970), 10. (F. Reeve) [See 861]
857 Choice, 7 (Jun 1970), 550.
858 LJ, 95 (15 Mar 1970), 1046. (E. Cohen)
859 Listener, 81 (9 Oct 1969), 491. (S. Hood)
860 NL, 53 (25 May 1970), 20. (A. Barralet)
861 NYHT (15 Jul 1970). (F. Reeve) [Poss. same as 856]
862 NYRB, 14 (26 Mar 1970), 31. (H. Muchnic)
863 SatR, 53 (21 Feb 1970), 43. (M. Friedberg)
864 Spectator, 223 (20 Sep 1969), 370. (R. Hingley)
865 Times (London), 17 Nov 1969. ("U. S. Outlet for S.")

For discussion of performance of play, see 696. For articles on and reviews of play, see 1111, 1116, 1125, 1137, 1140, 1305, 1412, 1419, 1425, 1426.

(viii) Reviews of Stories and Prose Poems

For information about trans. see 520. All of the reviews listed were published in 1971. Abbreviations: see p. 51.

866 Best Sellers, 31 (1 Oct), 305. (G. Snow)
867 Courier-Journal & Times (Louisville), 15 Aug, p. E7. (C. Shapiro)
868 Horn Book, 47 (Oct), 507. (M. Cosgrave)
869 LJ, 96 (1 Sep), 2672. (R. Neiswender)
870 Listener, 86 (8 Jul), 55. (P. Furbank)
871 Los Angeles Times (5 Sep), [Book section], p. 42. (R. Kirsch: "A. S.: More than a Symbol of Opposition")
872 NatR, 23 (8 Oct), 1123. (G. Davenport)
873 NS, 81 (18 Jun), 846. (F. Hope)
874 NYT (26 Jul), 22. (R. Locke)
875 Newsweek, 78 (26 Jul), 73A.
876 TLS (2 Jul), 752. ("Prized pravedniks")

(ix) Reviews of August 1914

For information about trans. see 537. Data about most of the reviews listed was obtained from a file of clippings at the Publicity Department of Farrar, Straus & Giroux Publishers, New York. Consequently, issue numbers and page numbers often are not indicated. Many of the newspaper reviews appeared in Sunday-magazine or book-review sections. The following dates fell on Sunday in 1972: 3, 10, 17 & 24 Sep; 1, 8, 15, 22 & 29 Oct; 5, 12, 19, 26 Nov, etc. All of the reviews listed were published in 1972. Abbreviations: see p. 51.

877 Atlantic, 230, iv (Oct), 65-9. (A. Kazin: "Few Speak for Freedom")
878 America, 127 (23 Sep), 206-09. (C. Hughes: "Hard Lot of Al. S.")
879 American Scene [News Bureau; Jersey City], Oct. (A. Vitkauskas)

880 Apartment Living (Nov), 20-21. (K. Lucas)
881 Arizona Republic (Phoenix), 22 Oct, p. N15. (F. Griffin)
882 Asheville [N.C.] Citizen Times (15 Oct), 11C. (L. Clark)
883 Atlanta Journal (Oct). (S. Sullivan)
884 Best Sellers (15 Oct), 336-7. (W. Parente)
885 Book-of-the-Month Club News (Sep). (J. Hutchens)
886 Books Abroad, 46, iii (Summer), 409-11. (J. Garrard)
887 Buffalo Courier-Express (8 Oct). (M. Russ)
888 Buffalo Evening News (30 Sep). (C. Brady)
889 Business Week (23 Sep).
890 Cedar Rapids Gazette (5 Nov). (P. Fleming)
891 Charlotte Observer (17 Oct). (H. Leland)
892 Chatanooga Times (8 Oct). (E. Ghignatti)
893 Chicago Daily News (8 Sep), Panorama, p. 8. (J. Friend)
894 Chicago Tribune Book World (17 Sep), 1. (H. Wolfe: "S.'s
Novel of the Decade")
895 Cincinnati Enquirer (14 Sep). (J. Weigel: "S.: Silenced in
Russia, May Be Overrated Here")
896 Citizen-Journal (Columbus, O.), 2 Oct, p. 4. (W. S. K.)
897 Clarion-Ledger (Jackson, Miss.), 29 Oct, p. 10D. (R. Isaacson)
898 Clearwater [Fla.] Sun (19 Nov), 3H. (A. McKenzie).
899 Cleveland Magazine (Nov), 93-4. (J. Amory)
900 Cleveland Press (15 Sep), 21. (K. Maxwell)
901 Coffeyville [Kan.] Journal (8 Oct). (R. M. S.)
902 Columbus [O.] Dispatch (1 Oct). (W. Harrington: "Prime S.
Pedestrian Reading")
903 Courier-Journal & Times (Louisville), 1 Oct, p. E7. (J.
Filiatreau)
904 Critic (Nov-Dec), 67-69. (P. Toynbee)
905 Daily Hampshire Gazette (Northampton, Mass.), 25 Oct. (L.
Tikos)
906 Daily Telegraph (London), 21 Sep. (D. Holloway: "Rivalling
Tolstoy?")
907 Dallas Morning News (24 Sep). (L. Tinkle)
908 Delaware Morning News (27 Sep). (P. Milford)
909 Delaware Valley Business Fortnight (9 Nov), 16. (J. Parks)
910 Denver Post (17 Sep). (S. Peckham)
911 Des Moines Sunday Register (17 Sep). (J. Bunke)
912 Detroit Free Press (17 Oct). (G. Whelan)
913 Detroit Jewish News (27 Oct), 7. ("Tsarist Anti-Semitism
as Well as World War I Russian Failures Reconstructed by S.")
914 Dominion-Post (Morgantown, W. Va.), 3 Dec, Panorama, p.
14. (J. Kershner)
915 Economist, 244 (23 Sep), 57. ("I am sorry for Russia")
916 Esquire, 78 (Nov), 30 & 32. (T. Solotaroff)
917 Express/News (San Antonio), 24 Sep. (S. Holmesby)
918 Fort Worth Star-Telegram (1 Oct), 6G. (L. Sanders)
919 Frederick [Md.] News-Post (16 Oct). (R. Lebherz)
920 Freedom News (Richmond, Cal.), Oct, p. 22. (T. Parkinson:
"Finest Fictional Narrative Since Thomas Mann")
921 Fresno Bee (17 Sep). (I. Olson)
922 Greenboro [N.C.] Daily News (8 Oct), E3. (R. Bulgin)
923 Groton [Conn.] News (18 Oct). (D. Stets)
924 Guardian (Manchester), 21 Sep, p. 14. (R. Williams: "Russia

Betrayed")
925 Hartford Courant (29 Oct). (R. Bolton)
926 Harvard Crimson (4 Oct). (D. Cramer)
927 Houston Chronicle (1 Oct). (D. Mares: "S....the Greatest?")
928 Houston Post (8 Oct), Spotlight, p. 34. (M. Brunsdale)
929 Independent-Journal (30 Sep), M20. (A. Dalbey)
930 Indianapolis Star (1 Oct). (R. Cady)
931 Jewish Daily Forward (N.Y.), 15 Oct. (M. Sticker) [In Yiddish]
932 Journal & Sentinel (Winston-Salem, N.C.), 1 Oct. (A. Tillett)
933 Kansas City Star (17 Sep). (T. Menn)
934 Kirkus (15 Aug), 973.
935 Labor Herald (Allentown, Pa.), 8 Nov. (T. Bruni)
936 LJ, 97 (15 Oct), 3334. (S. Haffner)
937 Lincoln [Neb.] Star (21 Sep). (C. Johnson)
938 Listener, 88, No. 2269 (21 Sep), 373-4. (J. Bayley: "The Guns of Tannenberg")
939 Long Island Catholic, 11, no. 20 (14 Sep), 1 & 13. (J. Murray: "'August 1914' will rewrite 'War and Peace'")
940 Los Angeles Times (24 Sep), [Book review section], p. 50. (R. Kirsch: "A. S. in Struggle with History") [Repr.: Roanoke Times (22 Oct), E17 and elsewhere]
941 Louisville Times (2 Oct), A13. (T. Pfeiffer)
942 Memphis Press-Scimitar (22 Sep). (V. Vawter)
943 Medford Mercury; Malden News; Melrose News (Mass.), 2 Oct. (A. Hayes & E. Hayes)
944 Mercury (Los Angeles), 15 Oct. (R. Seaton)
945 Miami Herald (24 Sep), 7H. (L. Donovan)
946 Milwaukee Journal (24 Sep). (M. Bikter: "A 'War and Peace' of 1917 and a New Biography Underscore the Importance of a Russian Writer" [also reviews Burg & Feifer (see 572)])
947 Minneapolis Tribune (17 Sep), 8D. (E. Gaines)
948 Minnesota Daily (25 Sep). (S. Suppan)
949 National Catholic Family Weekly (29 Oct). (J. Kennedy)
950 National Catholic Reporter (29 Sep), 9. (M. Murray: "S.: epic...but tedious")
951 National Fraternal Club News (15 Oct). (B. Stafford).
952 NatO (23 Sep). (B. Cook: "S.'s Earnest, but Tolstoy's Still on Top")
953 NatR, 24 (29 Sep), 1067-68. (F. Russell: "The Sweep of Greatness")
954 New Haven Register (17 Sep). (J. Childs)
955 NL, 55 (2 Oct), 16-17. (P. Bell: "S. Grappling with History")
956 NR, 167 (7 Oct), 27-32. (J. Laber: "Muted Echo of a Masterpiece")
957 NS, 84, No. 2166 (22 Sep), 391-92. (V. Pritchett: "War and the Futility of War")
958 New York Post (15 Aug). (J. Barkham) [Repr.: Daily Press (Newport News, Va.), 22 Oct.; Grand Rapids Press (17 Sep), and elsewhere]
959 NYRB, 19, v (5 Oct), 13-14. (P. Rahv: "In Dubious Battle")
960 NYT (6 Sep), 43. (C. Lehmann-Haupt: "S.'s War and Peace") [Repr., various titles: Seattle Post-Intelligencer (17 Sep); Norfolk Ledger-Star (15 Sep); Washington Star (15 Sep); This World

(Sunday magazine), 17 Sep; and elsewhere]

961 NYTBR (10 Sep), 1 & 48-51. (S. Karlinsky: "A New Departure for a Master")

962 New Yorker, 48 (14 Oct), 178-81. (N. Bliven: "Days that Shook the World")

963 News and Courier (Charlestown, S.C.), 1 Oct. (W. Thomas)

964 News and Leader (Springfield, Mo.), 17 Sep, p. A44. (C. Johnson)

965 News and Observer (1 Oct), IV, 6. (L. Hartley)

966 News-Journal (Daytona, Fla.), 5 Nov. (G. Pozetta)

967 Newsbeat (Queens Coll.), 19 Dec. (M. Cohen)

968 Newsweek, 80 (18 Sep), 105-06. (P. Prescott: "A Tolstoy of Our Time")

969 Observer Review (London), 17 Sep. (P. Toynbee: "Heavy Artillery") [see also 904]

970 Omaha World Herald (17 Sep). (V. P. H.)

971 Oregon Journal (Portland), 17 Sep, Sunday Oregonian, p. 17. (M. Bauer)

972 Orlando Sentinel (5 Nov), Florida Magazine, p. 38F. (G. Feifer)

973 Parade of Books (17 Sep). (R. Hollenbeck)

974 Patriot Ledger (Quincy, Mass.), 19 Oct, p. 42. (A. Hayes & E. Hayes) [Repr. of 943]

975 Peninsula Living (Redwood City, Cal.), 30 Sep. (M. Newman)

976 Philadelphia Sunday Bulletin (17 Sep). (E. Mossman)

977 Pittsburgh Post-Gazette (23 Sep). (J. Alexander)

978 Pittsburgh Press (17 Sep). (N. Knezevich)

979 Plain Dealer (Cleveland), 17 Sep. (C. McCarry)

980 Playboy, 19 (Nov), 24.

981 Post-Journal (Jamestown, N.Y.), p. 18. (L. Stanford)

982 Press Daily Enterprise (Riverside, Cal.), 3 Dec. (M. Schwartz)

983 Problems of Communism, 21 (Nov-Dec), 79-81. (R. Hingley: "Defeat at Tannenberg")

984 Providence Sunday Journal (17 Sep), H15. (M. Dolbier)

985 PubW (18 Sep), 43.

986 Sacramento Bee (24 Sep). (P. Freshwater)

987 Sacramento Union (8 Oct). (B. Forsyth: "A Rival for Tolstoy")

988 St. Louis Post-Dispatch (10 Sep), 4D. (E. Lehrman: "S.'s Masterful Story of a Russian Military Disaster")

989 San Francisco Chronicle (17 Jul). (W. Hogan: "S.--the New Tolstoy")

990 San Francisco Examiner (15 Sep), Book World. (J. Epstein)

991 SatR, 55 (Oct), 79-82, 88, 89-92, 96. (M. McCarthy: "The Tolstoy Connection")

992 Savannah News-Press (24 Sep), Sunday Magazine, p. 6F. (L. Powell: "S.'s 'War and Peace'")

993 Seattle Times (15 Oct). (M. Hermans)

994 Spectator, No. 7526 (23 Sep), 466-67. (R. Luckett)

995 Spectator, No. 7526 (23 Sep), 467-68. (Auberon Waugh)

996 Sun (Baltimore), 8 Oct. (L. Grant)

997 Sun-Times (Chicago), 10 Sep, Showcase-Book Week, p. 17. (G. Murray).

998 Sunday Chronicle Herald (Augusta, Ga.), 24 Sep, p. 10D. (R. Neal)

999 Sunday Journal & Star (Lincoln, Neb.), 1 Oct, Focus. (D. G.)

1000 <u>Sunday</u> <u>News</u> (Detroit), 10 Sep, p. 5F. (R. Werry)
1001 <u>Sunday</u> <u>Telegraph</u> (London), 17 Sep. (F. King: "In Tolstoy's
Shade")
1002 <u>Sunday</u> <u>Times</u> (London), 17 Aug. (J. Symons: "S.'s Requiem
for an Army")
1003 <u>Syracuse</u> <u>New</u> <u>Times</u> (9 Nov), 10. (E. Flaherty)
1004 <u>Tampa</u> <u>Tribune-Times</u> (15 Oct). (A. Holmes)
1005 <u>Tennessean</u> (Nashville), 1 Oct. (W. Parrill)
1006 <u>Time</u>, 100 (25 Sep), 89 & 93. (T. Foote: "Witness to Yesterday")
1007 <u>Times</u> (Erie, Pa.), 28 Sep. (E. Wellejus)
1008 <u>Times</u> (London), 21 Sep. (R. Holmes: "We must hold out un-
til evening")
1009 <u>TLS</u>, No. 3681 (22 Sep), 1086. ("Russia's Conscience")
1010 <u>Trentonian</u> (Nov). (O. Petrocelli)
1011 <u>Vermont</u> <u>Times-Reporter</u> (18 Sep). (A. Macneil)
1012 <u>Waco</u> <u>Tribune-Herald</u> (17 Sep). (G. Quill)
1013 <u>Wall</u> <u>Street</u> <u>Journal</u> (26 Sep). (E. Fuller: "S.: The Modern
Tolstoy?")
1014 <u>Washington</u> <u>Post</u> (17 Sep), <u>Book</u> <u>World</u>: M. Djilas, pp. 1 & 3;
J. Epstein, pp. 1 & 2.
1015 <u>Wesleyan</u> <u>Argus</u> (6 Oct). (D. White)
1016 <u>Women's</u> <u>Wear</u> <u>Daily</u> (13 Oct), 16. (R. Lesen)
1017 <u>Worcester</u> <u>Sunday</u> <u>Telegram</u> (1 Oct). (P. Edmunds)
1018 <u>World</u> (26 Sep), 54 & 56-7. (H. Gold: "S.: Question of Life
vs. Art")
1019 <u>Writers'</u> <u>Newsletter</u> (15 Sep), 3.

Additional reviews are to be expected in such journals as <u>Hud-
son</u> <u>Review</u>, <u>Russian</u> <u>Review</u>, <u>Slavic</u> <u>and</u> <u>East</u> <u>European</u> <u>Journal</u>,
<u>Slavic</u> <u>Review</u>, <u>Virginia</u> <u>Quarterly</u> <u>Review</u> and <u>Yale</u> <u>Review</u>. See
also review-articles and essays on <u>Avgust četyrnadcatogo</u>: 639,
647, 648, 670, 673, 677, 678, 681, 684, 685, 1286 (<u>TLS</u>) & 1461.
Also see 689a and: 1462-63, 1465-67, 1469-70, 1270, 1519-20.

7. Biography, news, "the Solzhenitsyn affair"

(i) Articles published in the <u>New</u> <u>York</u> <u>Times</u>

All articles listed in the <u>New</u> <u>York</u> <u>Times</u> <u>Index</u> as containing
references to S. are included here, with full titles; a dozen or
more additional articles mentioning S. were found and are listed
here as well, all in chronological order. Relatively unimport-
ant articles (with respect to S.) are so indicated if their titles do not make that fact clear. Some of the articles below are
listed elsewhere in this bibliography: book reviews, translations
of works by S. and so on. Usually the entry numbers of these
other listings are given.

1962

1020 Topping, S. "Easing of Curbs on Soviet Literature Is Attributed to Order by Khrushchev" (29 Nov), 4.
1021 "Magazine Ordered to Kill an Article" (14 Dec), 7. See 1673.

1963

1022 "2 Rival Publishers in N.Y. Offer New Soviet Novel"(16 Jan), 7.

1963

1023 Salisbury, H. "One Day . . ." (22 Jan), 7. [Rev., see 733]
1024 "Soviet Voids Pact for Sale of Novel" (1 Feb), 7.
1025 Slonim, M. "One Day . . ." (7 Apr), Book Rev., 4-5,34. [734]
1026 Underwood, P. "Hungarians Tell of Stalin's Camps: A Rash of Writings Follows 'Ivan Denisovich' Novel" (28 Apr), 31. [József Lengyel & Gyula Oszko]
1027 Salisbury, H. "'We Never Make Mistakes'" (1 Aug), 25. [Rev., see 762]
1028 Tanner, H. "Eased Line on Arts in Soviet Is Hinted by Two New Works" (18 Aug), 1 & 2. [Tvardovskij & S.]
1029 Shabad, T. "Russian Assailed for Short Story: S. Is Criticized for Portrayal of Official" (1 Sep), 7. [See 121]
1030 "Russian Defends Labor Camp Life" (13 Oct), 5. [See 125]
1031 Blake, P. "'We Never Make Mistakes'" (8 Dec), Book Rev., 6 & 40. [See 763]
1032 "69 Are Nominated for '63 Lenin Prize" (28 Dec), 4.

1964

1033 "Character in Novel Identified in Soviet" (15 Jan), 29. [See 151]
1034 "Russians Hint Novel Won't Get Big Prize" (12 Apr), 6. [See 168]
1035 Salisbury, H. "For the Good of the Cause" (12 Jul), Book Rev., 26. [See 779]
1036 "Soviet Magazine May Print New Novel by S." (5 Aug), 30.

1965

1037 Handler, M. "4 Russian Poems Introduced Here" (17 Jan), 68. [See 513]
1038 Shabad, T. "Soviet Author Scored on Prison Novel" (13 Mar), 5. [See 193]
1039 Carlisle, O. "Literary Life in Moscow" (14 Mar), Book Rev., 7, 52-53. (Brief mention of S.)
1040 "'Nihilist' Writing Worries Soviet: Press Rebukes Authors Who Are Popular with Young" (15 Aug), 21. (Brief mention)

1966

1041 "Russians Protest Writers' Jailings: 40 Petitioners Said to Include Prominent Figures" (16 Mar), 18. (Chiefly on Sinjavskij & Daniel)

1967

1042 Grose, P. "Soviet Liberal Poet Tells Foes: 'Don't Breathe Down My Neck'" (31 May), 10. (Brief mention of S.)
1043 Shabad, T. "Soviet Novelist Assails Censors: Letter to Writers' Session Urges the Abolition of All Restraints on Fiction" (5 Jun), 1 & 37. [See 30]
1044 "Quiet Soviet Author: Al. Is. S." (5 Jun), 36. (Biog.)
1045 "Text of S.'s Demand for End of Soviet Censorship" (5 Jun), 36. [See 547]
1046 "A Section Omitted from Soviet Text" (6 Jun), 4. [See 547]
1047 Grose, P. "Soviet Censors: A Writer Who Dared" (11 Jun), IV, 3. (Chiefly on S.)
1048 Handler, M. "Soviet May Bar Voznesensky Trip" (19 Jun), 29.
1049 Salisbury, H. "Russians Predicting End of Censorship" (14

Jul), 1 & 8.

1050 "Party is Accused by Czech Writers: 300 Intellectuals Reported to Implore West to Rescue Their 'Spiritual Freedom'" (4 Sep), 1 & 12. (S. among those appealed to)

1051 Kamm, H. "Soviet Is Silent on Any Widening of Freedoms" (16 Nov), 18. (S. pressed to sign disavowal of demands)

1052 Kamm, H. "Soviet Union: To Dissent, You'd Better Be Famous" (24 Dec), IV, 5.

1968

1053 Grose, P. "S. Again Defies Writers' Union" (13 Feb), 8. [See 550]

1054 "S. Work to Appear in London" (11 Apr), 11. [See 523]

1055 Gilroy, H. "Praeger to Issue New Soviet Novel" (26 Apr), 40. (Cancer Ward)

1056 Anderson, R. "S. Protests Plans for Publication of His Novel Abroad" (1 May), 18. [See 551]

1057 S[alisbury], H. "Moscow's Intellectuals: They Try to Make Themselves Heard, But the Regime Keeps Cracking Down" (5 May), IV, 8.

1058 Raymont, H. "S.'s Novels to Appear in West Over Russian's Protest" (11 Jun), 16.

1059 Marton, R. "S.'s Rights" (16 Jun), IV, 17. (Letter)

1070[sic] "Soviet Says Writer is Tool of the West" (27 Jun), 6. [See 207]

1071 Petrov, V. "Soviet Censorship of S." (30 Jun), IV, 13. (Letter)

1072 "S. Plea Sent to Podgorny" (15 Aug), 14. (Letter by Hochhuth and others)

1073 Lask, T. "First Circle" (11 Sep), 45. [Rev., see 805]

1074 Salisbury, H. "First Circle" (15 Sep), Book Rev., 1, 37-41. [See 806]

1075 Anderson, R. "Russia: At Home, Crackdown on the Intellectuals" (22 Sep), IV, 3. (Brief mention)

1076 Blake, P. "Cancer Ward" (27 Oct), Book Rev., 2-3. [See 842]

1077 Raymont, H. "Russian Émigrés Gain In Publishing: Religious Reprint House in Paris Carves a Niche" (30 Oct), 42. (Interview with I. Morozov, head of YMCA Press; ref. to Rak. korpus)

1078 Raymont, H. "Dial Press Faces Copyright Query: Its Edition of 'Cancer Ward' Disputed by Bodley Head" (12 Nov), 44.

1079 "Dial Press Defends Right to New Book" (14 Nov), 54.

1080 Kamm, H. "Soviet Is Denounced at Dissident's Rites" (15 Nov), 1. (Grigorenko also lauds S.)

1081 "First Circle" (1 Dec), Book Rev., 82. [See 806]

1082 "S. at Fifty" (11 Dec), 46. (Editorial)

1083 Grose, P. "Moscow Unrelenting in Blackout on S." (12 Dec), 4.

1969

1084 Lask, T. "Cancer Ward" (28 Feb), 37. [Rev., see 841]

1085 "Soviet Cancer Ward Novel Offered in 4 Versions Here" (1 Mar), 28.

1086 "S. Story Published by Time" (17 Mar), 2. [See 512]

1087 "American Academy of Arts Honors 3 Foreign Authors" (4 Apr), 31. (S. Spender, Yasunari Kawabata & S.)

1088 Fosburgh, L. "Art and Literary People Urged to Look Inward"

(22 May), 52. [See prev. entry; brief mention]

1089 Clarity, J. "Soviet Dissident Reported Moved" (5 Sep), 8. (Chiefly on Daniel)

1090 "3 Companies to Join in Film Production of 'Ivan Denisovich'" (2 Oct), 52.

1091 "S. Is Ousted by Soviet Writers' Local" (5 Nov), 3.

1092 "S. Ouster Is Denied by Union of Soviet Writers" (6 Nov), 4.

1093 Clarity, J. "S. Reported Ousted by Russian Writers: Action Follows His Removal from Hometown Local" (11 Nov), 12.

1094 "Soviet Confirms Ouster of Writer" (12 Nov), 18. [See 216]

1095 "Union Ousted a Defiant S." (13 Nov), 2. [See 556]

1096 Clarity, J. "S. Terms Soviet 'Sick Society'" (15 Nov), 1 & 11. [See 556]

1097 "Letter of Soviet Writer" (15 Nov), 11. [Text; see 556]

1098 "S. Play Banned by Russia, To Be Issued Here" (16 Nov), 13. [See 530]

1099 "No Problem" (16 Nov), 7.

1100 Clarity, J. "Russian Union Asserts 'No One' Bars S. Emigration" (26 Nov), 12. [See 218]

1101 Clarity, J. "Sholokhov Continues Soviet Attacks on S." (28 Nov), 3. [See 219]

1102 Clarity, J. "Russia: A Writer Is Told 'Get Out'" (30 Nov), IV, 7.

1103 "22 Soviet Writers Support Expulsion of S." (4 Dec), 9.

1104 "16 Western Intellectuals Score Soviet Attacks on S." (5 Dec), 47. [See Labedz (1285), pp. 197-8]

1105 Clarity, J. "Broadway Nudity Scored in Soviet" (12 Dec), 8. (Speaker S. Mixajlov also refers to S. [see 221a])

1106 "31 Writers Appeal to Soviet to Lift Bar to S." (19 Dec), 8. [See Labedz (1285), pp. 198-9]

1107 "Dissidents Protest S. Curb" (21 Dec), 18. [See 295]

1108 "Woman Dissenter's Arrest by the Russians is Reported" (25 Dec), 35. (N. Gorbanevskaja; brief mention of S.)

1109 "'Good Works' Urged for S." (27 Dec), 5. (Speech of Furtseva; also in Labedz [1285], 199-200)

1970

1110 Lee, J. "S. Novel Before Cameras" (13 Jan), 38.

1111 Funke, L. "Soviet Play Lives" (8 Feb), II, 1 & 8. [See 530 & note at 696]

1112 Gwertzman, B. "Soviet Quits European Writers' Group" (19 Feb), 8. [See 222]

1113 Gwertzman, B. "Soviet Halts Voznesensky Play Found Ideologically Unsound" (6 Mar), 10. (Brief mention of S.)

1114 Lewens, G. "Anti-Israeli Russians" (10 Mar), 42. (Letter)

1115 Bethell, N. "S. Can Still Write--He Just Can't Publish" (12 Apr), Magazine, pp. 36-7, 42, 44, 46, 50, 52, 54, 56, 59.

1116 Parry, A. "Samizdat? Da, Tovarich" (19 Apr), II, 1 & 3. (Ref. to "Love Girl", p. 3 [see 696])

1117 Kamm, B. "Re: Amalrik" (17 May), Magazine, p. 118. (Letter; brief mention of S.)

1118 Clarity, J. "Soviet Dissent Is Not Unified, But It Proves to Be Persistent" (14 Jun), 1 & 2. (Brief mention, p. 2)

1119 "S. Assails Detention of Medvedev in Mental Hospital" (17 Jun), 1 & 6. [See 531]

1120 "S.'s Statement" (17 Jun), 6. [Text; see 531]

1121 Gwertzman, B. "Soviet Yields on Dissenter But Not On Dissent" (21 Jun), IV, 2. (Release of Medvedev)

1122 "'Political Insanity'" (23 Jun), 42. (Editorial on above)

1123 Pontius, D. "Soviet Dissenters" (3 Jul), 24. (Letter)

1124 Szasz, T. "Psychiatry As Tactic" (25 Jul), 22. (Letter)

1125 Calta, L. "S. Play Coming" (7 Oct), 38. [See note at 696]

1126 "S. Is Awarded Nobel Prize in Literature" (9 Oct), 1 & 16.

1127 Gwertzman, B. "S. Is Willing to Go to Accept If Moscow Permits" (9 Oct), 16. [Quotes 557]

1128 "From the Prose of the Writer's Three Principal Works" (9 Oct), 16. [Brief excerpts from 500, 521 & 527]

1129 Clarity, J. "Unpublished at Home: Al. Is. S." (9 Oct), 16.

1130 Salisbury, H. "'The Only Living Soviet Classic'" (9 Oct), 16. (An appraisal; title quotes Evtušenko)

1131 "Biography Due Next Year" (9 Oct), 16. [See 573]

1132 "Nobel Award" (9 Oct), 36. (Editorial)

1133 "Nobel for a Soviet Author" (11 Oct), IV, 2.

1134 Clarity, J. " Dissidents Acclaim Award" (12 Oct), 5. [See 303]

1135 "Cablegram from S." (12 Oct), 5. [See 558]

1136 "Criticized at Home" (17 Oct), 2. (Brief quote from Novosti press agency under photo of S.)

1137 Barnes, C. "Stage: S.'s Play" (18 Oct), 94. [See note at 696; factual error in this review corrected by Barnes in his column of 19 Oct, p. 48.]

1138 "Novosti Press Agency on the Award of the Nobel Prize for Literature to Al. S." (24 Oct), 31.

1139 Mihajlov, M. "The Artist As the Enemy" (24 Oct), 31. [Mentions S.; Russ. tr. at 462]

1140 Kerr, W. "S.'s Vision of Man's Adaptability" (25 Oct), II, 1. [Review of première perf. of play; see note at 696]

1141 Weiler, A. "Filming Slated for 'First Circle' By S." (6 Nov), 50.

1142 Slonim, M. "Solzhenitsyn" (8 Nov), Book Rev., p. 56. (On reception of Nobel Prize announcement in Europe)

1143 Clarity, J. "Letter by Rostropovich Defends Nobel Award for S." (13 Nov), 1 & 8. [See 1146]

1144 Gwertzman, B. "Soviet Arts: Restraints Persist" (14 Nov), 6.

1145 Smith, R. "U.S.I.A Chief Sees a Soviet Ferment" (14 Nov), 6. (Frank J. Shakespeare, Jr.; includes comment on S.)

1146 Rostropovich, M. "An Open Letter to Pravda" (16 Nov), 37. [Text; see 305]

1147 "Imprisoned Soviet Words" (17 Nov), 44. (Editorial on above)

1148 Gwertzman, B. "Soviet Party Official Says the West Spurs Dissidence" (20 Nov), 3. [See 227a]

1149 Salisbury, H. "Soviet Union: Voice of an 'Unperson' Creates Worldwide Interest" (22 Nov), IV, 4. (Quotes Khrushchev more or less in support of S.)

1150 Gwertzman, B. "S. Shuns Nobel Trip" (28 Nov), 1 & 8. [See 559]

1151 "S.'s Hard Decision" (28 Nov), 26. (Editorial)

1152 Gwertzman, B. "S. Explains Change in Plans" (1 Dec), 10. [See 559]

1153 "Novelist's Letter on the Nobel Prize" (1 Dec), 10. [Text;

see 559]

1154 Gwertzman, B. "Why a Nobel Winner Will Stay at Home" (6 Dec), IV, 5.

1155 S. "City on the Neva" (10 Dec), 47. [See 515]

1156 Miller, A. "Banned in Russia" (10 Dec), 47. (Letter)

1157 Lewis, A. "S. Hailed Despite Absence At Presentation of 1970 Nobel Awards" (11 Dec), 3.

1158 Gwertzman, B. "S. Joins 'Rights Committee'"(11 Dec), 3. (Committee for Human Rights, founded 11 Nov by Andrej D. Saxarov with Andrej N. Tverdoxlebov and Valerij N. Čalidze)

1159 Lewis, A. "Notes from Underground" (12 Dec), 31. (Partly on book by Labedz [see 1285])

1160 "S. Said to Send Autobiography to Nobel Unit" (13 Dec), 84.

1161 Reston, J. "Pravda's 'Spiritual Emigrants'" (18 Dec), 39.

1162 "Dissidents in S. U. Are Facing a Crackdown" (18 Dec), 1 & 9.

1163 Sidorsky, D. "Miller Disputed on S." (26 Dec), 16. [See 1156]

1164 "New Attack Made on S." (27 Dec), 17. [See 230]

1165 "'Renegades...Begging Whisky': Pravda's Views on S. and Other Liberal Writers" (29 Dec), 29. [See 229]

1971

1166 "Rostropovich Drops 2 Helsinki Concerts Amid Air of Mystery" (14 Jan), 45. (Brief mention of S.)

1167 "Rostropovich Forced Again to Cancel Concert Abroad" (20 Jan), 7.

1168 Gwertzman, B. "6-Month Curb on Travel by Rostropovich Reported" (23 Jan), 7.

1169 "Concert by Rostropovich in Philadelphia Canceled," (30 Jan), 33.

1170 "Nobel Money Deposited in S. Account" (2 Feb), 6.

1171 "Rostropovich Cancels Again" (4 Feb), 6.

1172 Gwertzman, B. "Moscow Expels Foreign Newsman: Scandinavian Had Contact with S." (10 Feb), 7. (Per E. Hegge)

1173 "Leonid S. Sobolev, Critic, Conservative Leader Among Soviet Writers Dies" (18 Feb), 38. (Criticism of S. noted)

1174 "Rostropovich Is Expected at British Festival in 1972" (10 Mar), 10.

1175 Gwertzman, B. "S. Said to Seek Publisher for New Novel" (14 Apr), 6.

1176 Paper, H. "U.S.S.R. Limbo for Zand" (4 May), 46. (Letter to ed. on M. I. Zand; brief mention of S.)

1177 "Jewish Scholar to Leave Soviet" (11 May), 6. (M. I. Zand)

1178 Greenspun, R. "Film 'Ivan Denisovich' Best at Long Distance" (17 May), 40.

1179 Hess, J. "S.'s Novel Published in Paris" (12 Jun), 27.

1180 "The Writers" (13 Jan), IV, 5. (Note on Avg. čet.)

1181 "An Author's Appeal" (16 Jun), 45. [Text; see 533]

1182 Gwertzman, B. "Soviet Stand on S. Awaited" (19 Jun), 4.

1183 Krebs, A. "Notes on People: A Poet Remembered" (23 Jun), 53. (Chiefly on Tvardovskij; brief)

1184 Belliveau, D. [Letter] (25 Jun), 34. (On censorship in both U.S. & S.U.)

1185 Gwertzman, B. "Soviet Aide Calls for Orthodoxy in Arts" (30 Jun), 4. [See 231a]

1186 "S.'s Life" (4 Jul), IV, 11. [Text; see 534]

1187 Raymont, H. "Farrar Straus Gets S. Book" (6 Jul), 26.
1188 Blake, P. "' My Hands Are Burning '" (11 Jul), IV, 3. (On Avg. čet.)
1189 Locke, R. "S.'s Short Fiction" (26 Jul), 22. [Rev., see 874]
1190 Mihajlov, M. "Thoughts on Society: III" (28 Jul), 35. (Brief mention of S.)
1191 "London House Fights Copyright of S.'s 'August 1914'" (9 Aug), 26. (Flegon Press vs. YMCA Press, Paris)
1192 Gwertzman, B. "Sick of K. G. B. Spying, S. Says" (15 Aug), 1 & 24. [See 561; excerpts]
1193 "K.G.B. Spying and Brutality" (16 Aug), 26. (Editorial)
1194 Gwertzman, B. "Notes from the Russian Underground" (22 Aug), 1. (Western newsmen given 11 of more than 70 issues of samizdat periodical, Politiceskij Dnevnik, 1964-1971, some referring to S. [see 249a & 296a])
1195 Gwertzman, B. "The K.G.B. Says Local Police Beat Up S.'s Friend" (10 Sep), 12. (A. Gorlov; see 1192)
1196 "Swedish Rebuff to S. Scored" (13 Sep), 2. (On book by Hegge [see 2295])
1197 "Sweden and S." (14 Sep), 40. (Editorial; in Russ. at 475]
1198 Palme, O. "Sweden, S. and Diplomacy" (17 Sep), 42. (Letter replying to 1197 by Swed. Pr. Min.; in Russ. at 475)
1199 Clarity, J. "Notes on People" (18 Sep), 24. (Brief)
1200 Hegge, P. "The Rebuff of S." (24 Sep), 40. (Letter refuting 1198)
1201 Smith H. "Menuhin, at Moscow Music Congress, Calls for Open Emigration" (8 Oct), 10. (Also praises S.)
1202 "S. May Get Medal" (8 Oct), 10.
1203 Shabad, T. "Menuhin Reports Soviet Music Acquires a New Sophistication" (11 Oct), 2. (Brief mention of S.)
1204 "Neruda, Chilean Poet-Politician, Wins Nobel Prize in Literature" (22 Oct), 1 & 34. (Ref. to S. & controv. over Nobel award, p. 34.)
1205 S. "This Is How We Live" (7 Nov), Magazine, p. 116. [Reprint of 1120; see 531]
1206 Raymont, H. "Store Here Withdraws Pirated S. Book" (7 Dec), 54. (Ger. ed'n. [see entry 1963])
1207 Schonberg, H. "Rostropovich Cello Speaks Eloquently" (10 Dec), 50. (Brief mention)
1208 Shabad, T. "Defense of S. Seen in Two Works by Poet Who Voted to Expel Him from Writers' Union in '69" (12 Dec), 4. (E. Markin; see 231b)
1209 "Tvardovsky, Liberal Editor, Dies" (19 Dec), 60.
1210 Weiler, A. "Cinematic Circle" (19 Dec), 20. (On film Circle)
1211 Smith, H. "S. Goes to Tvardovsky Rites" (22 Dec), 1 & 9.
1212 Smith, H. "S. Suggests Small Nobel Ceremony Be Held in Moscow" (24 Dec), 2. [See 562]
1213 "Text of S. Letter to Swedish Academy" (24 Dec), 2. [See 562]
1214 "Poet Is Reported Curbed in Soviet: Writers' Union Said To Oust Backers of S." (30 Dec), 22. (Evg. Markin)
1215 "Solution for S.?" (31 Dec), 18. (Editorial)

1972

1216 "Soviet Playwright Expelled by Union" (4 Jan), 6. (A. A. Galič [Ginzburg])

1217 "S. to Get Nobel in Private in Moscow" (5 Jan), 3.
1218 "Writers' Union in Soviet Assails S. Novel" (12 Jan), 8.
[See 232]
1219 "Welcome to Miss Furtseva" (15 Jan), 30. (Editorial
urges F. to issue writings of S.)
1220 Smith, H. "Soviet is Said to Ban Dissident Journal" (4 Feb),
3. (On Xronika Tekuščix Sobytij)
1221 "New Attack on S. Reported" (9 Feb), 5. (By prosecutor in
trial of V. K. Bukovskij)
1222 "Yugoslav Writer Given Jail Term: Mihajlov Gets 30 Days for
Publishing in the Times" (10 Feb), 11. [See 1139]
1223 "Mihajlov Sentence Is Protested Here" (11 Feb), 10.
1224 S. "Lament for Tvardovsky" (12 Feb), 29. [See 535]
1225 Sosin, G. "Then Came Galich's Turn" (12 Feb), 29. (Brief)
1226 "5 Russians Protest Attacks on Dissenters" (9 Mar), 4.
(Brief mention)
1227 Smelyakov, Ya. "Tvardovsky--Man and Poet" (11 Mar), 28.
(Letter by Sov. poet protesting 1224)
1228 Zebot, C. "Stalinist Roots in Yugoslavia" (21 Mar), 40.
(Letter; chiefly on Mihajlov)
1229 "Church Accused by S: He Says Russian Orthodoxy Neglects
Its Flock" (23 Mar), 7. [See 536]
1230 "A Russian Speaks Out Again" (26 Mar), IV, 7. [See 536]
1231 Raymont, H. "S. to Get '70 Nobel in Private in Moscow April
9" (28 Mar), 2.
1232 Smith, H. "S. Tells of Struggle to Write Despite Soviet
Pressures" (3 Apr), 1 & 10. [See 563]
1233 "Writer Shows Reliance on Advice from Wife" (3 Apr), 10.
1234 "Excerpts from the Transcript of the Conversation with S.
in Moscow" (3 Apr), 10. [See 563]
1235 "S. Speaks" (4 Apr), 42. (Editorial)
1236 "Moscow Refuses Swede a Visa to Give Award to S." (5 Apr),
1 & 7. (K. R. Gierow)
1237 "Still No Nobel" (6 Apr), 42. (Editorial)
1238 Nicholson, M. "Soviet Writers" (6 Apr), 42. (Letter; protests 1227)
1239 "S. May Get Nobel Prize in Embassy" (6 Apr), 87. (Statement by Swed. For. Min. K. Wickman)
1240 Smith, H. "S. Still Hopes to Receive His Nobel Prize in
Ceremony" (7 Apr), 3.
1241 Smith, H. "Attacks Renewed on S.: New Book Insults Russians,
Soviet Press Asserts" (8 Apr), 7. [See 234]
1241a "'It's a Shame'" (8 Apr), 7. [See 564]
1241b "Lawyer's Visa Cancelled" (8 Apr), 7. (Fritz Heeb)
1242 "S. Hints Hope Gone on Nobel" (9 Apr), 5. [See 565]
1243 Smith, H. "S.: Again the Penalty of Frank Talk" (9 Apr),
IV, 4.
1244 "S. Rules Out Nobel Award in Private" (10 Apr), 22. [See
565]
1245 "Press Attacks on S. Go On" (13 Apr), 6. [See 235]
1246 Raymont, H. "S.'s Nobel Dispute Called 'a Big Bore' by Neruda" (16 Apr), 10.
1247 Lelyveld, J. "3 Soviet Debaters Begin U. S. Tour" (20 Apr),
47. (Brief mention)
1248 Lask, T. "Poets' Group Here Assails Neruda: Chilean Criti-

cized for Stance on Plight of S." (21 Apr), 23.

1249 Epstein, Julius. "Neruda's Comments" (5 May), 40. (Letter)

1250 Brown, L. "Writers and Governments" (24 May), 46. (Letter)

1251 Semple, R. "Soviet Minister of Culture Says S. Opposes 'Our Entire Society'" (25 May), 13. (Furtseva on S.)

1252 Tsevat, M. "Decision on Ezra Pound" (7 Jun), 44. (Brief mention of S.)

1253 Van Gelder, L. "Notes on People" (7 Jul), 13. (Brief)

1254 Clarity, J. "Notes on People" (18 Jul), 39. (On recent statement of V. Turkina [see 1264])

1255 "S. Nobel Lecture Published; It Denounces Soviet Union and the UN" (25 Aug), 1 & 2.

1256 "Excerpts from Nobel Lecture by S." (25 Aug), 2.

1257 "The Nobel Speech Is Reported to be Redraft of Mild Version" (25 Aug), 2.

1258 "S.'s Credo" (27 Aug), IV, 14. (Editorial)

1259 "Group Formed in U.S. to Protest Soviet Treatment of S." (29 Aug), 2.

1260 Lehmann-Haupt, C. "S.'s War and Peace" (6 Sep), 43. (Rev. of Aug. 1914 [see 960]

1261 Karlinsky, S. "A New Departure for a Master" (10 Sep), Book Review, pp. 1, 48-51. (Aug. 1914; see 960)

1262 "S.: Writer Caught Between" (10 Sep), Book Rev., p. 49. (Signed: Editor)

1263 Shub, A. "The Escalation of Soviet Dissent--and of Soviet Repression" (10 Sep), Magazine, pp. 31, 92-94. (On samizdat)

1264 Turkina, V. "The Subject Objected: The Guest Word" (17 Sep), Book Rev., p. 55. (Trans. by A. Klimoff from Russ. [492])

1265 Jellinek, R. "August 1972: The Last Word" (24 Sep), Book Rev., p. 63. (Quotes M. Glenny, defending self against criticism of Karlinsky [see 1261])

1266 S. "Art for Man's Sake [Parts I & II]," tr. T. Whitney (30 Sep), 31 & (7 Oct), 33. [Nobel lecture; see 540]

1267 Clarity, J. "Notes on People" (3 Oct), 53. (Notes birth of S.'s son, Ignat)

1268 Feifer, G. "S." (8 Oct), Book Rev., p. 36. (Reply to 1264)

1269 Clarity, J. "Notes on People" (21 Oct), 41. (Metropolitan Juvenaly of Tula, at a meeting in Athens, criticizes S.'s letter to Pimen [see 536])

1269a Leyfell, A. "S.'s SOS--Is It Falling on Deaf Ears?" (25 Oct), 46. (Letter)

1270 Smith, H. "S.'s New Book is Reviewed by the Russian Underground" (20 Nov), 14. [See 243]

1271 "Excerpts from Unofficial Reviews of 'August 1914'" (20 Nov), 14. (Includes quote from letter of Ž. Medvedev to I. Melež on Larni's article about Avg. čet. [see 233]) [See 318a]

1272 Smith, H. "Soviet Annual Honors Silenced Poets" (6 Dec), 40. (Brief mention of S.)

1273 "S. Would Take Loan from American" (18 Dec), 14. (Albert Maltz offers S. royalty money; see 53a)

1273a Gent, G. "Two More U. S. Novelists Come to Aid of S." (21 Dec), 28. (R. P. Warren & B. Malamud)

1973

1273b Vladimirov, S. "S.: A Financial 'Statement'" (8 Jan), 39.

(Letter; S. V. is a commentator for Novosti Press Agency)
  1274 Smith, H. "S. Is Denied a Divorce, But Renews Attempt" (9
Jan), 8.
  1274a Medvedev, Zhores. "In Defense of S." (26 Feb), 31. (Letter sent from London, where engaged in research, in reply to
1273b)

(ii) Biography, news, "the Solzhenitsyn affair": a. Articles and
    documents in books stressing politics over literature

  1275 Hayward, M. & E. Crowley, eds. Soviet Literature in the
Sixties: An International Symposium [Sep 1963]. New York/ Lon-
don: Praeger (for the Institute for the Study of the USSR), 1964.
221 pp. Contents include the following:
  Rzhevsky, L. "The New Idiom," 55-80 [see pp. 68, 75-77].
  Rubin, B. "Highlights of the 1962-63 Thaw," 81-99 [see pp. 89,
    92-93, 95 & 97].
  Benno, P. "The Political Aspect," 178-202 [see pp. 179, 183,
    189, 191-3, 196, 200-201].
  Also see pp. 12, 14, 45, 48, 50, 118, 139 & 206.

  1276 Whitney, T. "Russian Literature and Soviet Politics," pp.
3-51, as an introduction to: The New Writing in Russia, tr. T.
Whitney. Ann Arbor: U. of Michigan Press, 1964.
  1277 Conquest, R. Russia After Khrushchev. New York: Praeger,
1965. 267 pp. (see pp. 62, 100).
  1278 Johnson, Priscilla. Khrushchev and the Arts: The Politics
of Soviet Culture, 1962-1964. Cambridge, Mass.: MIT Press, 1965.
Contents include:
  "L'affaire Solzhenitsyn," 70-78.
  "Controversy over Solzhenitsyn," 271-88:
  V. Chalmaev, "Saints and Devils," 272-75 [tr. of 122]
  V. Lakshin, "Ivan Denisovich, His Friends and Foes," 275-88
    [tr. of 145].
  See also pp. 4-6, 10, 20, 25, 36, 70, 95, 118, 124, 156, 187,
195, 212, 213 & 216.

  1279 Mihajlov, M. "Lakshin and Solzhenitsyn," pp. 126-28 in his
Moscow Summer, tr. editors of New Leader. New York: Farrar,
Straus & Giroux, 1965. (See also pp. 23, 33, 66, 202) Repr.:
Labedz (1285), pp. 55-56. [Tr. of 2433; in Russian at 437]
  1280 Linden, C. Khrushchev and the Soviet Leadership, 1957-1964.
Baltimore, Md.: Johns Hopkins Press, 1966. See pp. 148, 160,
217, 223-24.

  1281 Vladimirov, L. The Russians. New York: Praeger, 1968. See
pp. 176-8 [repr. in Labedz (1285), pp. 59-60] and pp. 106 & 218.

  1282 Shub, A. The New Russian Tragedy. New York: W. W. Norton,
1969. 128 pp. See pp. 19, 21, 61, 63 & 112.

  1283 Werth, A. Russia: Hopes and Fears. New York: Simon and
Schuster, 1969. See pp. 83, 142-4, 186, 265, 271-74, 278-83,
285, 287, 293, 299, 332; in particular: "Literature in Transi-
tion," pp. 255-305.

  1284 Brumberg, A., ed. In Quest of Justice: Protest and Dis-

sent in the Soviet Union Today. New York: Praeger, 1970. 476pp.
The following chapters, all translations of Russian documents,
relate to S. [all but Chap. 90 are repr. from 1347]:
  49. S. to the Fourth Congress of Soviet Writers, 245-50 [tr. of
      250].
  50. Antokolsky to Demichev, 251 [tr. of 253].
  51. S. to Writers' Union (12 Sep 1967), 252-3 [tr. of 261].
  52. Secretariat Meeting with S. (22 Sep 1967), 253-69 [tr. of 262].
  53. Zimianin on S. et al, 269-71 [tr. of 263].
  54. Writers' Union to S. [25 Nov 1967], 271 [tr. of 265].
  55. S. to Writers' Union [1 Dec1967], 271-72 [tr. of 266].
  56. Tvardovsky to Fedin [7-15 Jan 1968], 272-79 [tr. of 267].
  57. Kaverin to Fedin [25 Jan 1968], 279-81 [tr. of 269].
  58. S. to Lit. Gazeta [21 Apr 1968], 281 [tr. of 273].
  59. S. to Writers and Newspapers [18 Apr 1968], 282 [tr. of 272].
  60. S. to Writers' Union Members [16 Apr 1968], 283 [tr. of 271].
  61. Speech by G. Svirsky [16 Jan 1968], 283-90 [tr. of 268].
  90. Attack on S. (from Lit. Gazeta), 391-98 [tr. of 207].

1285 Labedz, L., ed. Solzhenitsyn: A Documentary Record. New
York: Harper & Row; Canada: Longman, 1971. 229 pp. "Foreword"
by H. Salisbury, pp. ix-xv; "Introduction" by Labedz, pp. xvi-
xxiv; comments and notes throughout text, esp. pp. 1, 39, 57,
145, 161, 209. (Also, London: Allen Lane The Penguin Press,
1970. xvi, 182 pp.; 1972. 264 pp.; and Bloomington: Indiana Uni-
versity Press, 1973--with Nobel lecture and other new material.)
[French translation: see 1919]
Contents, 1971 ed'n. [note: most trans. items are excerpts only]:
"S.'s rehabilitation (6 Feb 1956)," 3 [tr. of 238].
"A biographical note on S. (28 Nov 1962)," 5 [tr. of 59].
"Visiting S. in Ryazan (25 Jan 63)," 5-9 [tr. of 88].
"One Day With S.--An Interview, by Pavel Ličko (31 Mar 1967),"
   10-14 [tr. of 1604].
"Alexander Tvardovsky's Preface to One Day (Nov 1962)," 15-16
   [tr. of 54].
"Soviet reviews of One Day," 17-20 [tr. of 55, 84, 57, 87, 90].
"How people read One Day: A survey of letters, by Al. S.," 21-
   37 [tr. of 246]
"Khrushchev on S. (12 Mar 1963)," 41 [tr. of 97].
"Meeting of Moscow writers (19 Mar 1963)," 41-42 [tr. of 99].
"Attacks on S. (22 Mar & 2 Apr 1963)," 42-43 [tr. of 101, 109].
"Tvardovsky on S. (12 May 1963)," 43-4 [tr. of 115].
"The battle over S. reopens (31 Aug-26 Dec 1963)," 44-53 [tr.
   of 121, 127, 128, 123, 134, 136].
"The Lenin Prize for S.? (28 Dec 1963-11 Apr 1964)," 53-54 [tr.
   of 138 & 168].
"Tvardovsky looks back (Jan 1965)," 54-5 [tr. of 190].
"Mihajlo Mihajlov: 'Moscow Summer 1964' An Interview with V. I.
   Lakshin (Jan 1965)," 55-56 [see 1279].
"S.'s manuscripts seized (Oct 1965)," 59-60 [repr. of 1281].
"Moscow writers on Cancer Ward (17 Nov 1966)," 60-80 [tr. of 248].
"Jaures Medvedev on the fate of S.'s wife," 80-81 [tr. of 447,
   I, pp. 31-33].
"S.'s open letter to the Fourth Soviet Writers' Congress (16
   May 1967), " 82-87 [tr. of 250].

1285 (contents, cont'd.)

"S.'s statement (8 Oct 1970)" 211 [tr. of 42].
"French communists on S. (9 & 14 Oct 1970)," 211-212 [tr. of
    1888 & 1898].
"Sympathy from Italian communists (9 & 16 Oct 1970)," 212-13
    [tr. of 2207 & 2211].
"S.'s telegram to Dr. Karl Ragnar Gierow (11 Oct 1970)," 214
    [tr. of 43].
"Letter from 37 Soviet intellectuals congratulating S. (10 Oct
    1970)," 214-15 [tr. of 303].
"Soviet official reactions (10, 14 & 17 Oct 1970)," 215-18 [tr.
    of 223, 224 & 225; repr. of 1415a; tr. of 226].
"The Swedish Academy to Literaturnaya Gazeta (19 Oct 1970)," 218
    [LG did not publish the letter].
"Congratulations from a prison camp, 219 [tr. of 302].
"Lukacs on S. (15-21 Oct 1970)," 219-20 [tr. from Fr. (see 1907)
    itself an excerpt from a text written much earlier (see 1871 &
    2052)].
"Rostropovich's open letter (31 Oct 1970)," 220-223 [repr. of
    1146 (tr. of 305)].
"S. to the Swedish Academy (27 Nov 1970)," 223-4 [repr. of 1153
    (tr. of 44); Labedz has 1 Dec by mistake].
"Message from S. (9 Dec 1970)," 225 [tr. of 45].
"Address at the Nobel Festival by Dr. Karl Ragnar Gierow (10 Dec
    1970)," 225-7 [in Russ. at 429; not listed elsewhere in this
    bibliography in English].
"A renewed attack (17 Dec 1970)," 228-9 [tr. of 229].

1286 Reviews of Labedz:
  Economist, 237 (12 Dec 1970), 61.
  Louisville Times (2 Sep 1971), A9. (T. Pfeiffer)
  LJ, 96 (1 Sep 1971), 2645. (H. Kublin)
  NR, 165 (16 Oct 1971), 30. (P. Blake)
  RusR, 31, ii (Apr 1972), 200-01. (N. Pashin)
  SatR, 54 (4 Dec 1971), 54-58. (M. Friedberg)
  TLS (15 Oct 1971), 1271-2. ("Peace and war: S.'s New Novel":
    also reviews Avg. čet. & Nivat & Aucouturier [see 1918])

1286a Aleksandr Solzhenitsyn, Rabrindranath Tagore, Sigrid Und-
set, William Butler Yeats. New York: Gregory (Nobel Prize Library), 1971. 360 pp. Biography. [Have not seen this]

1287 Koutaissoff, E. The Soviet Union. London: Ernest Benn,
1971. 288 pp. See pp. 239-40.

1288 Medvedev, Zhores. The Medvedev Papers: Fruitful Meetings
Between Scientists of the World; Secrecy of Correspondence is
Guaranteed by Law, tr. V. Rich (foreword by J. Ziman). London:
Macmillan; New York: St. Martins Press, 1971. [Russ. tr. at 447]
See pp. 35-43, 289, 292, 379-380 & elsewhere [pp. 35, 36, 38 cor-
respond to excerpt in Labedz (1285), pp. 80-81; on pp. 379-80 is
letter by S. with reply (see 554a)]

1289 Medvedev, Zhores A. & Roy A. Medvedev. A Question of Mad-
ness, tr. Ellen de Kadt. New York: Alfred A. Knopf; London: Macmillan, 1971; New York: Random House (Vintage), 1972. All 223 pp.
See pp. 135-36 (letter by S. [see 531]). [Book is in Russ.: 464]
1290 Reddaway, Peter, tr. & ed. Uncensored Russia. New York:

American Heritage Press, 1972 (also pub. in England). 496 pp.
Text includes trans. of first eleven issues of samizdat periodical, The Chronicle of Current Events [Xronika Tekuščix Sobytij].
See pp. 335-349: "Alexander Solzhenitsyn"; contents: Comment by
Reddaway, pp. 335-6; tr. of 279, pp. 336-8; tr. of 286, pp. 338-
39; tr. of 286a, p. 339; tr. of 297, pp. 339-349. [Have not seen
this; information from H. Hatfield [see 699)]

1291 Rothberg, A. The Heirs of Stalin: Dissidence and the Soviet
Regime, 1953-1970. Ithaca: Cornell U. Press, 1972. See following chapters:
  5 "Denisovich's Day," 55-60.
  8 "Matryona's House," 85-102.
  9 "For the Good of the Cause," 103-116.
  10 "The Lenin Prize," 117-123.
  16 "Solzhenitsyn and Glavlit," 192-203.
  18 "Solzhenitsyn's Ordeal," 218-32.
  27 "The Nobel Prize," 349-59.
See also pp. 13, 29, 33, 73, 127, 134, 159, 165-66 & 189.

1292 Reviews of Rothberg:
  Choice, 9 (Jun 1972), 568.
  LJ, 97 (1 Jan 1972), 70.
  NYTBR (23 Jul 1972), 6.
  PubW, 210 (17 Jan 1972), 51.
  RusR, 32, i (Jan 1973), 85-6. (W. Leonard)

See also 1329, 1355, 1397 and Rothberg (569), Björkegren (570),
Burg & Feifer (571) and Scammell (573). For books in languages
other than English which deal wholly or in part with the "Solzhenitsyn affair" see: 237, 428-431, 1918-19, 1955, 1957-59, 2053,
2119, 2190 (plus translations), 2295, 2397 and 2455.

(ii) Biography, news, "the Solzhenitsyn affair": b. Articles and
    documents in periodicals other than the New York Times

    Most of the information listed below was taken from secondary
sources; for probable content of many of the items, see notes at
New York Times entries (1020-1274) near the same date. For likely dates of important articles not listed here, in such periodicals as the Washington Post or the London Times, see New York
Times entries. Abbreviations used: BISUSSR: Bulletin of the In-
stitute for the Study of the USSR; CSM: Christian Science Moni-
tor; IHT: International Herald Tribune (Paris); NatO: National
Observer; NatR: National Review; NYHT: New York Herald Tribune;
PC: Problems of Communism; PubW: Publishers' Weekly; RusR: Rus-
sian Review; SatR: Saturday Review; TLS: Times (London) Literary
Supplement. Note that the following, as listed here, are all
London newspapers: Daily Mail; Daily Telegraph; Sunday Times; &
Times; and that Guardian indicates the Manchester Guardian.

1962

1293 "One Day," New Statesman, 64 (23 Nov), 729.
1294 Hingley, R. "A New Voice Out of Siberia," Sunday Times
(2 Dec).
1295 "Connoisseur Speaks," Time, 80 (14 Dec), 26.

1296 "A Newer World," TLS (4 Jan), 3.
1297 "Rival Versions of Russian Novel Go Down to the Wire," PubW, 183 (14 Jan), 47.
1298 "Neck and Neck," TLS (1 Feb), 77. (Same as 1297)
1299 "Soviets Say Contract for S. Novel is Void," PubW, 183 (4 Feb), 48-49.
1300 "Out in the Cold (Complexities Stirred Up by the Publication of 'One Day in the Life of Ivan Denisovich')," TLS (8 Feb), 93.
1301 Jaesrich, H. "'One Day'," TLS (8 Feb), 93. (Letter)
1302 Grosvenor, Peter. "Khrushchev's blue-eyed boy teaches Russia a new Stalin lesson," Daily Express (London), 13 Feb.
1303 Bukhanov, V. "Visiting Al. S. in Ryazan," Moscow News (16 Feb). [Tr. of 88]
1304 "Three (at least) paperback S.'s on the market," PubW, 183 (25 Feb), 38-39.
1305 "Soviet Author Must Rewrite First Play," NYHT (26 Mar). (Olen' accepted by "Sovremennik" Theater in Moscow, pending revision.)
1306 Gaev, A. "Telling the Grim Truth," BISUSSR, 10 (Apr).
1307 Labedz, L. "'Soviet Art Must Be Beautiful': A Chronicle of the Chill," Partisan Review, 30, i (Spring), 99-108. (On Khrushchev and the arts; mentions S. pp. 100-01)
1308 Johnson, P. "The Regime and the Intellectuals," PC [Special Suppl.], 4 (Jul-Aug), pp. ii-x.
1309 "Soviet Critics on Al. S.," Soviet Literature, 9 (Sep), 141-44. (Brief quotes from a dozen or more critics)
1310 "A Kind of Teaching," TLS (27 Sep), 747. (On PD)
1311 "Russia's Writers: After Silence, Human Voices," Time, 82 (20 Dec), 82-3.

1312 Conquest, R. & R. Hingley & G. Urban. "Khrushchev and the Intellectuals: A Discussion," East Europe, 13, ii, pp. 2-14.
1313 "Prison Camp Book Controversy," Times (22 Feb), 7.
1314 "Pravda blow to 'Denisovich': Chance of Lenin Prize fades," Times (16 Apr), 12.
1315 Pallon, V. "Hello, Commander," USSR (Jun), 54-55. [Tr. of 150]

1316 Marchenko, A. "New Features in Contemporary Literature (Review of Discussions)," Soviet Literature, 2 (Feb), 148-54. (See pp. 149-50)
1317 "Russian Writers Under Fire," Times (16 Aug), 6.
1318 "'Pravda' Hits 'Izvestia' on Arts Policy," Times (10 Sep), 8.
1319 Kariakin, Iu. "An Episode in the Current Battle of Ideas," Soviet Review, 6, iii (Autumn), 21-31. [Tr. of 180]

1320 Daily Telegraph (1 Jun). (Report that KGB has seized S.'s manuscripts)
1321 "Protest over censorship: A. S.," Guardian (3 Jun), 7.
1322 "Soviet writer challenges the censor," Sunday Times (4 Jun), 1 & 3.

1323 "Writers Join in Soviet Protest," Times (10 Jun), 4.
1324 "Man of Courage," Newsweek, 69 (12 Jun), 44.
1325 "One Day with S.--An Interview," Survey, 64 (Jul), 181-5. (P. Ličko; tr. of 1604)
1326 Salisbury, H. "Soviet Literary Censorship May End: Banned Novel to Appear," Times (13 Jul), 4.
1327 "Soviet Censors on the Defensive," Life, 63 (28 Jul), 4.
1328 "Protest by Russian Author," Times (25 Sep), 4.

1968

1329 "S., Al. I.," pp. 598-99 in Prominent Personalities in the USSR: A Biographic Directory (Compiled by the Institute for the Study of the USSR, Munich). Metuchen, N. J.: Scarecrow Press, 1968.
1330 "Soviet Writer Defiant," Times (14 Feb), 5.
1331 "Letter from Pavel Antokolsky to the Secretary of the Central Committee of the CPSU, P. N. Demichev," Survey, 67 (Apr), 127-8. [Tr. of 253] Also in this issue: "S. Then and Now," pp. 128-30, tr. of 59, 263, 265 & 266.
1332 "Commentary," TLS (11 Apr), 379. (On Cancer Ward)
1333 "More from S.," Times (11 Apr), 8.
1334 "Safeguarding 'Cancer Ward'," Times (16 May), 12.
1335 Gaev, A. "Writers and Critics in the USSR," BISUSSR,15 (Jun).
1336 "New War and Peace," Newsweek, 77 (6 Jun), 45-46.
1337 Raymont, H. "Western Publishers to Print Two Books Banned by Russians," NYHT (12 Jun).
1338 "Dial, Harper Both to Issue S. Novels," PubW, 193 (17 Jun), 45.
1339 "Soviet Writer Accused of Aiding West," Times (27 Jun), 4.
1340 "Russia's Forbidden Novel--Praise from Prague," Atlas, 16, i (Jul), 57-58. (Tr. of 1588, with ed. note)
1341 Smith, R. "Politics, Publishing and Russian Novels," PubW, 194 (15 Jul), 39.
1342 Blumenfeld, F. "Another Pasternak?" Newsweek, 72 (29 Jul), 92.
1343 "Writer More Dangerous than Pasternak," Times (20 Aug).
1344 Glenny, M. "S.: No Compromise," Times (21 Sep), Sat. Rev.
1345 "The Writer as Russia's Conscience," Time, 92 (27 Sep), 22-27. (Artemova [429] gives the actual author of this anon. cover story as A. Belinkov; she gives pp. as 24-31 [foreign ed.])
1346 "Writer's Pen Should Not Be Stopped," Time, 92 (27 Sep), 25. (Excerpts of letter by S. [see 547])
1347 "L'Affaire S.," PC, 17, v (Sep-Oct), 37-51. (Repr.: Brumberg [1284], pp. 245-290, which see for list of contents.)
1348 Tvardovsky, A. "A Letter to the Secretary of the Soviet Writers' Union, Konstantin Fedin . . .," Survey, 69 (Oct), 112-121. (Tr. of 267; repr. in Labedz [1285], pp. 128-40)
1349 "S.: A Bibliographic Note," Radio Liberty Dispatch (2 Oct), 1-12.
1350 "Al. S.," Soviet Literary 'Criminals': Radio Liberty Research Paper, No. 20, p. 12.
1351 Cuneo, P. "New Fall Books," America, 119 (12 Oct), 328.
1353[sic] Vizinczey, S. "How Brainwashing Succeeds," Times (16 Nov), 25.
1354 Smith, R. "Publishers Trade Charges on S. Novel," PubW, 194 (23 Nov), 20. (With ed. comment)

1355 "S., Al. Is.," Current Biography (Feb); repr.: pp. 410-13 in Current Biography Yearbook, 1969. New York: H. W. Wilson Co., 1970.

1356 "Commentary," TLS (13 Feb), 156.

1357 "A Big One," Times (8 Mar), 8. [Artemova (429) has p. 20]

1358 Louis, V. "S. Lives Martyr's Role," Washington Post (16 Mar), 131 & 134. (With introd. note by A. Shub)

1359 Louis, V. "A Conversation with Russia's Most Controversial Writer," NYHT (17 Mar).

1360 Louis, V. "S.," Survey, 70/71 (Winter-Spring), 257-60; with introd. material on Louis titled, "S.: Is He Nice?", pp. 251-57 [repr.: Labedz (1285), 152-7].

1361 "A Visit to S. by the Czech Writer Pavel Ličko," Listener, 81 (20 Mar), 372. [Tr. of 1604]

1362 "Russia: Four New Works," Time, 93 (21 Mar), 28.

1363 Marin, Y. "Soviet Writers in the Struggle for Intellectual Freedom," BISUSSR, 16 (Apr).

1364 Bushman, I. "S., Al. Is.," Portraits of Prominent USSR Personalities, 2, ii (Apr), 101-106.

1365 Letcher, S. "End of the Procession," Time, 93 (4 Apr), 13. (Letter noting omission of last 3 paragraphs of "Easter Procession"; see 512.)

1366 Crankshaw, E. "Voice the Kremlin Wants to Silence," Observer (6 Apr), 9.

1367 Crankshaw, E. "S.'s 'Easter Spirit'," Toronto Mail & Globe (8 Apr).

1368 "The Times Diary," Times (9 Apr), 8.

1369 Esam, I. "Conscience of a Nation," New Zealand Listener, 60, No. 1540 (18 Apr), 8.

1371 [sic] "Planned Encyclopedia Treatment of Literature Alarms Oktyabr," Current Abstracts of the Soviet Press, 2, ii (May), 19-20. [Tr. of 212]

1372 "A. V. Belinkov's Defense of S.'s The Cancer Ward at a Special Meeting of the Writers' Union, November 17, 1966," RusR, 28 (Oct), 453-58; with introd. note by D. von Mohrenschildt, p. 453. (Tr. of 343) [Also see samizd., 248]

1373 Webb, W. "Russian Writer Not Expelled," Guardian (6 Nov).

1374 Saikowski, C. "Lid Clamped: S. Ouster Reflects Tougher Soviet Ideological Stance," CSM (14 Nov), 4. [Radosh & Tikos (674) have p. 8]

1375 "Silence for S.," Time, 94 (14 Nov), 36.

1376 "One Black Day in the Life of Al. S.," Economist (15 Nov).

1377 Bonavia, D. "Russia's Demand to Be Free," Times (15 Nov).

1378 "S.," Times (17 Nov).

1379 "Commentary," TLS (20 Nov), 1336.

1380 "Russia: Courageous Defender," Time, 94 (21 Nov), 34.

1381 "Soviet Writer's Appeal," Guardian (21 Nov).

1382 "A. I. S. (A Bibliography," Radio Liberty Library (24 Nov), 1-7. (Mimeographed; for internal use.)

1383 "One Day in the Life," Newsweek, 74 (24 Nov), 57-58.

1384 Wohl, P. "S.'s Letter to Union Circulated: Writer's Expulsion Reverberates in Soviet Union," CSM (26 Nov), 11.

1385 Bonavia, D. "S. May Live in the West," Times (26 Nov).

1386 Levy, D. "Politics of Soviet Literature," Montreal Star

(28 Nov).

1387 "Writer 'Excused': Russian Literary Union Hints that S. Leave USSR," CSM (28 Nov), 4.

1388 "Noted Russian Author Joins in Attacks on S.," NYHT (28 Nov). (Sholokhov)

1389 "Misused," Times (29 Nov).

1390 Dutton, G. "S.," TLS (4 Dec), 1405. (Letter; includes cable sent to Writers' Union in support of S., signed by several Australian writers.)

1391 Saikowski, C. "Soviet Writers Under Fire: Moscow Puts on the Pressure to Bring Back Socialist Realism," CSM (5 Dec), 2.

1392 "Threat of Exile," Time, 94 (5 Dec), 49+.

1393 "Invitation to Leave," Newsweek, 74 (8 Dec), 66.

1394 Times (16 Dec). (Open letter of 31 western writers to Writers' Union in support of S.; also at 1106; repr. in Labedz [1285], pp. 198-9; in Russ. at 428, pp. 193-4)

1395 Ashanin, C. "Open Letter to the Union of Soviet Writers," Christian Century, 86 (17 Dec), 1617-18.

1396 "Russian's Protest on S.," NYHT (22 Dec).

1397 Smogorzewski, K. "S., Al. Is.," p. 165 in Britannica Book of the Year, 1969 (Enc. Brit., Inc., 1969) [Also brief additional references to S. in yearbooks for 1968 & 1970 (indexed).]

1970

1398 Pismenny, G. "The Exclusion of Al. S. from the Writers' Union," BISUSSR, 17, ii (Feb), 21-32.

1399 "S.: A Candle in the Wind," Time, 95 (23 Mar), 25.

1400 Wilsworth, D. "Lawyer Says He Acts for S.," Times (14 Apr).

1401 Bookseller (18 Apr). (Has statement by S.'s lawyer, F. Heeb; repr. in Labedz [1285], pp. 159-60.)

1402 "Soviet Section Quits European Writers' Group," Current Abstracts of the Soviet Press, 2, v (May), 25. (Tr. of 222)

1403 Gwertzman, B. "Medvedev Detention Brings Bitter S. Protest," NYHT (17 Jun).

1404 "Protesting Spiritual Murder," Time, 95 (29 Jun), 30-31.

1405 Scammell, M. "The Faces of S.," Observer (30 Aug), 21-22.

1406 Philpot, T. "Persecution of a Soviet Novelist," Humanist, 85 (Sep), 274-7.

1407 "S.: A New Novel," Times (30 Sep).

1408 Wakeford, G. "Will New Dr. Zhivago Get His Prize?" Daily Mail (9 Oct).

1409 Zorza, V. "The Nobel Bridge," Guardian (9 Oct), 13.

1410 "Nobel Award to Soviet Writer Deplored," Scotsman (Edinburgh), 10 Oct.

1411 Feifer, G. & D. Burg. "The Tough Rebel the Kremlin Faces," Sunday Times (11 Oct), 16.

1412 Snyder, L. "S. Play a First in Minneapolis," CSM (14 Oct).

1413 "Commentary," TLS (16 Oct), 1194. (Criticizes awarding of Nobel Prize to S.; polemical exchange follows--see: 1421, 1430, 1436, 1441, 1442, 1444, 1445, 1446, 1448, 1450, 1452, 1453, 1454, 1456.)

1414 Hingley, R. "S.-Prize Here," Spectator (17 Oct), 432 & 434.

1415 Zorza, V. "The Right to Write," Guardian (17 Oct).

1415a Soviet Weekly (17 Oct). (Has statement critical of Nobel award to S.; repr. in Labedz [1285], pp. 216-17.)

1416 "Prize and a Dilemma," Time, 96 (19 Oct), 38-9.
1417 "S. Wins Nobel Prize in Literature," PubW, 198 (19 Oct),
30-31.
1418 Wolff, G. "I Accept the Prize," Newsweek, 76 (19 Oct), 67.
1419 Barnes, C. "S. Play in Minnesota," NYHT (20 Oct).
1420 Foote, T. "Novelist Al. S.: Nobel Prize Winner Who Deserved
It," Life, 69 (23 Oct), 58. (Tr. into Russ. at 462)
1421 Kenedy, R. "S.," TLS (30 Oct), 1276. (Letter; see 1413)
1422 Saikowski, C. "S.: The Kremlin Still Hunts a Way Out," CSM
(23 Oct).
1423 "Writer in the Eye of the Storm," Economist (26 Oct).
1424 "Dissent in the USSR," Nation, 211 (26 Oct), 389.
1425 Kroll, J. "The Witness," Newsweek, 76 (26 Oct), 85. (Play
review)
1426 Kalem, T. "The Invisible Nation," Time (2 Nov). (Play rev.)
1427 "Nobel for Outcast," Senior Scholastic, 97 (2 Nov), 5.
1428 Stevens, E. "S. Collecting the Nobel Prize," Newark Evening
News (4 Nov).
1430 [sic] Thomson, R. "S.," TLS (27 Nov), 1390-91. (Letter; see
1413)
1431 "Rostropovich Appeals for S.," SatR, 53 (28 Nov), 28.
1432 Hegge, P. "A Telephone Call to S.," Atlas, 19 (Dec), 31-32.
(See 557a)
1433 Saikowski, C. "A Nobel Solution for S.," CSM (2 Dec).
1434 "Newsmakers," Newsweek, 76 (7 Dec), 42.
1435 Critchlow, J. "Episode in the Life of S.," Commonweal, 93
(11 Dec), 278-80.
1436 Dewhirst, M. "S.," TLS (11 Dec), 1466-7. (Letter; see 1413)
1437 Crankshaw, E. "A Voice for Russia," Observer (13 Dec), 7.
1438 "S.," NatR, 22 (15 Dec), 1337.
1439 "S.'s Day," Newsweek, 76 (21 Dec), 52.
1440 "Attack on S.," Time, 96 (28 Dec), 18.

1971

1441 R. "Column," Encounter, 36 (Jan), 35-8. (See 1413)
1442 "Commentary," TLS (1 Jan), 12. (Reply to 1441; see 1413)
1443 Bartlett, K. "Lightning Rods of Freedom," CSM (6 Jan), 8.
1444 Bloch, L. "S.," TLS (8 Jan), 41. (Letter; see 1413)
1445 "S.," TLS (15 Jan), 68: letters by R. Conquest & W. Weather-
by, with reply by ed. (See 1413)
1446 Bazarov, K. "S.," TLS (29 Jan), 126. (Letter; see 1413)
1447 "Dissent in Russia: The Thin Wedge," Newsweek, 77 (1 Feb),
29-31.
1448 "S.," TLS (5 Feb), 158: letters by A. de Figueiredo & R. Conquest. (See 1413)
1449 Markmann, C. "What Is Right?" Nation (8 Feb), 185-6.
1450 "S.," TLS (12 Feb), 182-3: letters by L. Bloch & K. Bazarov. (See 1413)
1451 "S.," Vogue, 157 (15 Feb), 90-93. (Chronology, p. 90)
1452 Bazarov, K. "S.," TLS (19 Feb), 213. (Letter; see 1413)
1453 "Commentary," TLS (26 Feb), 242. (See 1413)
1454 R. "Column," Encounter, 36 (Mar), 27-9. (See 1413)
1455 Saikowski, C. "Moscow Melts for Rostropovich," CSM (1 Mar), 4.
1456 Bloch, L. "S.," TLS (5 Mar), 271. (Letter; see 1413)
1457 "Not to Provide Lecture," CSM (25 Mar), 3.

1458 Thomas, E. "The Crimnals Are Also Victims," London Magazine, 11 (Apr/May), 83-8.
1459 Zimmerman, P. "Prisoner's Base," Newsweek (24 May), 97. (Rev. of movie "One Day")
1460 S. K. "Witness," Time (31 May), 86. (Movie rev.)
1461 Shub, A. "S.'s New Book," Washington Post (19 Jun); IHT (19-20 Jun). (On Avg. čet.)
1462 "S.'s Story," Sunday Times (20 Jun), 25.
1463 "God Is Upper-Case," Time, 97 (21 Jun), 29.
1464 "Newsmakers," Newsweek, 77 (21 Jun), 42.
1465 "New War and Peace," Newsweek, 77 (28 Jun), 45-6.
1466 Findsen, O. "S. Novel Published in Paris," Cincinnati Enquirer (15 Jul).
1467 "Big Prize," Newsweek, 78 (19 Jul), 55.
1468 Prescott, P. "A Life Worth Loving," Newsweek, 78 (26 Jul), 73-74.
1469 Bannon, B. "The Story Behind the Book: The Battle of 'August 1914'," PubW, 200 (16 Aug), 37.
1470 "S.'s August Fourteen," Bookseller (21 Aug), 1300.
1471 "S. Complains of Secret-Police Harassment," PubW, 200 (23 Aug), 28.
1472 "Beyond Endurance," Time, 98 (30 Aug), 26-7.
1473 Kirsch, R. "Al. S.: More than a Symbol of Opposition," Los Angeles Times (5 Sep), Calendar, p. 42.
1474 "Embarrassing Award," Time, 98 (13 Sep), 30.
1475 Barry, N. "Tom Courtenay in 'Ivan Denisovich': A Film with Legs," Times (6 Nov), Sat. Rev., p. 9.
1476 "August Fourteen: Bodley Head Granted an Interim Injunction," Bookseller (4 Dec), 2412-15.

1972

1477 "S.'s Tributes," Newsweek, 79 (3 Jan), 23.
1478 "Soviet Comment," CSM (13 Jan), 2.
1479 "Intolerance," Newsweek, 78 (17 Jan), 39.
1480 "The Prophet Writer," CSM (28 Mar), 18.
1481 "Slowness of Reward," CSM (30 Mar), 14.
1482 "Lenten Letters," Time, 99 (3 Apr), 31.
1483 "Newsmakers," Newsweek, 79 (3 Apr), 48.
1484 Kaiser, R. "S. Complains of Police Harassment, Surveilance," Washington Post (3 Apr), A16; repr. in Guardian in 3 parts: "Days in the Life Of," 3 Apr., p. 8; "Soviet Spirit in State of Siege," 4 Apr., p. 5; "Running Water Only When It Rained," 5 Apr., p. 13. (See 563)
1485 Smith, H. [On interview with S.] IHT (4 Apr.?).
1486 Kaiser, R. "Russia's Cultural Thorn: The Cross of S. Just Refuses to Go Away," Courier-Journal (Louisville), 14 Apr., p. A11. (L. A. Times-Washington Post Service)
1487 "S.'s Witness," America, 126 (15 Apr), 386-7.
1488 "S. Speaks Out," Time, 99 (17 Apr), 46.
1489 "Unsilenced Voice," Newsweek, 79 (17 Apr), 49-50; also: "What S. Had to Say," p. 49 (excerpts of interview [see 563].)
1490 Saunders, G. "The Kremlin's Campaign Against S.," Militant (21 Apr), 12-13. (Also in Intercontinental Press, 3 Apr.)
1491 "S.: Lenten Letter," NatR, 24 (28 Apr), 445-7. (See 536)

1492 Hegge, P. "S. and the Nobel Prize," Survey, 18, ii (Spring), 100-111. (Excerpts in trans. from 2295)

1493 [The Press on S.] Novosti Press Agency, 1972. (English tr. of 237; only 500 copies printed, according to Artemova [429].)

1494 "Will S. Get His Nobel?" Senior Scholastic, 100 (1 May),11-12.

1495 Wagner, S. "Washington Press Corps Supports S.," PubW, 201 (29 May), 22.

1496 Glenny, M. "A Major Russian Novelist Refuses to Be Silenced: 'No Regime Loves Great Writers'," Life, 72 (23 Jun), 42-44B.

1497 Kraft, J. "Letter from Moscow," New Yorker, 48 (24 Jun), 58.

1498 "S. Speaks," CSM (26 Aug), 14.

1499 "S. Nobel Prize Lecture Assails Censorship," CSM (31 Aug), 8.

1500 Goldsborough, J. "Books: Soviet Diplomat's View of S.'s Work," IHT (? Sep).

1501 "Newsmakers," Newsweek (4 Sep), 52.

1502 "One Word of Truth," Time, 100 (4 Sep), 33.

1503 "Notes and Comment," New Yorker, 48 (9 Sep), 29.

1504 "A Voice from the Depths," Wall Street Journal (6 Sep), 12.

1505 Green, A. "Book Business: Trade Winds," SatR (9 Sep), 81.

1506 Grannis, C. "S. Speaks for All of Us," PubW, 202 (11 Sep),40.

1507 "Ninth Circle?" NatR, 24 (15 Sep), 995.

1508 "S. on Scientists," Science, 177 (15 Sep), 972.

1509 "S. the Man, His Fate and His Country," Vogue, 160(15 Sep), 98+.

1510 "Al. Is. S.," SatR, 55 (16 Sep), 80.

1511 "One Word of Truth," CSM (18 Sep), 14.

1512 "Against Compromise," Listener, 88 (21 Sep), 368. (Quotes Graham Greene on Nobel lecture.)

1513 Romanowski, J. "Al. S.'s August 1914, or the Truth about Book and Myth," Soviet Studies in Literature, 8 iv (Fall), 315-340. (Tr. of 234; see orig. Polish: 2322)

1514 Mok, M. "Michael Glenny," PubW (25 Sep), 24.

1515 "Milestones," Time (16 Oct), 74.

1516 Seeger, M. "The Russian Who Is a Stranger in His Own Land," Los Angeles Times (22 Oct).

1517 Driscoll, J. "Observations: Clashing Yardsticks," NatO (4 Nov).

1518 "Minnesota to Publish New S. Play," PubW (6 Nov), 30. (See 542)

1519 Barkham, J. "Here Are 1972's Best," New York Post (7 Dec).

1520 Foote, T. "Modest Proposals from a Spent Book Reviewer," New York (11 Dec), 54, 55, 57. (See p. 57)

1521 "The Year in Pictures; S.: Under Heavy Attack, the Writer Stands Firm," Life, 73 (29 Dec), 43. (Brief note with photo)

1973

1522 Kael, P. "The Current Cinema: Poetry and Politics," New Yorker, 48 (20 Jan), 80-81, 85-86. (Rev.-art. on movie "Circle")

1523 "People," Time, 101 (22 Jan), 35.

1524 "Soviet Union: In An Alien Fog," Newsweek, 81 (22 Jan), 40-41. (S.'s divorce problems; pub'n. of Guns of August in USSR)

1525 "Honorary Members and Fellows," MLA Newsletter, 5, i (Feb), 5. (S. elected honorary member of MLA at 28 Dec. meeting.)

1525a Runyon, K. "In Concentration Camps for 18 Years," Courier-Journal (Louisville), 10 Mar, p. A13. (About Th. Dollefeld, survivor of Nazi & Stalinist camps, who speaks of his affinity for S.)

1525b Iswolsky, H. "S. and the Artist's Vocation," Catholic Work-

er, 39, iii (Mar-Apr), 7. [Rev. of 540; this entry out of place]
See also 497, pp. 153-6 (note); 1762; & 2143.

(iii) Translations of Russian articles published in Current Digest of the Soviet Press

1526 "Stalin Labor Camp Tale Hailed as 'Needed', 'Influential'," XIV, 45 (5 Dec 1962), 13-14:
Baklanov, G. "That this May Never Happen Again" [tr. of 56; full].
1527 "Literature," XIV, 46 (12 Dec 1962), 24-25:
Simonov, K. "About the Past in the Name of the Future" [tr. of 55; excerpt]
1528 "Ilyichev's Talk on Policy in Literature and the Arts," XIV, 51 (16 Jan 1963), 16-21: "Create for the People, for the Sake of Communism" [tr. of 73].
1529 "How Much Does Russian Literature Owe to Europe? XV, 1 (30 Jan 1963), 26-28:
Ermilov, V. "Ignominious Flight of the Slavic Review" [tr. of 74].
1530 "Ilyichev States Policy for Young Writers and Artists," XV, 2 (6 Feb '63), 7-13, 40: "Young Writers and Artists Should Serve Great Ideals" [tr. of 84; full text]
1531 "S. Tale, Yevtushenko Life Story Under Fire," XV, 12 (17 Apr 1963):
Poltoratsky, V. "Matryona's House and Its Environs," 8-9 [tr. of 103; full text].
1532 "Tvardovsky Denies Restrictions in Literature and Art," XV, 19 (5 Jun 1963), 11-13: Tvardovsky, A. "The Literature of Socialist Realism Has Always Gone Hand in Hand with the Revolution" [tr. of 115; full text].
1533 "What Is Injustice? Critic of S. Story Asks," XV, 36 (2 Oct 1963), 15-16:
Barabash, Yu. "What Is Justice?" [tr. of 121; full text].
1534 "Life in the Prison Camp: A Challenge to S.," XV, 41 (6 Nov 1963), 11-12:
Gudzenko, A. "We Remained Human Beings" [tr. of 125; full text].
1535 "Controversy Over S.'s Work Continues," XV, 44 (27 Nov 1963):
Granin, D. "Is the Critic Right?" 12-13 [tr. of 127].
Seliverstov, N. "'Today's' Is More Like 'Yesterday's'," 13-14 [tr. of 128, including editor's note].
Chalmayev, V. "'Saints' and 'Devils'," 14-15 [tr. of 122].
1536 "The Real-Life Prototype of a S. Character," XVI, 3 (12 Feb 1964):
Pallon, V. "Greetings, Commander," 12-13 [tr. of 150; full text].
Ivanov, V. "Hasn't the Main Character Been Embellished?" 13 & 35 [tr. of 137; condensed text].
1537 "Who Voices Readers' Verdict on S. Story?" XVI, 4 (19 Feb 1964): "Readers' Forum: Concerning A. S.'s Story 'For the Good of the Cause'," 18 [tr. of 123: E. Yampolskaya, L. Reznikov, V. Sheinis].
"Enthusiastic Affirmation, Pointed Arguments," 18-19 [tr. of 134].
"To the Editors of Literaturnaya Gazeta," 19-20 [tr. of 136].
1538 "Readers and Critics Discuss S. Works," XVI, 5 (26 Feb 1964):
"A Lenin Prize for S.?" 8 [tr. of 149: M. Lezinsky, N. Molchanyuk].
"Marshak, S. "A Truthful Story," 8-9 [tr. of 154].
Bushin, V., p. 9 [tr. of 148].
Zhukhovitsky, L. "Co-Author Wanted" & G. Brovman, p. 9 [tr. of 146].
1539 "Disputes Continue Over S., Young Poets," XVI, 6 (4 Mar 1964),

p. 24: "More on S.'s 'Matryona'":
 "The Readers Speak":
  Trufanova, V. "Politician, Citizen, Artist" [tr. of 155].
  Gazizov, R. "Depth and Freshness of Critical Thought" [tr. of 156].
 1540 "Ivan Denisovich's Friends and Foes Continue Debate," XVI, 12 (15 Apr 1964):
 "Exactingness," 3 [tr. of 159].
 Lakshin, V. "Ivan Denisovich, His Friends and Foes," 3-8 [tr. of 145].
 "The General Work of Criticism," 8-9 [tr. of 162].
 1541 "High Exactingness," XVI, 16 (13 May 1964), 23 [tr. of 168].
 1542 "Literature," XVI, 45 (2 Dec 1964), 25: Tvardovsky, A. "Novy Mir in 1965" [tr. of 182].
 1543 "From Speeches at the Russian Writers' Conference," XVII, 10 (31 Mar 1965), 18-19: Egorychev, N. "Lofty Duty of the Artist" [tr. of 193].
 1544 "Novy Mir at 40—Tvardovsky Reaffirms Its Policies," XVII, 11 (7 Apr 1965), 8-13: Tvardovsky, A. "On the Anniversary" [tr. of 190].
 1545 "The History of Novy Mir," XVII, 13 (21 Apr 1965), 12-18: Dementyev, A. & N. Dikushina. "The Path Traversed" [tr. of 190].
 1546 "A Rejoinder to Tvardovsky Anniversary Article," XVII, 15 (5 May 1965), 19-19: Vuchetich, Ye. "Let Us Clarify Matters" [tr. of 194].
 1547 "'Small' vs. 'Big' Truth: Literaturnaya vs. Novy Mir," XVII, 47 (15 Dec 1965), 9-11: "From the Editors" [tr. of 195].
 1548 "Bodyul," XVIII, 17 (18 May 1966), 13-15: "Speech by I. I. Bodyul, First Secretary of the Central Committee of the Communist Party of Moldavia" [tr. of 198].
 1549 "'Big' and 'Little' Truth in Art: Lakshin and His Critics," XVIII, 46 (7 Dec 1966):
 Lakshin, V. "The Writer, the Reader and the Critic," 9-12 [tr. of 202].
 Ivanov, V. "Realism Today," 13 [tr. of 206; excerpts].
 1550 "Literaturnaya Warns S. to Repudiate His Works," XX, 26 (17 Jul 1968): "The Ideological Struggle: The Writer's Responsibility," 3 [tr. of 207]; "To Literaturnaya Gazeta," 3-5 [S.'s letter of 21 Apr 1968; see 36 & 207].
 1551 "Press and Publishing," XX, 47 (11 Dec 1968), 29: "Life and the Newspaper's Position" [tr. of 209; excerpts].
 1552 "Russian Writers' Union Expels S.," XXI, 46 (10 Dec 1969), 3: "In the Russian Republic Writers' Union" [tr. of 217].
 1553 "Writers' Union Hints S. Should Emigrate," XXI, 47 (17 Dec 1969), 3: "From the Secretariat of the Board of the Russian Republic Writers' Union" [tr. of 218].
 1554 "Reaction to S.'s Nobel Prize," XXII, 41 (10 Nov 1970), 3-4: "Unseemly Game" [tr. of 223]; "The Writer's Word at the Service of the Times" [tr. of 225]; "Where does the Nobel Committee Look for Literary Talent and Glory?" [tr. of 226].
 1555 "Party Plenums Set Ideological Tightening," XXII, 46 (15 Dec 1970), 3-4: Kozhanov, N. & G. Kondratenko. "Powerful Means of Upbringing" [tr. of 227; condensed text].
 1556 "Pravda Attacks Amalrik, S.," XXII, 49 (5 Jan 1971), 16-18: Alexandrov, I. "The Poverty of Anti-Communism" [tr. of 229].

1557 "Krasnaya Zvezda on Literary Truth," XXII, 52 (26 Jan 1971),
13: Sinelnikov, M. "Following the Compass of Communist Party Spirit" [tr. of 230].
1558 "Tracing the S. Genealogy," XXIV, 1 (2 Feb 1972), 9-10, 16:
"The Magazine Stern About the S. Family" [tr. of 232].
1559 "S. Assailed for 'August 1914'," XXIV, 14 (3 May 1972), 1-2:
"When History Is Stood in the Corner" & "In a Distorting Mirror"
[tr. of 233].

(3) Afrikaans. Translation.

1560 Die dag van Ivan Denisowitsj: die egte beeld van Stalin se
strafkampe, tr. L. van der Westhuijzen. Kaapstad: H.A.U.M.,
1963. iii, 194 pp.

(4) Albanian. Translation.

1561 "Nji dite e Ivan Denisoviçit," Rilindja, 2 deri, 31, xx
(1964), 1908-2009. (Translation serialized in Albanian newspaper published in Priština, Yugoslavia. Bibliographical data,
taken from Rolland [see 701], seems partially erroneous; have not
been able to verify. The full name of the periodical is: Rilindja: Organ i lidhjes socialiste te populit punues të kosovës e
metohisë [Prishtinë].)

(5) Arabic. Translation.

   Information from Charles Raad, Dar an-Nahar Pub., Beirut.

1562 Janah assarataane. Beyrouth: Dar an-Nahar. Part 1, 1970,
346 pp., tr. by a group of translators; Part 2, 1971, tr. Yous-
sef el-Khal.

(6) Bulgarian. Translation.

1563 Edin den na Ivan Denisovič, tr. V. Rajčev. Sofija: Narod-
na Kultura, 1963. 156 pp.

(7) Chinese. Translation.

1564 Pei ts'ang ti ling hun, tr. Tao-Shan Huang. Tapei: Chih
Wen Pub., 1970. 229 pp. [OD]

(8) Czech. (Czechoslovakia)

   Abbreviations: S.: Solženicyn. Periodicals: ČsR: Českoslo-
venská Rusistika; KT: Kulturní Tvorba; LN: Literární Noviny; RP:
Rudé Pravo.

Translations:

1564 "Jeden den Ivana Děnisoviče," tr. G. Laub. Plamen, r. 5
(1963): č. 1, 14-20; č. 2, 51-61; č. 3, 137-145; č. 4, 149-171
(with introduction by A. Tvardovskij: "Místo úvodu").
1565 "Na stanici Krečetovka," tr. G. Laub. RP (13 Jan 1963), 3.
1566 "Oběd," tr. J. Tafel. KT, r. 1, č. 4 (1963), 8-9. (Chapter
from OD)
1567 "Případ ze stanice Krečetovka," tr. G. Laub. Československý Voják, r. 12 (1963): č. 4, 8-9; č. 7, 10-12; č. 10, 6-8.

1568 Jeden den Ivana Děnisoviče, tr. S. Machonin. Praha: NPL, 1963. 96 pp.
1569 Ve vyšším zájmu, tr. A. Nováková. Praha: Svět Sovětů, 1964. 146 pp. [Contents: PD (title story), SK, MD; title story appeared earlier in: ZZ, I, 3 (1964), 4-45 & Čtení o Sovět, r.13 (1964): č.4, 36-52; č.5, 37-52; č.6, 37-44.]
1570 Jeden den Ivana Děnisoviče a jiné prózy, tr. S. Machonin & A. Nováková. Praha: Svět Sovětů, 1965. 295 pp. With foreword by J. Franěk. (Contents: OD, SK, MD, PD)
1571 "Zachar Kalita," tr. D. Pohorská. Plamen, r.8, č.4 (1966), 28-34.
1572 "Stražný duch Kulikova pole," tr. A. Nováková. KT, r.4, č. 27 (1966), 8-9. [ZK]
1573 "Pravá ruka," Listy, VI (12 Dec 1968), 6. [Tr. not named; Eng. tr. at 511]
1574 Odsouzenci, tr. J. Krbec. Praha: Nakl. Dilia, 1968. 59 pp. [Contains tr. of SK by S. & "Nočnoj razgovor" by L. Andreev]

Criticism:

1575 Honzík, J. "Nejen znamenitá próza," KT, r.1, č.1 (1963),16.
1576 "Ze sovětské kultury," Rovnost (27 Jan 1963), 5. [On SK]
1577 Putík, J. "Věc života a smrti," Plamen, r.5, č.6 (1963),1-4. [On OD]
1578 Sekora, O. "Muž, o kterém se mluví," Svět Sovětů, r.26, č. 7 (1963), 8-9. [On OD]
1579 Drozda, M. "Bolestná pravda S-nova," LN, r.12, č.8 (1963), 5. [On OD]
1580 Rákos, P. "O jednom dni a jeho násobcích," LN, r.12, č.20 (1963), 9. [Also on József Lengyel]
1581 Očadlíková, M. [has note on S. in]: Současná sovětská literatura, vol. 1: Ruská próza. Praha: Svět Sovětů, 1963-64.
1582 Fojtíková, E. "Realismus S-novy novely 'Jeden den Ivana Děnisoviče'," ČsR, IX, 1 (1964), 34-38.
1583 Lukács, G. "O literatuře i tvůrčím marksismu," LN, 3 (1964). [Tr. of 1972]
1584 Lukács, G. "Solženicyn," Plamen, 8, vi (1966), 76-83.
1585 Drozda, M. "Solženicyn, Ivan Suchov a Pavel Korčagin," pp. 147-83 in his Babel, Leonov, Solženicyn. Praha: Československý Spisovatel, 1966.
1586 Reviews of Drozda:
ČsR, 1 (1966), 50-52. (T. Brablik)
LN, 39 (24 Sep 1966), 5. (V. Svaton: "Svědectví ruské prózy")
Slavica Slovaca (Brno), 3 (1966), 286-88. (T. Ivanová: "Nová podnatná koncepcia")
1587 Ličko, P. "O setkáni se S-nem," Světová Literatura, 4 (1968). [Tr. of 1604]
1587a "S. je náš bratr," Literární Listy, r.1, č.12 (16 Apr 1968), 10. (Interview of Jan Procházka in Paris)
1588 Literární Listy (Jun or Jul 1968). (Has editorial article on RK; tr. into Engl. at 1340)
1589 Student (Jun or Jul 1968). (Has ed. article on RK, according to inform. given at 1340)
1590 Listy, 6 (12 Dec 1968), 7: Honzík, J. "V prvním kruhu"; & Koževníková, K. "Mistr stylu" [Ger. tr. at 2118].

1591 Drozda, M. "Románové umění Al. S-na," Plamen, 11, iv (1969), 76-81.
1592 Sobotka, I. "První kruh," Reportér, 4 (1969).
1593 RP, 16 (20 Jan 1970). [Interview with S. Mixalkov, N. Gribačev, L. Sobolev & N. Voronkov by corresp. for Novosti; same interview in other languages: 1876, 2060, 2455; info. from Artemova (429), who notes also that this was not published in USSR.]

(9) Slovak. (Czechoslovakia)

Abbreviations: same as for Czech; see p. 83.

Translations:

1594 Jeden deň Ivana Denisoviča, tr. J. Ferenčík. Bratislava: SVKL, 1963. 144 pp.
1595 Tri poviedky, tr. Z. Jesenská & V. Hegerová. Bratislava: SVKL, 1964. 186 pp. With foreword by Jesenská. [Contents: SK, MD, PD]
1596 Matrionina chalupa, tr. J. Ferenčík, Z. Jesenská & V. Hegerová. Bratislava: Slovenský Spisovatel, 1966. 270 pp. [Combines 1594 & 1595]
1597 Pravda (Bratislava), 7 Jan 1967. (Excerpts from RK)

Reviews of "Stanice Krečetovka", performance of Slovak adaptation of "Slučaj na stancii Krečetovka" over Bratislava TV, Dec. 1963; (not all of the reviews are in Slovak language):
1598 KT, r.1, č.50 (1963), 13. (D. Havlíček: "S.")
1599 Lidová Demokracie (10 Dec 1963), 3. (pp [V. Poppova]: "Televisní vydání S-na")
1600 LN, r.12, č. 50 (1963), 8. (M. Schulz: "Vážně i rozmarně")
1601 RP (7 Dec 1963), 4. (Z. Bláha)
1602 VP[Výtarná Práce?] (3 Dec 1963), 3. (Z. Bidlo: "Bratislava Krečetovka")
1603 Zdravotnické Noviny (11 Dec 1963), 2. ([Jiří] Led[erer]: "Bolestné drama dneška")

Interview of S.:
1604 Ličko, Pavel. "Jedného dňa u Alexandra Isajeviča Solženicyna (literárná tvorba a umelecké názory)," Kulturný Život (Bratislava), No. 13 (31 Mar 1967), 1 & 10 (Rjazaň-Moskva, Marec 1967). [Translations: 438; 1285, pp. 10-15; 1325; 1361; 1587; 1673a; 1751; 1918, pp. 113-18; 2044; 2190 (in turn tr. at: 1840, 2347, 2349, 2365-66); 2320; 2455]

(10) Danish.

Source for several items: Artemova (429). Two spellings noted of S.'s name: Solsjenitsyn & Solzjenitsyn.

Translations:

1605 En dag i Ivan Denisovitjs liv, tr. E. Frey. København: Gyldendal, 1963; 1965; 1968. 154 pp.
1606 To fortaellinger: Et møde på Kretjetovka station; Matrjonas gård, tr. E. Frey. København: Gyldendal, 1964. 134 pp.
1607 Kræftafdelingen, tr. O. Jensen. Kòbenhavn: Gyldendal, 1969; 1970. 2 v.: 362 & 300 pp. [RK]

1608 <u>I den første kreds</u>, tr. S. Rachlin. København: Gyldendal, 1970; 1971. 2 v.: 366 & 380 pp.

1609 <u>For sagens skyld og andre noveller</u>, tr. E. Frey, O. Jensen & S. Rachlin. København: Gyldendal, 1971. 247 pp. [Contents: same as 520; "Hans høre hånd," tr. Jensen, had appeared earlier: <u>Gyldendals Magasin</u>, 1 (1970), 94-108.]

1610 <u>August 1914</u>, tr. O. Jensen. København: Gyldendal, 1972. 2 v.: 356 & 314 pp.

Criticism:

1611 Nag, M. <u>Sovjetlitteraturen 1917-1967</u>, tr. F. Martner. København: Hasselbach, 1968. See pp. 223-4, 235-6, 262. [Tr. of 2278a]

1612 Lukács, G. <u>Solsjenitsyn</u>, tr. K. Nielsen. København: Gyldendal, 1971. 140 pp. [Tr. of 2052, with biog. note & bibl. by translator; in note on contents, Artemova (429) has: "Al. S. tegnet af A. Sidur, Moskva".]

1613 Steffensen, E. "Aleksandr Solzjenitsyn: Identitet og etik. Om nogle centrale problemer i Solzjenitsyns forfatterskab," <u>Dansk Udsyn</u> (Askov), 51 (1971), 140-61.

(11) Dutch. (Netherlands; Belgium)

Special source: Theun de Vries; the following entries were selected from clippings of 150 short articles & news items supplied by him: 1626-37, 1639, 1641-45. Important items: 1622, 1638, 1640 & 1646. Abbreviations: S.: Solzjenitsin or Solzjenitsyn (both spellings about equally common).

Translations:

1614 <u>Het verhaal van een dag: Uit het leben van Iwan Denisowitsj</u>, tr. T. de Vries. Amsterdam: Pegasus, 1963. 223 pp.; 1971. 180 pp.

1615 "Matrjona's huis," tr. C. Timmer, in: <u>Halverwege: Zeven moderne Russen</u>. Amsterdam: Van Oorschat, 1963.

1616 <u>In de eerste cirkel</u>, tr. P. Grashoff. Baarn: De Boekerij, 1969. 590 pp. [Tr. from English]

1617 <u>Kankerpaviljoen</u>. Baarn: De Boekerij, 1969. 2 v.: 288 & 229 pp. [Tr.?; foreword by H. Böll; possibly this is a tr. from Ger.; see 1950]

1618 <u>In het belang van de zaak</u>, tr. P. Waszink, C. Willemse, E. Gütlich & T. Rammelt. Baarn: De Boekerij, 1971. 222 pp. [Contents same as 520]

1619 <u>De kamphoer en de simpele ziel</u>, tr. M. Weijers. Baarn: De Boekerij, 1971. 168 pp. [Olen']

1620 <u>Augustus veertien</u>, tr. D. Peet. Baarn: De Boekerij, 1971. 2 v.: 320 & 320 pp.

1621 "In memoriam Twardowski," <u>Haagse Post</u> (12-18 Jan 1972).

Criticism:

1622 Eekman, T. "De dag van een dwangarbeider," <u>Nieuwe Stem</u>, 19 (1964), 46-52.

1623 E. C. "Al. S.: The First Circle," <u>Het Vaderland Weekjournal</u> (16 Nov 1968), 5.

1624 Schreurs, A. "Met A. S. naar nieuw literair process?" <u>Spectator</u> (9 Nov 1968). [See note top of p. 89, this bibliography.]

1625 Liedmeier, J. "S. heilzame kranker," <u>Standaard</u> (20 Dec 1968).

1626 van het Reve, K. "Ziekenhuisroman van Al. S. het boek van een mens," Vrij Nederland (? 1969). [Exact date not known; rev. of Eng. tr. of Cancer Ward]

1627 Liedmeier, J. "S., de Tolstoj van het nieuwe Rusland," Tijd (15 Feb 1969).

1628 Hendrikse, H. "Een ex-gevangene werd de meest besproken schrijver van Rusland," Trouw (25 Nov 1969).

1629 Hendrikse, H. "Als vijand van het sowjetsystem aangeklaagd," Trouw (27 Nov 1969).

1630 R. F. "S.: de grootheid van de kleine feiten," Limburgs Dagsblad (7 Aug 1970).

1631 Oerlemans, J. "Die macht van S.," Algemeen Handelsblad (9 Oct 1970).

1632 Scheepmaker, N. "De tweede regering," Volkskrant (9 Oct 1970), 9.

1633 Gans, J. "S.'s Nobelprijs," Telegraaf (15 Oct 1970).

1634 Ros, M. "Literair Logboek," Algemeen Handelsblad (16 Oct 1970).

1635 Ros, M. "S.: Symbol van de strijd tegen de corruptie," Algemeen Dagblad (17 Oct 1970).

1636 Verheul, K. "Nobelprijs voor geniale autodidact," Vrij Nederland (17 Oct 1970).

1637 Ferguson, M. "S. dissident maar ook geestverwant?" Het Vaderland (31 Oct 1970).

1638 Verheul, K. "S. en zijn publiek," Maatstaf, 18 (1970), 537-44.

1639 Stommels, F. "S. over vrij zijn achter prikkeldraad," Gelderlander-Pers (? 1971).

1640 Hotz, R. "Al. S.," Streven, 1, ii (1971), 161-74. (Ger. tr. at 2118)

1641 Spierdijk, J. "Kultuurkul," Telegraaf (3 Feb 1971).

1642 van Noord, J. "S. . . . nieuw boek," Het Vaderland (4 Sep 1971).

1643 Brandenburg, A. "Bundel verhalen S.," Haarlems Dagblad (20 Nov 1971).

1644 Ferguson, M. "Gekunstelde Kohout en rechtstreekse S.," Het Vaderland Weekjournal (18 Dec 1971), 3.

1645 Verhaar, H. "Geen Russische wet verbiedt de oppositie-krantjes...," NRC/Handelsblad (24 Dec 1971).

1646 Demets, G. Aleksandr Solzjenitsyn. Brugge [Bruges]: Orion (N. V. Desclee de Brouwer), 1971. 53 pp. [Listed by Artemova (429)]

1647 van den Heuvel, Martin. "S.: de grootste en de lastigste," Studio KRO (13-19 Feb 1972).

1648 A. J. O. "Het Kankerpaviljoen krijgt in TV-stuk beter gestalte," Volkskrant (16 Feb 1972).

(12) Estonian. (USSR) Translations:

1649 Üks päev Ivan Denissovitši elus, tr. L. Meri & E. Sarv. Tallin: Gaz.-žurn. izd., 1963. 114 pp.

1650 Asja huvides, tr. O. Jõgi. Tallin: Gaz.-žurn. izd., 1964. 108 pp. [PD]

See also 313.

(13) Finnish.

Information about most of the critical articles and several of the translations was provided by Esa Adrian. Abbreviations: S.: Solzhenitsyn or Solženicyn; HS: Helsingin Sanomat; SS: Suomen Sosialdemokraatti.

Translations:

1651 "Ivan Denisovitšin päivä," tr. M. Lahtela. APU [Helsinki weekly], 49-51 (1962) & 1-10 (1963).
1652 "Päivä Stalinin keskitys leirissä," tr. E. Adrian. Suomen Kuvalehti, 50-51 (1962) & 1-6 (1963). [OD]
1653 Ivan Denisovitšin päivä," tr. M. Lahtela. Helsinki: Tammi, 1963. 250 pp. (And 4 later editions) [Contents include SK & MD]
1654 Syöpäosasto, tr. E. Adrian [Anisimoff]. Helsinki: Tammi. v. 1, 1968, 323 pp; v. 2., 1969, 268 pp. (And 3 later editions) [RK]
1655 Ensimmäinen piiri, tr. E. Adrian. Helsinki: Tammi, 1970. 690 pp. (And 3 later ed'ns.) [KP]
1656 "Valo joka sinussa on," tr. E. Adrian. (Tr. of "Svet, kotoryj v tebe [Sveča na vetru]", broadcast over Finnish radio in Sep. 1971.)
1657 Elokuu-14, tr. E. Adrian. Helsinki: Tammi, 1972. [Avg.čet.]

Criticism:

1658 Laitinen, Kai. "Päivä elämää," Parnasso, 3 (1963).
1659 Polkunen, M. "Varhaiskevättä," Uusi Suomi (7 Apr 1963).
1660 Piirto, P. "Päivä Stalinin varjossa," HS (11 Apr 1963).
1661 Ekman, R. "Uusia tuulia keskitysleirilta," Sosialistinen Aikakauslehti, 8 (1963).
1662 Pihlström, B. "Stalineran i litteraturens ljus," Nya Pressen (10 Dec 1963). [In Swedish]
1663 Tapiola, K. "Uuden luokan byrokraatti ja Tolstoin opetuslapsi," HS (29 Dec 1968). [On RK, part I]
1664 Tapiola, K. "Tyrannit, kavaltajat, vangit," HS (6 Apr 1969). [On RK, part II]
1665 Adrian, E. "S. Stalinin ympyröissä," HS (15 Nov 1969). [On KP]
1666 Adrian, E. "Al. S. sairaalasta," SS (? 1969). [On RK]
1667 Adrian, E. "Kybernetiikkako lamppu?" HS (25 Jul 1970). [On Sveča]
1668 Koskimies, R. "Vuosisatamme 'Sota ja rauha'," Uusi Suomi (9 Oct 1970). [On KP]
1669 Tarkka, P. "Kokonaisen puheen romaani," HS (15 Nov 1970). [On KP]
1670 Lehtonen, R. "Byrokratian tilaus," SS (13 Dec 1970). [On KP]
1671 Mikkola, M. "Tyrannit, kavaltajat ja vangit," Parnasso, 5 (1971). ["Tyrants, traitors & prisoners": general article]
1672 Adrian, E. "S. Tannenbergissä," HS (18 Jul 1971). [On Avg. čet.]
1672a Björkegren, H. Al. S., 1971. [Tr. of 2397; information incomplete]
Also see 2407.

(14 Flemish. (Belgium) Criticism

See entries 1624 and 1625. D'argent (see 1918, p. 510) indicates that these are in Dutch language, whereas Artemova (429) labels them as Flemish, appearing in Belgian periodicals. [Discrepancy noted at last minute, too late to resolve conclusively.]

(15) French. (France, Belgium, Canada, Luxemburg, Switzerland)

Basic source: the annual bibliography in Cahiers du Monde Russe et Soviétique. Special sources: about 150 entries taken from D'Argent (see 1918, pp. 493-511) without verification (but several minor articles listed by D'Argent were not incorporated into the present bibliography); about 20 additional items were taken from Artemova (see 429). Abbreviations: S.: Soljénitsyne (most common) or Soljénitsyn (rare). Periodicals: CN: Croix du Nord (Lille); ES: Études Soviétiques; FAN: Feuille d'Avis de Neufchâtel; FL: Figaro Littéraire [also used by MLA]; FN: France Nouvelle; FO: France Observateur; LF: Lettres Françaises; LN: Lettres Nouvelles [MLA uses LetN]; NCan: Nouvelle Candide; NCr: Nouvelle Critique (Revue du Marxisme Militant); NL: Nouvelles Littéraires [also MLA]; NO: Nouvel Observateur; QL: Quinzaine Littéraire; RDM: Revue des Deux Mondes [also MLA]; TM: Temps Modernes [also MLA]. Other: Dim.: Dimanche; Gaz.: Gazette; Lit.: Littérair(e); Mag.: Magazine; Nouv.: Nouvel(le); Rép.: Républicaine; Rev.: Revue; Trib.: Tribune.

Translations:

1673 "Le document que Kroutchev paraphe: La Sibérie sous Staline voici ce que c'était," Paris Match, 713 (8 Dec 1962), 98-101. (Excerpt from OD; tr. not named; a second excerpt, planned for issue of 15 Dec., was ordered killed by courts.)
1673a Une journée d'Ivan Denissovitch, tr. Léon & Andrée Robel & M. Decaillot. Paris: Julliard, 1963; 1967; 1970. 223 pp. With "Préface" by P. Daix [which had appeared earlier in LF, 967 (28 Feb 1963), 1 & 6]. Other ed'ns: Paris/Lausanne: La Guilde du Livre, 1968; Paris: Le Club Française du Livre, 1970; Éditions 10/18, 1970; Union Générale, 1970. 191 pp.; Rombaldi, 1971. 255 pp. [with tr. of 1604 as preface].
1673b "La maison de Matriona," tr. C. Ligny. TM, 202 (Mar 1963), 1542-83.
1674 "Pour le bien de la cause," tr. C. Ligny. TM, 209 (Oct 1963), 650-80; 210 (Nov 1963), 853-67.
1674a "Un incident à Kretchetovka," tr. C. Ligny. LN (Apr-May 1964), 17-42; (Jun-Jul-Aug), 97-122; (Nov-Dec), 102-29.
1674b La maison de Matriona. L'inconnu de Kretchetovka. Pour le bien de la cause, tr. Léon & Andrée Robel. Paris: Julliard, 1966. xii, 246 pp. "Préface" by L. Robel. Other ed'ns.: Paris: Club Français du Livre, 1969; Paris/Lausanne: Guilde du Livre, 1970.
1675 "Esquisses et petits récits," tr. V[éronique] T[issot]. LN (May-Jun 1966), 13-29. [15 etudes]
1675a "Dix contes d'Al. S.," tr. O. Djorjadzé. Synthèses, 23 (Apr 1968), 16-23.
1675b Le premier cercle, tr. Henri-Gabriel Kybarthi. Paris: Laffont, 1968. 576 pp.; 1972. 825 pp.
1676 Le pavillon de cancéreux, tr. Alfreda & Michel Aucouturier,

Lucile & Georges Nivat & Jean-Paul Sémon. Paris: Julliard, 1968.
738 pp. 2nd ed., 1969. Introd. by G. Nivat. Other ed'ns: Paris:
Livre de Poche, 1970. 704 pp.; Le cercle du bibliophile, [1971].
539 pp., with preface by A. Lanoux.
  1676a "La main droite," tr. V. Fosty. FL, 1190 (24 Feb 1969), 7.
(with introd. by J. Martin-Chauffier)
  1676b "La Procession Pascale," tr. A. Aucouturier. Gazette Littéraire (Switzerland), 22 Mar 1969.
  1677 "L'inconnu de Kretchetovka," A la Page [Ed. Tallandier], 60
(Jun 1969), 4-28; 61 (Jul 1969), 58-72. [Tr. not named]
  1677a "La procession de la nuit de Pâques," FL, 1197 (14-20 Apr
1969), 16-17. [Tr.?]
  1677b "Prière," tr. Tatiana & Gabriel Matzneff. Combat, 8163 (15
Oct 1970), 1.
  1678 "Le souffle," tr. V. Fosty. FL, 1274 (19-25 Oct 1970), 10.
[Tr. of "Dyxanie" (prose poem)]
  1678a "Le feu de bois et les fourmis. En suivant la rive de
l'Oka," tr. L. Nivat. Monde (23 Oct 1970), 18. [Prose poems]
  1678b "Le main droite," tr. E. Lesseps. NO, 318 (14 Dec 1970),
41-43.
  1679 Zacharie l'Escarcelle, et autres récits, tr. Lucile and
Georges Nivat & Alfreda Aucouturier. Paris: Julliard, 1971. 139
pp.; Paris: U.G.E., 1972. 128 pp. Contents: "Études et Miniatures" [16 prose poems, incl. "Le vieux seu" (see 5b)]; "Zacharie
l'Escarcelle"; "La Main droite"; La Procession pascale"; "Lettre
à trois étudiants"; "Lettre ouverte du 15 juin 1970"; "Flamme au
vent (la lumière qui est en toi". [These works appear in same
order on pp. 17-99 of Soljénitsyne, ed. Nivat & Aucouturier (1918)]
  1679a La fille d'amour et l'innocent: pièce en 4 actes et 11
tableaux, tr. A. Préchac. Paris: R. Laffont, 1971. 288 pp. Bibliography, pp. 281-3. [Olen']
  1679b "La main droite," pp. 3-13 & "Procession pascale," pp. 13-
16 in:Littérature russe clandestine, tr. C. Lopez. Paris: Éd.
A. Michel, 1971. xi, 342 pp. "Préface" by Jean-François Revel.
  1680 Août quatorze, tr. Alfreda & Michel Aucouturier, Georges
Nivat & Jean-Paul Sémon. Paris: Éd. du Seuil, 1972. 512 pp.
  1680a "Le cri: le discours du prix Nobel," Express (4-10 Sep
1972), 96-103. [Note: full text of Nobel speech in translation
also incl. in 1972 ed. of Les droits de l'écrivain (see 1840)]

  For letters and samizdat documents by and about S., see 1840 &
1918.

Criticism:

  This section includes biography and important news articles as
well as criticism, in both periodicals and books; the order is
chronological; reviews are listed in separate subsections at appropriate locations within the chronological sequence. Abbreviations used are given on p. 89. For books, theses and articles
in books, see 1713, 1840, 1870-73, 1918-19 & 1928a. Important
articles in periodicals include the following: 1689, 1690, 1848,
1852, 1854, 1887, 1907, 1911, 1912, 1914, 1915 (and other articles at Oct-Nov 1970), and some of the reviews of Aug. 1914 (see
entries 1929-1940).

1680b Triolet, E. "Pour l'amour de l'avenir," <u>LF</u>, 955 (7 Dec),
1-4. [Polish tr.: 2311]
1681 "Une journée dans un camp de mort sous Staline," <u>NCan</u>, No.
84, pp. 1, 9-10.
1681a Cathala, J. " Une journée d'I. D.," <u>FN</u>, 895 (12 Dec), 28-9.
1681b Samaret, V. "Une journée d'I. D.," <u>FO</u>, 658 (13 Dec), 12-13.

1682 Kouznetsof, M. "Une victoire de l'humain et la naissance
d'un écrivain de talant," <u>Libération</u> (18 Jan). [Tr. of 77]
1682a "Lettre de la commission pour la verité sur les crimes de
Staline à A. S.," <u>NCan</u> (24 Jan); also in <u>Démocratie 63</u> , 170, p.
11. [Tr. of 238?]
1682b Minaev, G. "Autour de roman d'Al. S.," <u>LF</u>, 964 (1 Feb), 1
& 9. [Tr. of 87]
1683 Daix, P. "Rien n'est jamais acquis à l'homme," <u>Libération</u>
(26 Feb).
1683a Villalaur, A. "L'Univers d'I. D.," <u>LF</u> (Mar).
1684 Martin-Chauffier, L. "Un scandale," <u>Figaro</u> (20 Mar), 1.
1685 Boukhanov, V. "A Riazan chez S.," <u>LF</u>, 970 (21 Mar), 1 & 4.
[Tr. Of 88]
1686 Féron, B. "Un écrivain sans complaisance: Al. S.," <u>Monde</u>,
754 (30 Mar), 2.
1687 Michel, J. "Le roman de Nikita Serguéievitch," <u>FO</u>, 675
(11 Apr), 16. [On OD]
1688 Riquet, R. "Quand Buchenwald était en Sibérie," <u>FL</u> (27 Apr).
1689 Herling, G. "De Tchékhov à S.," <u>Preuves</u>, 148 (Jun), 46-49.
1690 Zamoyska, H. "S. et la grande tradition," <u>Table Ronde</u>, 185
(Jun), 61-81.
1691 Lamarque, J. & M. Merlier. "Les Soviétiques sous Staline,"
<u>Partisans</u> (Oct-Nov), 162-73.

Reviews of <u>Une journée d'Ivan Denissovitch</u> (Mar-Jul 1963):

1692 <u>Arts</u>, 907 (13 Mar), 4. (S. Lescaut)
1693 <u>Avenir</u> du Luxembourg (Arlon), 7 May. (L. D.)
1694 <u>Candide</u> (18 Apr), 14. (K. Haedens: "Il n'y a pas de quoi
crier au génie")
1695 <u>Carrefour</u> (27 Mar), 12. (C. M.)
1696 <u>CN</u> (5 Apr), 1-2. (L. Guissard)
1697 <u>Débat Communiste</u>, 14, p. 16.
1698 <u>Dépêche du Maine</u> (5 May). (B. Garach)
1699 <u>Études</u> (Jul), 154. (R. Bosc)
1700 <u>Éducation Nationale</u> (2 May). (O. Wormser)
1701 <u>ES</u>, 178, pp. 64-65. (A. Avdeienko: "Un événement littéraire: Une journée d'I. D.") [Ger. tr. (?) at 1967a]
1702 <u>Express</u>, 616, pp. 36-7. (P. Rawicz)
1703 <u>FL</u>, 885 (6 Apr), 5. (G. B[ortoli])
1704 <u>France-U.R.S.S.</u> Mag., 202, pp. 10-13. (J. Champenois)
1705 <u>Gauche</u> (14 Jun). (A. Franklin)
1706 <u>LF</u>, 971 (28 Mar), 2. ("L'Univers d'I. D.")
1707 <u>Libre Belgique</u> (Brussels), 16 May. ("Haro sur Staline")
1708 <u>NCr</u>, 144 (Apr), 131-36. (B. Taslitzky)
1709 <u>NL</u> (4 Apr). (E. Leguèbe)
1710 <u>Paris-Normandie</u> (Rouen), 19 Apr. (Y. Hecht)

1711 Phare Dimanche (Brussels), 7 Apr. (J. Bertrand)
1712 Trib. de Genève (11 May). (G. Bratschi)

1964

1713 Borel, P.-L. "De Péguy à Sartre" in Paradoxes du XXe siècle. Neufchâtel: Messeilles, 1964. (On S., pp. 132-33)
1714 "Pour le Bien de la Cause," FO (24 Jan).
1715 Tatu, M. "La Pravda prend indirectement position contre la candidature de S. au Prix Lénine," Monde, 808 (14 Apr), 5.
1716 Daix, P. "Si nous reparlions de S.," LF, 1029 (14 May), 1 & 11.
1717 Kariakine, Yu. "Une journée d'I. D. de S. et le culte de la personalité," Nouv. Rev. Internationale, 9, pp. 178-94. [Tr. of 180].
1718 Forgues, P. "Novy Mir," Mercure de France, 1212 (Oct), 332-37. (On Tvardovsky, NM & S.)

1965

1720 [sic] Brice, J. "A. Tvardovsky est l'eminence grise du dégel soviétiques," FL, 1023 (25 Nov), 7.

1966

1721 Robel, L. "S.: Un grand écrivain et une grande conscience," LF, 1117 (3 Feb), 3.
1722 Stil, A. "Pour le bien de la cause," Humanité (3 Mar).
1723 Nyssen, H. "Al. S.," Marginales (Brussels), Sep, 53-56.

Reviews of La Maison de Matriona [see 1674b] (Jan-Jun 1966):

1724 Berry (17 Feb). (P.-G. Michel)
1725 CN (4 Feb). (L. Guissard)
1726 Ecole et la Nation, 150 (Jun), 44-46. (J. Spangare)
1727 Esprit, 349 (May), 1119-20. (C. Audejean)
1728 Europe, 444-445 (Apr-May), 236-39. (P. Gamarra)
1729 FN, 1060 ((Feb), 21. (G. Ziegler)
1730 Gauche (5 Feb), 10. (A. Franklin)
1731 Gaz. de Lausanne (19 Feb). (J. Bloch-Michel)
1732 Humanité-Dim. (3 Apr). (M. Monod)
1733 Légion Violette (Blancmesnil), May-Jul. (A. Blanc) [see 1743]
1734 LF, 1119 (17 Feb), 8. (A. Villelaur)
1735 LN (24 Feb). (G. d'Aubarède)
1736 Liberté (Lille), 11 Mar. (A. Stil) [Same as 1722?]
1737 NCan (21 Jan). (P. Rosset:"Après l'autocritique, la critique")
1738 Nouv. Gaz. (Charleroi), 24 Feb. (M. Prist)
1739 NO, 69 (9 Mar), 29-30. (C. Roy)
1740 Paris-Normandie (Rouen), 4 Feb.
1741 Petit Varois-Marsellaise (Toulon), 1 Mar. (A. Remacle)
1742 Phare Dim. (Brussels), 6 Feb. (J. Bertrand)
1743 P.T.T.-Informations (Mar). (A. Blanc) [Same as 1733?]
1744 QL, 1 (15 Mar), 10. (P. Rawicz: "La souffrance des humbles")
1745 Ski Français (Dec). (M. Melou)
1746 Trib. de Genève (12 Mar). (G. Bratschi)
1747 Trib. de Lausanne (6 Feb). (P. Descargues)

1967

1748 Radine, S. "La maison de Matriona," Cité Nouv. (9 Feb).

1749 "Sur A. S.," QL, 23 (1 Mar), 15.

1750 "Le J'accuse de S.," Contrat Social, 3, pp. 153-56.

1751 [Ličko, P.] "Une journée chez S.," QL, 52 (15-31 Jul), 6-7.
[Tr. by S. Kocik of 1604 (excerpts)]

1752 "L'Éclat de S.," Courrier des Pays de l'Est, 81, pp. 44-45.

1753 Fosty, V. "Cinquante ans de littérature soviétique (1917-67)," FL (6 Nov), 8-10.

1754 Monde, 7133 (20 Dec), suppl.:
Marie, J.-J. "Une génération qui retrouve le sens du tragique,"
  p. iv.
Féron, B. "A. S.," p. v.

1755 Thoorens, L. Panorama des littératures. Verviers, Belgium:
Ed. Gérard (Marabout Université, No. 140), 1967. (See v. 5, p. 213)

1968

1756 "Le 'Times' publie les extraits du roman S.," Monde (13 Apr).

1757 Cathala, J. "U.R.S.S., une renaissance, la littérature pay-sanne," Monde, 7255 (11 May), suppl., p. vii.

1758 Fosty, V. "Voici le nouveau roman de S.," FL (20-26 May), 14.

1759 Nantet, J. "Le dossier de la littérature soviétique," NL
(25 Jul).

1760 Slavinsky, M. "Le cas S.," Est et Ouest, 414, pp. 15-18.

1760a Ganne, G. "Un nouveau Pasternak," Aurore (10 Sep). [See
1804]

1761 M. P. "Une journée d'I. D.," RDM (Oct), 222-24.

1762 Bethell, N. "Le scandaleux 'procès' d'Al. S.," FL, 1170
(7-13 Oct), 9-11. [See later articles by B. at 1115 & 2062]

1763 France-Dufaux, P. "La clef de voûte du message de S.," Sol-eil (Quebec), 19 Oct.

1764 Bielski, N. "La moitié du monde et dans cette moitié un
châteaux dont 'l'enchanteur' est Staline," NO (4 Nov).

1765 Malry G. "S. et le 'Printemps de Prague'," Matin (Anvers);
Métropole; Flandre Libérale (8 Nov).

1766 Jacob, A. "Al. S. a rejeté les arguments de ses accusateurs,"
Monde (12 Nov).

1767 Warsz, A. "Les clandestins de la contestation en U.R.S.S.,"
FL (18 Nov).

1768 Vigneaux, J. "Ce sont toujours les crucifiés qui gagnet,"
Pourquoi Pas?(Belgium) (21 Nov), 173-9.

1769 Olivier, D. "Un monde de soupirs," Réforme (23 Nov).

1770 de Kerchove, A. "Patrie de la souffrance, S., M. C. Blais,
Clavel," Rev. Générale Belge (Dec), 105-08.

1771 Kyria, P. "Ecrivains étrangers," Rev. de Paris (Dec),109-10.

1772 Stil, A. "Vents d'Est," Humanité (19 Dec).

1773 Nantet, J. "Les héritiers de Tolstoi," NL (26 Dec).

1774 Journal de Genève-Samedi Littéraire, 52 (28 Dec):
Aucouturier, N. "Honneur à S. . . ."
Biro, Adam. "En droite ligne de Tolstoi".

Reviews of Le premier cercle (Sep. 1968-Dec. 1969):

1775 Beaux-Arts (Brussels), 19 Oct 1968). (A. Miguel)

1776 Bulletin Bibliographie des Armées (1er trimestre 1969).

1777 Bulletin des Lettres (Lyon) (Oct 1968), 15.

1778 Combat (3 Oct 1968). (P. Kyria)

1779 Cri du Monde (Oct 1968), 52. (V. Hamryluk)

1780 Critique, 25 (1969), 624-28. (F. Galichet: "Un géomètre au cachot")
1781 CN (29 Sep 1968). (L. Guissard)
1782 Eaux Vives (Feb 1969), 17. (Ch. Burucoa)
1783 Études (5 Feb 1969). (F. Devalière)
1784 FAN (12 Nov 1968). (P. Borel: "Un grand roman russe")
1785 FL, 1170 (7-13 Oct 1968), 11. (V. Fosty: "Un témoin qui revient de l'enfer")
1786 France Catholique (6 Dec 1968), 1 & 8. (J. de Fabrègues)
1787 Livres et Lectures (Dec 1968). (M. Guillet)
1788 Matin (Anvers) (25 Sep 1968). (G. Malry)
1789 Monde, 7470 (18 Jan 1969), suppl., pp. i-ii. (H. Zamoyska)
1790 Paris-Normandie (Rouen) (25 Oct 1968). (Y. Hecht)
1791 Populaire du Centre (17 Oct 1968). (Kenett)
1792 Profession Dentaire (Oct 1969). (V. Volmane)
1793 IVe [Quatrième] Internationale, 35 (Feb 1969), 56-57. (M. Lequenne)
1794 QL, 58 (1 Oct 1968), 3-4. (M. Nadeau)
1795 Rencontres (Sep 1968). (L. Emery)
1796 Rép. Lorrain (28 Sep 1968). (C. Fleury)
1797 Révolution Prolétarienne (Dec 1969). (B. Giauffret)
1798 Sélection des Libraires, 62 (Oct 1968). (R. Laffont)
1799 Soir (Brussels) (16 Oct 1968). (V. Fosty)
1800 Témoignage Chrétien (19 Dec 1968). (J. Madaule)
1801 Trib. de Genève (16 Oct 1968). (G. Bratschi)
1802 Trib. de Lausanne (22 Sep 1968). (P. Descargues)
1803 Villes Nouvelles (Apr 1969). (H. Jaoui)

See also 1878 & 1881.

Reviews of both Le premier cercle and Le pavillon des cancéreux (Oct 1968-May 1969):

1804 Aurore (15 Oct 1968). (G. Ganne: "La revanche de S.") [See also 1760a]
1805 Contacts Electriques (May 1969). (P. R.)
1806 Echos (15 Nov 1968). (A. C.)
1807 Economie en France et dans le Monde, 1080 (11 Jan 1969), 31. (K. de Rosbo)
1808 Express, 901 (14 Oct 1968), 121-23. (A. Bercoff)
1809 Gaz. Lit. (Switzerland) (12 Oct 1968), 23. (M. Aucouturier)
1810 LF, 1260 (4 Dec 1968), 8. (A. Villelaur)
1811 Mag. Lit., 28 (Apr-May 1969), 26-29. (M. Del Castillo)
1812 NO (18 Nov 1968), 38-39. (C. Roy: "Vu du bagne")
1813 Spectacle du Monde (Dec 1968), 98-99. (J. Mabire: "Sous la lune noire")

Reviews of Le pavillon des cancéreux (Aug 1968-Apr 1969):

1814 A la Page (Mar 1969). (C. Melchior-Bonnet).
1815 Aspects de la France (16 Jan 1969). (J. Valmont)
1816 Canard Enchaîné (30 Oct 1968). (M. Lebesque)
1817 Cri du Monde (Dec 1968), 51-52. (X. Grall: "Une montée au calvaire soviétique") [See also 1838]
1818 CN (4 Nov 1968). (L. Guissard)
1819 Dépêche de Saint-Etienne (9 Nov 1968); Echo et Liberté

(Lyon) (10 Nov 1968). (J. Davranches)
1820 Echo Rép. de la Beauce et du Perche (17 Apr 1969). (C. Dox)
1821 FAN (22 Feb 1969). (P. Borel)
1822 Figaro (2 Dec 1968). (C. Jardin).
1823 France Catholique (20 Dec 1968). (A. Palante)
1824 France-U.R.S.S. Mag. (Jan 1969). (M. W.)
1825 Humanité-Dim. (5 Jan 1969). (M. Monod)
1826 Lectures Pour Tous, 180 (Jan 1969), 83. (P. Dumayet)
1827 LF, 1251 (2 Oct 1968), 3. (P. Daix: "Sous le signe de S.")
1828 Monde, 7344 (24 Aug 1968), suppl., p. vi. (H. Zamoyska)
[Pt. I]
1829 Monde, 7404 (2 Nov 1968), suppl., p. v. (H. Zamoyska) [Pt.
II]
1830 NCr, 203 (1969), 60-63. (A. Stil)
1831 Nouv. République du Centre-Ouest (Tours) (28 Mar 1969).
(C. Melchior Bonnet)
1832 Omnipracticien Français (Apr 1969), 327-33. (P. Befort)
1833 IVe [Quatrième] Internationale, 36 (Mar 1969), 60-64. (M.
Lequenne) [Also reviews Les droits de l'écrivain (see 1840)]
1834 QL, 61 (16 Nov 1968), 3-4. (J.-J. Marie: "Le mensonge en
miettes")
1835 Résonances (Feb 1969), 11-14. (M. Dargent: "Un cancérologue
juge")
1836 Semaine des Hôpitaux (26 Apr 1969), 22-31.
1837 Soir (Brussels) (11 Sep 1968). (V. Fosty)
1838 Témoignage Chrétien (12 Dec 1968). (X. Grall: "Le pavillon
des cancéreux: la Russie a-t-elle une âme leucémique?")
1839 Voix du Nord (10 Dec 1968). (R. Ramet)

See also 1758, 1874, 1877-78, 1883 & 1885.

1969

1840 Les droits de l'écrivain. Paris: Ed-ns. du Seuil, 1969. 96
pp.; 1972. 128 pp. (with "Discours de Stockholm"). [Tr. of Tra
autoritarismo (see 2190 for list of contents)]
1841 Reviews of Les droits de l'écrivain:
  Combat (16 Jan 1969). (P. Kyria: "Le cas S.")
  Figaro (25 Jan 1969). (C. J.)
  LF, 1266 (15 Jan 1969), 1 & 4. (P. Daix: "L'affaire S.")
  Monde, 7470 (18 Jan 1969), suppl., p. i.
  Paris-Normandie (Rouen) (24 Jan 1969). (Y. Hecht)
  Réforme (15 Feb 1969), 13-14. (D. Olivier: "L'écrivain et son
    destin")
  Trib. des Nations (7 Feb 1969). (P. Cazenave)
  See also 1833.
1842 Tvardovski, A. "L'affaire S.," Preuves, 214 (Jan), 3-10.
[Tr. of 267]
1843 Sion, G. "A. S.," Phare-Dim. (Brussels) (19 Jun 1969), 5.
1844 Smorlarski, H. "Un veilleur appelé A. S.," Trib. Juive
(23 Jan).
1845 Audejean, C. "Des millions de S.," Esprit, 2 (Feb), 306-14.
1846 Dumon, M. "A. S.," M' (Belgium), Feb.
1847 Frioux, C. "Le 'Progressisme' dans la littérature soviétique,"
Politique Aujourd'hui (Feb), 115-117.

1848 Zamoyska, H. "S.," Table Ronde, 253 (Feb), 141-45.
1849 Guéhénno, J. "Les devoirs de l'écrivain," Figaro (20 Feb),1.
1850 Parias,L.-H."Faut-il 'aller vers de peuple'?" France Catholique (7 Mar).
1851 Laloux, I. "La vie et la mort, l'insolite et le réel," Vers
l'Avenir (Namur) (11 Mar).
1852 Gillès, D. "S., ou l'écrivain réduit au silence," Revue de
Paris, 76, iv (Apr 1969), 37-42.
1853 Lacarrière, J. "La maison de Matriona," Liens (Apr).
1854 Amette, J. "Al. S.," Nouv. Rev. Française, 17, No. 198 (Jun),
1164-69.
1855 Fosty, V. "'La bougie dans le vent' de S.," FL, 1213 (18
Aug), 26.
1856 Fosty, V. "La curée," FL (10 Nov).
1857 Jacob, A. "Al. S. a rejeté les arguments de ses accusateurs,"
Monde (13 Nov).
1858 Rebatet, L. "S., un grand écrivain persecuté," Rivarol, 983
(14 Nov), 5-6.
1859 M. B. "S. bâillonné," Construire (Zurich) (19 Nov).
1860 LF, 1309 (19-25 Nov):
"Une déclaration du comité National des Ecrivains," p. 3.
"En marge de l'exclusion d'Al. S.," pp. 3-4, 6 [see also 1865;
in Russian at 428, p. 129 & 429].
1861 "Aragon et Sartre condamnent l'exclusion de S.," France-
Soir (20 Nov).
1862 Cournot, M. "Les 'tolerances' de la police soviétique," NO
264 (1-7 Dec), 24-25.
1863 Benoit, R. "Un autre auteur soviétique défie les autorités;
il parle de la 'décrépitude du régime' après l'exclusion de S. de
l'Union des Ecrivains," France-Soir (5 Dec). [A. Amal'rik]
1864 Kahn, J.-F. "S. rallume des cierges," Express (8 Dec).
1865 "La déclaration du Comité National des Ecrivains Français
en faveur de S.," Monde (13 Dec). [New list of signatures (see
1860)]
1866 Léger, Y. "S., la Russie, l'exil," QL, 85 (15 Dec), 5.
1867 "'L'Unita' (Rome) déclare: Même les adversaires des plus
acharnés de S. reconnaissent son génie," Monde (25 Dec).
1868 "Mme. Fourtseva, Ministre de la Culture soviétique dit:
'Que S. écrive de bons ouvrages et ils seront publies'," Aurore
(27 Dec). [A similar report of Mme. F.'s Paris statement appeared in Le Monde, 28 Dec., which appears in trans. in Labedz
(1285), pp. 199-200.]
1869 "Un communiqué de l'Union des Ecrivains d'URSS sur la dif-
fusion d'un pièce de S.," Monde (31 Dec). [Contains communiqué
from French Union of Writers cautioning publishers against publishing "Pir pobeditelja" (see 24) against S.'s wishes. (Pub. in
Labedz [1285], p. 158.)]

1970

1870 Chaix-Ruy, Jules. A. Soljénitsyne ou la descente aux en-
fers: Etude. Paris: Del Duca, 1970. 159 pp.
1871 Lukács, G. Soljénitsyne, tr. S. Bricianer. Paris: Galli-
mard, 1970. 192 pp. [Tr. of 2052]
1872 Bersani, J., D. Autrand, G. Lecarme & B. Vercier. La littérature en France depuis 1945. Paris: Bordas, 1970. (See pp.

728-29; also has excerpt from Une journée d'I. D.)

1873 Fischer, E. "Fin de Partie et Une journée d'Ivan Denisso-vitch," in his: A la recherche de la réalité: Contribution à une esthétique marxiste moderne, tr. J.-L. Lebrave & J.-P. Lefebvre. Paris: Denoël, 1970. 344 pp. [Beckett & S.; tr. of 1979]

1874 Bouilly, J. "Le Pavillon des Cancéreux," Présences (Draveil), 1er trimestre.

1875 Fosty, V. "A. S. dramaturge, un théâtre du désespoir," FL (5 Jan). [Olen']

1876 "Pour quoi S. a-t-il été exclu de l'Union des Ecrivains?" ES, 263 (Feb). [Same as 1593]

1877 Crousse, J.-L. "Le pavillon des cancéreux," Rev. Nouv. (Tournai) (Feb).

1878 Jeunes Femmes (Feb), 92-95:
Chevallier, M. "Le pavillon des cancéreux".
Jeanette, C. "Une journée".
Hatzfeld, G. "Le premier cercle".

1879 "A. S. charge un avocat Suisse de défendre ses intérêts à l'étranger," Monde (10 Mar). [F. Heeb]

1880 "Un film anglo-américano-norvégien sera tiré d'Une Journée d'Ivan Denissovitch," Monde (21 Mar), suppl., p. vii.

1881 Jorens, R. "'Le premier cercle' de S.," Union (22 Mar), 10-11.

1882 Porquerol, E. "La maison de Matriona," Bull. Mensuel de la Guilde du Livre (Lausanne) (4 Apr), 105-07, 128.

1883 Crespin, R. "Le pavillon des cancéreux," Cité Nouv. (16 Apr), 6.

1884 Piatier, J. "Littérature concentrationnaire," Monde, 7863 (25 Apr), suppl., p. v.

1885 George, R. "Le pavillon des cancéreux," A l'Ecoute du Monde (Lyon) (May), 11.

1886 "Cinquante écrivains français demandent le Prix Nobel pour S.," Figaro (20 Jul).

1887 Jacquemin, G. "Autour de S.," Marginales (Brussels) (Aug), 1-11.

1888 Wurmser, A. "S.: Prix Nobel," Humanité (9 Oct), 1 & 10. [Excerpt in English in Labedz (1285), pp. 211-12]

1889 Berner, P. "S. le persécuté couronné par le Prix Nobel," Aurore (9 Oct), 1 & 8.

1890 Simon, S. "Fragile et indomptable," Figaro (9 Oct), 32. (Other stories on S., same page.)

1891 Bosquet, A. "Mieux qu'un martyr," Combat (9 Oct), 16.

1892 Rawicz, P. "Un héros couronné," Monde (10 Oct), 2.

1893 Wenger, A. "A. S. croyant," Croix (11-12 Oct), 20. (Other stories on S., same page.)

1894 Martin-Chauffier, J. "S.: Prix Nobel," FL (12 Oct).

1895 Kahn, J. "Dites que S. est le plus grand," Express, 1005 (12 Oct), 125-26.

1896 Gordey, M. "Le Nobel à S., les soviétiques en font un affaire," France-Soir (12 Oct).

1897 Roy, C. "Un homme à aimer," NO, 309 (12 Oct), 41-42.

1898 Daix, P. "Au plus grand écrivain russe vivant," LF, 1355 (14 Oct), 1, 3, 4. [Excerpt in Eng. in Labedz (1285), p. 212]

1899 Robel, L. "Mais tout dépend des moyens qui sont ceux de l'artiste," LF, 1355 (14 Oct), 6.

1900 Gamarra, P. "S.," FN (14 Oct).

1901 Gauthier, J. "Et le Prix Nobel de la trique," Canard Enchaîné (14 Oct).
1902 Stil, A. "Grandeur et limite d'un humanisme," Humanité (15 Oct).
1903 Chavardes, M. "Nous appartenons à l'humanité," Hebdo-Témoignage Chrétien (15 Oct).
1904 Duranteau, J. "S.: Prix Nobel," Education (15 Oct), 25.
1905 Matzneff, G. "Sur une prière de S.," Combat, 8163 (15 Oct),1.
1906 Lanoux, A. "S. dans les pas de Dostoievski," NL, 2247 (15 Oct), 1 & 7.
1907 Politique Hebdo, 2 (15-21 Oct):
Frioux, C. "S.: Le prophète et son pays," 25.
Mark[stein], E. "La littérature soviétique en tutelle," 26-27 [also see her articles at 683 & 1918, pp. 389-99].
S. [facsimile of letter to Juliard, 18 Jun 1969], p. 26.
S. "Flamme au vent (ou La lumière qui est en toi)," tr. A. Aucouturier [excerpt].
Lukács, G. "Soljénitsyne" [excerpt from 1871; appears in Eng. tr. in Labedz (1285), pp. 219-20].
1908 Michel, M. "Le pavillon des cancéreux," Monde (17 Oct). [On forthcoming radio presentation]
1909 Parias, L.-H. "Le message de S.," France Catholique, 1244 (16 Oct), 13.
1910 Olivier, D. "Un homme de vigeur et de sérénité," Réforme (17 Oct).
1911 FL, 1274 (19 Oct):
Fosty, V. "Un soviétique à visage humaine," 9-10.
S. "Le souffle," tr. V. Fosty, 10.
Lanoux, A. "L'écrivain et le secrétaire," 11-12.
Rousset, D. "Le porte-voix 'des cancéreux'," 12-13.
London, A. "Combattant de la vérité," 13.
1912 Monde des Livres (23 Oct):
Nivat, G. "S. et l'esthétique marxiste," 18-19.
Nivat, L. "Introd. à 'Etudes et Miniatures'" and tr. by her: "Le feu de bois et les fourmis", "En suivant la rive de l'Oka" & "Zacharie l'escarcelle" [excerpt].
Palmier, J.-M. "Les mésadventures du 'réalisme socialiste'," 18.
1913 Kiejman, C. "S. 'recompense'," Jeune Afrique (27 Oct), 53.
1914 Moreau, J.-L. "Littérature soviétique: Le Pari de Stockholm," RDM, 11, pp. 478-84.
1915 Nivat, G. "Au tocsin de l'histoire," QL, 105 (1 Nov), 12-14.
1916 "La voix de S.," Alpha-Le Million, 90 (10 Nov), 345-46.
1917 Fosty, V. "L'affaire S.," Rev. Nouv. (Dec), 500-510.

1971

1918 Nivat, Georges & Michel Aucouturier, eds. Soljénitsyne. Paris: Les Éditions de l'Herne (Série Slave, No. 16), 1971. 519 pp. [For reviews, see 396, 682 & 1286 (TLS)]
Contents:
Aucouturier, M. & G. Nivat. "Avant-Propos," 9-10.
"Chronologie," 13-16.
"Textes de Soljénitsyne," 17-99 [repr. from 1679; see contents there]. (Other items by S. in this book: "Comment on lit 'Ivan Denissovitch," 212-223; "Prière," p. 345: Letter to Juliard of 18 Jun 1969, p. 416b; and other letters & documents from samiz-

1918 (cont'd):
dat [see pp. 225-63, 272, 287-8, 298-306, 319-20 & 323].)
"Documents" [all items in this section are translations from
Russian; numbers given in brackets below are entry numbers in
this bibliography; the translations usually are just excerpts]:
1. "L'homme," pp. 103-118:
P. Kossolapov [59], 104; V. Boukhanov [88], 104-09; You. Koun-
gourtsev [191], 110-13; P. Ličko [1604], 113-18.
2. "S. et la presse soviétique, 1962-1966," pp. 119-223:
A. Tvardovski [54], 120-22; C. Simonov [55], 122-23; V. Ermilov [57], 123-25; G. Baklanov [56], pp. 125-27; A. Dymschitz
[58], 127-8; N. Kroujkov [64], 128; E. Broido [63], 128-9; N.
Zorine [69], 129; B. Kagane [70], 129; A. Astafiev [72], 129;
M. Nolmane [76], 129; I. Tchitcherov [65], 129-30; L. Fomenko
[85], 130-31; G. Minaev [87], 132-3; F. Tchaptchakov [78], 133-
35; Editorial in Kommunist [81], 135; I. Droutze [79], 135-7;
F. Kouznetsov [80], 137; N. Goubko [93], 137-8; excerpt from
brochure Que les étoiles se rapprochent [104], 139-40; S. Pavlov [101], 141; V. Poltoratski [103], 142-3; A. Dymschitz [105],
143-4; N. Sergovantsev [107], 144-7; V. Pertsovski [131], 147-
48; V. Bouchine [114], 148-9; Iou. Barabach [121], 150-51; M.
Sinelnikov [126], 151; D. Granine [127], 151; Editorial note
in LG [128], 152; N. Pouzanova [129], 152-3; letter of E. Iampolskaia, I. Okounieva & M. Goldberg [123], 153; L. Reznikov
[123], 153-4; V. Cheinis & R. Tsimerinov [123], 154; Editorial
note in LG [134], 154-5; letter from ed's. of NM to LG, with
reply [136], 155-7; A. Makarov [135], 157-8; A. Ovtcharenko
[130], 158-61; V. Sourganov [144], 161-3; V. Ivanov [137], 164-
66; M. Lezinski [149], 166-7; N. Moltchaniouk [149], 167; V.
Pallon [150], 167-9; V. Pankov [152], 169-70; A. Stavitski [153],
170-71; S. Marchak [154], 171-3; article in LG [159], 173-4; V.
Lakchine [145], 174-9; editorial in LG [162], 179-82; V. Skoui-
bine [157], 182; S. Savine [164], 182-3; edit. in Pravda [168],
183-5; edit. in Trud [170], 185; L. Grekov [169], 185-6; Iou.
Barabach [174], 186-190; V. Lakchine [175], 190-91; edit. in
LG [175], 191-2; N. Volguine [181], 192-3; Iou. Kariakine [180],
193-201; A. Tvardovski [190], 201; G. Brovman [188], 201; N.
Egorytchev [192], 201-02; E. Voutchetich [194], note: name er-
roneously given as "Bouketitch"], 202; S. Pavlov [196], 202;
Iou. Barabach [186], 202-03; S. Mojniagoune [203], 203; A. Makarov [197], 203-4; M. Alekseiev [199], 204; V. Kojevnikov [201],
204-05; V. Lakchine [202], 205-08; B. Grigoriev [205], 209-10;
enquette in VL [200], 210; H. Mikoulina [208], 211-12.
3. "L'affaire S.," pp. 224-323:
[247], pp. 225-259; [250], 259-63; [255], 263; [251], 264; [252],
264; [256], 264-5; [257], 265-6; [258], 266-8; [253], 268-9;
[251], 269-70; [254], 270-71; [261], 272; [262], 272-86; [265],
286; [266], 287-8; [263], 287-8 (note); [267], 289-96; [269],
297-8; [271], 298-9; [272], 299-300; [273], 300; [207], 300-06;
[278], 306-12; [287], 313-319; [289], 319-20; [218], 320-23;
[43], 323.
"Études et Témoignages":
del Castillo, M. "Al. S.: La littérature retrouvée," 327-43.
Laffitte, S. "Lettre à l'éditeur," 344-45.
Aucouturier, M. "L'art de S.," 346-51.
Nivat, G. "Essai sur la Symbolique de S.," 352-64.

1918 (cont'd):

Niebolsyne, A. "S.: Une vision tragique et héroique," tr. J. Lafond, 365-9.

Kopelev, L. & R. Orlova. "La verité de la vie et la liberté de l'artiste," tr. J. Lafond [from samizdat], 370-81.

Frioux, C. "S. et son temps," 382-88.

Markstein, E. "De la difficulté d'étudier la littérature soviétique," tr. G. Nivat [see 619], 389-99.

Katkov, G. "La perversité dans l'homme," tr. J. Lafond, 400-11.

Adamovitch, G. "Une mise en garde: A propos d'un entretien," 412-416.

Labriolle, F. "S. entre le stoicisme et la révolte," 417-22.

Denoix, P. "La médecine face à la liberté de l'homme," 423-25.

Zamoyska, H. "A la recherche du bonheur," 426-35.

de Proyart, J. "La femme, l'Amour et l'Enfer," 436-490.

"Bibliographie":

d'Argent, F. "Essai de Bibliographie d'Al. S.," 493-511.

"Index," pp. 512-519.

[Note: This book measures about 8 by 11 inches and has small type; it is equivalent to a conventionally-sized book of 1000 pages.]

1919 Soljénitsyne accuse. Paris: Dominique Wapler, 1971. 268 pp. Foreword by A. Lanoux; introduction and notes by L. Labedz; translations by G. Piquemal. [Probably has most of the same documents as in Labedz (1285), with some additions through May 1971] Review: see 481.

1971-72

1920 Nivat, G. "S.: La justice est la conscience de l'humanité," Journal de Genève, Samedi Lit. (29 May 1971).

1921 Fosty, V. "Vera Fosty a lu le dernièr S. 'Août 1914', interdit en U.R.S.S.," Figaro (2 Jul 1971), 1-3.

1922 Nantet, J. "Mendel Mann présente Août 1914: La dernière bataille de S.," NL (2 Jul 1971), 12.

1923 Rawicz, P. "Al. S.: Son nouveau roman," Monde (2 Jul 1971), 13 & 15.

1924 Ierunca, V. "S. ou le réalisme nécessaire: La civilisation a l'épreuve," France Catholique (9 Jul 1971).

1925 "S. s'attaque au K.G.B.," QL (1-15 Sep 1971), 31.

1926 Aragon, L. Express (21-28 Sep 1971). (Interview; comments on S. & Šoloxov; Russian tr.: 477.)

1927 Jardin, C. "Al. S. fustige la Russie contemporaine," Figaro (4 Oct 1971).

1927a Bory, J.-L. "Un hymne à la terre russe et au passé russe," Paris Match (12 Oct 1971), 67. [Rev. of 1679]

1928 [The Press on S.] French tr. of 237. 1972. (Only 200 copies published, according to Artemova [see 429].)

1928a Schardt, M. [Mrs. Magnon]. "La technique du récit dans l'oeuvre de S. Une journée d'Ivan Denissovitch et dans celle de Camus La Chute," Master's Thesis, Université d'Aix-Marseille, Fac. des lettres, juin 1972.

Reviews of Août quatorze (Sep-Oct 1972):

1929 FL (16 Sep). (C. Baigneres: "La 'tragédie humaine' de S.")

1930 Gaz. de Lausanne (14-15 Oct). (A. Bosquet: "S. et la Saint Russie")

1931 Journal de Genève, Samedi Lit.(21 Oct). (J.-C. Gateau: "Entretien avec les traducteurs") [See also 1932, same issue]
1932 Journal de Genève, Samedi Lit.(21 Oct). (J.-L. Kuffer: "L'histoire, ce n'est pas la raison qui la dirige")
1933 Monde (15 Sep), 14. (M. del Castillo: "Une épopée spirituelle") [See also 1934-36 in same issue]
1934 Monde (15 Sep), 14. (P. Pascal: "Le livre devant l'histoire")
1935 Monde (15 Sep), 15. (M. Aucouturier: "Une maîtrise romanesque")
1936 Monde (15 Sep), 15. (B. Féron: "Un artiste taillé dans le roc")
1937 NL, 2350 (9-15 Oct), 3-4. (J. Nantet: "S.: écho sonore du 'tocsin muet'")
1938 Pourquoi Pas?, 2811, pp. 168, 173-5. (J. Vigneaux: "Retrouver le plaisir de lire 'comme au IXe siècle'")
1939 QL (16-30 Sep), 3-5. (M. Nadeau: "Le mémoire d'un peuple")
1940 Soir (22 Sep). (P. Me.)

For other articles in French (or tr. from Fr.) see: 642, 2082 & 2228.

(16) German. (Germany, Austria, Switzerland)

Special sources (aside from standard reference works): information about many of the book reviews was supplied by Karin Busch of Luchterhand Verlag and Lionel von dem Knesebeck of S. Fischer Verlag; about 50 of the entries were taken from Artemova (see 429). Abbreviations: S.: Solschenizyn (most common spelling, esp. in recent years) or Solshenizyn (occasional usage, esp. first several years). Periodicals: CW: Christ und Welt; DAS: Deutsches Allgemeines Sonntagsblatt; FAZ: Frankfurter Allgemeine Zeitung; FH: Frankfurter Hefte; FNP: Frankfurter Neue Presse; FR: Frankfurter Rundschau; HAZ: Hannoversche Allgemeine Zeitung; MM: Münchener Merkur; NatZ: National-Zeitung (Basel); NF: Neues Forum: Internationale Zeitschrift für den Dialog (Wien); NN: Nürnberger Nachrichten; NZ: Nürnberger Zeitung; NZZ: Neue Zürcher Zeitung; RM: Rheinischer Merkur (Köln); SaZ: Saarbrücker Zeitung; SH: Sowjetunion heute: Zeitschrift über Leben u. Arbeit, Kultur, Wirtschaft, Wissenschaft, etc. i. d. UdSSR; StN: Stuttgarter Nachrichten; StZ: Stuttgarter Zeitung; SdZ: Süddeutsche Zeitung.

Translations:

1941 Ein Tag im Leben des Iwan Denissowitsch, tr. W. Löser, T. Friedrich, I. Hanelt & E.-M. Kunde. Berlin/ Grunewald: F. A. Herbig Verlag & Non-Stop Bücherei, 1963. 126 pp. Other ed'ns: Gütersloh: Bertelsmann Lesering, 1964. 190 pp.; 1970 ed. incl. under another title [see 1957].

1942 Ein Tag im Leben des Iwan Denissowitsch, tr. G. Kurz & S. Summerer. München & Zürich: Droemer/Knaur, 1963 & 1968. 143 pp. Also: Berlin/Darmstadt/Wien: Deutsche Buchgemeinschaft, 1968. 238 pp. (Tr. from Eng. of Hayward&Hingley, with introd. by Hayward & Labedz [see 500])

1943 "Matrjonas Hof," pp. 146-181 in Nach dem Tauwetter: Neue russische Erzählungen, ed. & tr. I. Tinzmann. München: Kindler,

1964.
1944 "Im Interesse der Sache," Sowjetliteratur, 2 (1964). [Tr.?]
1945 ...den Oka-Fluss entlang: 15 Kurtzgeschichten und eine Erzählung.* Frankfurt/M: Possev Verlag, 1965. 76 pp. [With MD]
1946 NZZ (4 Feb 1967), tr. M. Humbert: "Atmen", "Der Segender See", "Das Entchen", "Spiegelbild im Wasser" & "Der Scheiterhaufen und Die Ameisen".
1947 [S.'s letter of 16 May 1967 (see 30)] in: Welt (1 Jun 1967); Ost-Probleme, 12 (16 Jun 1967); & Sowjet Studien, 22 (1967), 85-90.
1948 "Die rechte Hand," tr. E. Marin. FAZ (22 Jun 1968).
1949 Der erste Kreis der Hölle, tr. E. Mahler & N. Nielsen-Stokkeby. Frankfurt/M: S. Fischer, 1968. 669 pp. (other ed'ns in 1969,-70,-71).
1950 Krebsstation, tr. C. Auras, A. Jais & I. Tinzmann (under eds. G. Drohla & E. Borchers). Neuwied & Berlin: Luchterhand. 2 vols.: 1968. 408 pp. (with foreword by H. Böll); 1969. 326 pp. Also: Wien: Molden, 1968-69; Gütersloh: Bertelsmann Lesering,1970.
1951 "Osterprozession in Peredelkino," CW (4 Apr 1969), 13 & 17.
1952 "Die Osterprozession: Bericht aus dem Jahre 1966," tr. E. Marin. FAZ (5 Apr 1969). Also under title "Prozession in Peredelkino," Neue Presse am Sonntag (11 Apr. 1971).
1953 "Wollen Sie Ihre Schande noch vergrössern?" Welt (17 Nov 1969). (S.'s letter of 12 Nov 1969 [see 41])
1954 "Preussische Nächte," tr. R. Drommert. Zeit, 47 (9 Dec 1969), 10. (Excerpts from "Pir pobeditelja" [see note at 24])
1955 Von der Verantwortung des Schriftstellers, ed. F. Ingold. Zürich: Die Arche. 2 vols.: 1969. 47 pp.; 1970. 62 pp. (Contains texts by S. & other materials by Gribačev, Kaverin, Mixalkov, Sobolev & Tvardovskij)
1956 Im Interesse der Sache: Erzählungen, tr. M. von Holbeck, L. Labas, E. Marin, C. Meng & I. Tinzmann. Neuwied & Berlin: Luchterhand, 1970. 456 pp. (Contents: same as 520, plus OD). Same contents except for MD also under title: Ein Tag im Leben des Iwan Denissowitsch und andere Erzählungen. Frankfurt/M: Büchergilde Gutenberg, 1970. 430 pp. (with essay by G. Lukács, pp. 399-428 [see 1971]).
1957 Gegen die Zensur: Kommentare und Briefe [tr. I. Herbert & I. Weyer]; Ein Tag im Leben des Iwan Denissowitsch [tr. W. Löser et al (see 1941)]. München/Wien: Herbig, 1970. 200 pp. With introd. by H. von Ssachno: "Der Fall Al. S.," pp. v-xiii.
1958 Der Fall Solschenizyn: Briefe, Dokumente, Protokolle, comp. B. Nielsen-Stokkeby. Frankfurt a.M./Hamburg: Fischer-Bücherei, 1970. 171 pp. Bibliography, pp. 170-71. (Contents about the same as in 428)
1959 Bestraft mit Weltruhm: Dokumente zu dem Fall Alexander Solshenizyn, ed. & comp. E. Guttenberger; tr. I. Herbert & I. Weyer. Frankfurt/M: Possev Verlag, 1970. 370 pp. With foreword by J. Train and bibliography of works of S., pp. iii-xxiv. (Contents probably identical with 428)
1960 Zwischenfall auf dem Bahnhof Kretschetowka: Erzählungen, tr. A. Jais & A. Kaempfe. München: Herbig, 1971. 217 pp. [SK, MD & PD]
1961 Matrjonas Hof, tr. I. Tinzmann. Stuttgart: Reclam, 1971. 125 pp.; Frankfurt/M: Suhrkamp, 1972. 101 pp. With brief bib. & afterword by K. Borowsky.

───────
* tr. M. von Holbeck

1962 Nemow und das Flittchen: Theaterstück, tr. G. Drohla. Neuwied & Berlin: Luchterhand, 1971. 130 pp. [Olen']
1963 August neunzehnhundertvierzehn, tr. A. Kaempfe. München:
Langen-Müller, 1971. 765 pp. [Pirated edition]
1964 August vierzehn: Roman, tr. S. Geier. Darmstadt & Neuwied:
Luchterhand, 1972. 780 pp.
1965 "Wozu die Gabe der Kunst," tr. E. Lehmann-Braun. FAZ (15
Sep 1972), 7-8. [Also have ref. for this at FAZ, 214 (13 Sep
1972); possibly it was pub. in two parts.] (Nobel lecture)

See also 2053 (documents on S. affair), 2118 ("Autobiography" &
Nobel lecture) & 2119 (Lenten letter, etc.).

Criticism:

This section includes some biography and news; books are listed
together with periodicals in approximate chronological order; reviews are grouped in separate sections within the chronological
sequence. Abbreviations used are listed on p. 101. For books &
articles in books, see 1973-75, 1979, 1982-84, 2052-54, 2083,
2096, 2118-19; note also that several books in the preceding section have documents relating to the S. affair: 1955, 1957-59. Important articles in periodicals include the following: 1968,1971-
72, 1977, 2036, 2039, 2061, 2063, 2085, 2087, 2098 & some of the
reviews of Aug. 1914 (see entries 2099-2117).

1963-68

1966 Mathewson, R. "Betrachtungen über russische und westliche
Prosa," Sowjetstudien, 15 (1963), 30[-?].
1967 Buchanow, V. "Ein realistischer Schriftsteller: Al. S.,"
SH, 5-6 (1963), 28. [Tr. of 88]
1967a Awdejenko, A. "S-ns Erstlingswerk," SH, 5-6(1963), 29.
[Tr. of 1701?]
1968 von Ssachno, H. "Von Tauwetter zu 'Tauwetter'," Merkur,185
(Jul 1963), 690-98; in same issue:
Bienek, H. "Die Maden im Fleisch," 698-700.
1969 Bode, B. [pseud. of Tarasova]. "Über Ästhetik, Ethik und
ähnliche Nutzlosigkeiten," Osteuropa, 9 (Sep. 1963), 637-38.
1970 Bode, B. "Sowjetliteratur 1962/63: Al. S.," Osteuropa, 10
(Oct 1963), 7-6-11.
1971 Lukács, G. "S.: 'Ein Tag im Leben des Iwan Denissowitsch',"
Neue Rundschau, 75, iii (Mar 1964), 401 ff. Repr. at 1956 & 2052;
also repr.: pp. 545-65 in: Lukács, G. Werke, v. 5: Probleme des
Realismus, II. Der russische Realismus in der Weltliteratur. Neuwied & Berlin: Luchterhand, 1964; and pp. 296 ff. in: Lukács, G.
"Ausgewählte Schriften, III. Russische Literatur--russische Revolution," Rowohlts deutsche Enzyklopädie, Bd. 314-16. Reinbek b/
Hamburg: Rowohlt, 1969. [Translations: see 567, 581, 1584, 1612,
1871, 1907 (excerpt), 2146, 2149, 2183, 2256, 2371, 2394, 2444]
1972 Lukács, G. "Lukács über Literatur und Marxismus," Ost-Probleme, 11 (29 Mar 1964). [Czech tr. at 1583]
1973 Kindler-Literatur-Lexikon. Zürich: Kindler Verlag, 1965:
Bd. IV. "Matrenin dvor," sp. 2224-25; Bd. V. "Odin den' Ivana
Denisoviča," sp. 800-02; Bd. V. "Rakovyj korpus," sp. 3009-10.
[Not sure what this is; info. from Artemova (429)]

1974 Maurina, Z. Die Aufgabe des Dichters in unserer Zeit. München: Jolis Verlag, 1965. 168 pp. (Essays; includes at least some mention of S.)

1975 von Ssachno, H. "Die Ära S.," pp. 338-56 in her Der Aufstand der Person: Sowjetliteratur seit Stalins Tod. Berlin: Argon Verlag, 1965. [Spanish tr.: 2372]

1976 Fesenko, Andrej & Tatiana. "Charakteristische Besonderheiten der russischen Sprache: Die 'Lagersprache'," Osteuropa, 1/2 (Jan-Feb 1965), 42-44.

1977 Bode, B. [pseud of N. Tarasova]. "Die Diskussion um S. als Zentrum der Auseinandersetzungen in der Sowjetunion," Osteuropa, 10 (Oct 1965), 679-694; 11/12 (Nov-Dec 1965), 784-96. [Orig. russ. text: see 363]

1978 NZZ (10 Nov 1965). (Article in this issue on seizure of S.'s papers and manuscripts by KGB)

1979 Fischer, E. "Das Endspiel und Iwan Denissowitsch," pp. 7-32 in his Kunst und Koexistenz: Beitrag zu einer modernen marxistischen Ästhetik. Reinbek b/Hamburg: Rohwolt, 1966. 253 pp. (Beckett & S.) [Translations: Eng.: 587; Fr.: 1873]

1980 Bode, B. [pseud. of N. Tarasova]. "Umschau: Sowjetliteratur 1964: 'Zum Nutzen der Sache'," Osteuropa, 1 (Jan 1966),40-42.

1981 Mayer, H. "Ein imaginäres Romanmuseum des 20. Jahrhundert," Weltwoche (Zürich), 1701 (17 Jun 1966), 25.

1982 Opitz, R. "Al. S.," pp. 280-87 in: Moderne sowjetische Prosa, vom Beginn der fünfziger Jahre bis zur Gegenwart: Übersicht und 22 Porträtsstudien. Berlin: Volk & Wissen, 1967. 327 pp. [Artemova (429) gives relevant pages as 278-290]

1983 Holthusen, J. Russische Gegenwartsliteratur, 2. (1941-1967). Bern und München: Francke, 1968. (See pp. 94 ff.)

1984 Maurina, Z. "Al. S.: Der tragische Lebensbejaher," pp. 195-210 in her Porträts russischer Schriftsteller. Memmingen/Allgäu: Dietrich, 1968. 253 pp.

1985 Hartmann, R. "Die Welt im Krankensaal," FNP, 8 (10 Jan 1968).
1986 Schult, H. "Phase des Stillstandes," FH, 2 (Feb 1968), 125-26. [On OD]

1987 Mihajlow, M. "Das 'Totenhaus' Dostojewskis und S-ns," Orientierung, beih. 4 (1968), 55. [Tr. of 2430]

1989 [sic] Ingold, F. "Der Fall S.: Vor- und Nachgeschichte," NZZ, 489 (11 Aug 1968), 49-50.

1990 "Man hält mir den Mund zu," Spiegel, 44 (28 Oct 1968), 188. [Subject: see 262]

Reviews of Der erste Kreis der Hölle (Aug 1968-Nov 1970):

1991 CW (30 Aug 1968), 10. (W. Bronska-Pampuch: "Der Teufelskreis")

1992 DAS (26 Jan 1969), 24. (G. Hartlaub: "Gleichheit nur im Sterben") [Also on Krebsstation]

1993 FAZ, 220 (21 Sep 1968). (K. Korn: "Mawrino, Allegorie der Hölle")

1994 FR (11 Jan). (H. Pross-Weerth: "Ein Trotzdem-Ja-Sager")

1995 HAZ (23/24 Nov 1970). (I. Priess: "Zeitlose Fragen--aktuell gestellt") [Note: year could be in error]

1996 Monat, 245 (Feb 1969), 81-84. (W. Werth: "Im Teufelskreis")

1997 NatZ, 509 (8 Dec 1968). (W. Kraus: "Bedrohte Stimme der

Wahrheit")
 1998 NZZ, 197 (30 Mar 1969). (F. Ingold)
 1999 RM, 19 (9 May 1969), 22. (E. von Kuehnelt-Leddihn: "Schwarz-
er Himmel über roter Hölle")
 2000 SaZ, 50 (28 Feb/1 Mar 1970), 33. (H. Böll: "Die verhaftete
Welt") [Early version of 2039?]
 2001 StN (25 Jan 1969). (W. Hehl)
 2002 StZ (18 Jan 1969). (M. Szenessy: "Die Physiker--nicht von
Dürrenmatt")
 2003 SüZ (5 Dec 1968). (H. von Ssachno: "Die gescheiterte Revolution")
 2004 Welt (19 Dec 1968), 5. (J. Rühle: "Präzeptor des sozialen
Gewissens: Nicht nur politische Fabel, auch existentielles Gleichnis")
 2005 Welt am Sonntag (26 Jan 1969). (H. Schlewe: "Erschütternd:
Report aus der Hölle")
 2006 Zeit (3 Jan 1969), 14. (M. Reich-Ranicki)
 See also: 2010, 2024, 2029, 2039-40 & 2055.

Reviews of Krebsstation (Sep 1968-Feb 1970):

 2007 Badische Zeitung, 285 (10 Dec 1968). (H. Fehr: "Wovon die
Menschen leben")
 2008 Bremer Nachrichten, 169 (21 July 1969). (W. Kraus: "Kosto-
glotows zweite Geburt")
 2009 CW (18 Apr 1969), 14. (W. Bronska-Pampuch: "Wer schreibt
die Tragödie? S., ein Moralist seines Volkes")
 2010 DAS, 22 (1 Jun 1969). (G. Hartlaub: "Brücken der Sympathie")
[Also on Der erste Kreis der Hölle]
 2011 FAZ (12 Nov 1968). (K. Korn: "Opfer des Systems, Überwinder
des Systems")
 2012 FH, 3 (Mar 1969), 210-11 & 2.(Feb 1970), 144-46. (H. Schult)
 2013 FR, 188 (16 Aug 1969). (H. Ungureit: "Rebellion eines Un-
politischen")
 2024 [sic] MM (30 Nov 1968). (F. Meurer) [On Krebsstation, pt.1
& Der erste Kreis]
 2025 MM, 74 (27 Mar 1969). (F. Meurer: "War es ein politischer
Krebs?") [On pt. 2]
 2026 Neue Rundschau, 3 (1969), 556-60. (H. Bienek)
 2027 NZ, 271 (20 Nov 1969). (G. Schramm: "Knüppel bei der Hand")
 2028 RM (22 Nov 1968), Literaturbeilage. (H. Schreiber: "Mensch-
en im Tauwetter: Schicksale im nachstalinistischen Russland")
[Pt. 1]
 2029 Spiegel, 44 (28 Oct 1968), 185-6. ("Am Schnittpunkt") [Also
on Der erste Kreis]
 2030 StN, 97 (26 Apr 1969). (D. Schmidt: "Das Krankenzimmer als
Gesellschaftsmodell")
 2031 StZ (1968). (M. Szenessy: "Die Symptome des Optimismus")
[Bibl. data incompl.]
 2032 SüZ, 228 (21/22 Sep 1968). (M. Grunert: "Finde sich damit
ab, wer kann")
 2033 Weltwoche, 1380 (1968), 25. (F. Schonauer)
 2035 [sic] Zeit (20 Sep 1968), 16. (H. von Ssachno)
 See also: 1992, 1985, 2040-41, 2078, 2084, 2087.

2036 Bienek, H. "Literatur des Infernos: Al. S. und der neue kritische Realismus," Neue Rundschau, 80, i, pp. 147-58. [Repr. in 2096?]

2037 Tvardowski, A. "Solschenizynismus," NF, 183/1, pp. 149-52. [Tr. of 267]

2038 Reinhold, W. "Al. Is. S.: Leben und Werk," Leserzeitschrift (Karlsruhe), 3, pp. 1-7.

2039 Böll, H. "Die verhaftete Welt in S-ns 'Erster Kreis der Hölle'," Merkur, 5 (May), 474-83. [Longer version of 2000?; excerpts in tr. at 297 & 1290]

2040 Weidman, B. "Das Verdrängte erwacht: Gedanken zu den Romanen von Al. S.," Deutsche Kulturelle Monatsschrift, 29, v (7 Jun), 390.

2041 Schult, H. "Station des Leids," FH, 7 (Jul), 515-17.

2042 Ingold, F. "Die Auseinandersetzungen um S-ns 'Krebsstation' in der Sowjetunion," NZZ (20 Jul), 49-50.

2043 Radda, F. "Russlands verlorene Söhne: Der russische Erzähler Al. Is. S.," Österreichischer Rundfunk (12 Aug). [Broadcast]

2044 Ličko, P. "Ein Tag bei Al. Is. S.," NZZ (12 Oct), 51-52. [Tr. of 1604]

2045 von Ssachno, H. "Finale im Fall S.?" SdZ (14 Nov).

2046 Pörzgen, H. "S. schreibt einen offenen Brief," FAZ (17 Nov). [S.'s letter of 12 Nov 1969]

2047 Schiller, U. "Schicksale unter Stalins Schatten: Ein Stück unbewältigter Vergangenheit: Der Fall S.," Zeit, 47 (21 Nov), 6.

2048 Laub, G. "Das Gewissen der Sowjetunion: Zum Ungezeifer degradiert: Al. S.," Zeit, 49 (5 Dec 1969), 17-18. [Excerpts in tr.: 298 & 1285, pp. 202-03]

2049 Peschler, E. "Der Fall S.," Weltwoche, 1882, p. 35.

2050 Krättli, A. "Der Fall S.," Schweizer Monatshefte, 49, ii (1969-70), 193 ff.

2051 Lukács, G. "S-ns Romane," pp. 31 ff. in his Soziologische Essays. Neuwied & Berlin: Luchterhand, 1970. (Written 1969) [Repr.: 2052]

2052 Lukács, G. Solschenizyn. Neuwied: Luchterhand, 1970. 88 pp. Bibliography, pp. 86-88. Contents: "S.:'Ein Tag im Leben des Iwan Denissowitsch'," 5-29 [repr. of 1971] & "S-ns Romane," 31-84 [repr. of 2051]. Reviews: see 568. [Translations of book: see 567, 1612, 1871, 2149. 2256, 2394; for tr. & repr. of first essay, see 1971.]

2053 "Die Auseinandersetzung um Al. S.," pp. 87-182 in: Literatur und Repression: Sowjet. Kulturpolitik seit 1965, ed. & tr. H. von Ssachno & M. Grunert. München: Deutscher Taschenbuch-Verlag, 1970. 196 pp.

2054 Nordmeyer, B. "Der freie Mensch in der Apokalypse der Gegenwart," pp. 112 ff. in her: Profile des Jahrhunderts: Durchblicke. Stuttgart: Verlag Urachhaus, 1970.

2055 Froitzheim, D. "Religiöse Fragen in Al. S-ns Roman 'Der erste Kreis der Hölle'," Pastoralblatt für die Diözösen Aachen, Berlin, Essen, Köln, Osnabrück (Köln), 23, i, pp. 22-26.

2056 Geiger, H. "Gerechtigkeit für S.," Evangelische Kommentare, 3, i, pp. 44-48.

2057 Huber, E. "Haben Sie S. schon gelesen?" Stimmen der Zeit,

95, i, pp. 62-66.

2058 "Al. S.: Unterdrückter," NF, 193, pp. 23-25.

2059 Hilsbecher, W. "Die Sowjetgesellschaft auf der Krebsstation," Merkur, 262 (Feb), 179-81.

2060 "'Unsere Wege trennten sich': Schriftsteller zum Ausschluss S-ns aus dem Autorenverband," SH, 3 (1 Feb), 18-19. [See note at 1593]

2061 Lukács, G. "Die manipulierte Wirklichkeit: S. vor dem Hintergrund des sozialistischen Realismus," FAZ (11 Mar).

2062 Bethell, N. "Ein Symbol für Russlands Leid und Grösse," Welt, 231/259 (20 Mar). (Long article on Der erste Kreis)

2063 Böll, H. "Leiden, Zorn und Ruhe," Spiegel (30 Mar), 198-200. (On Im Interesse der Sache)

2064 Reich-Ranicki, M. "S. und wir: Ans Anlass seines Buches 'Im Interesse der Sache'," Zeit, 18 (1 May), 34-35.

2065 "Die offizielle Erklärung zum Fall S.," Osteuropa, 20, Archiv, pp. 502-05. [Tr. of 220]

2067 [sic] Ingold, F. "Der Wirklichkeit ins Gesicht sehen: S. und der Sozialistische Realismus," NatZ, Nr. 570.

2068 Schult, H. "Ein Mann geht," FH, 9 (Sep), 671-78. (On Im Interesse der Sache)

2069 Korn, K. "Literatur als ethisches Potential: Der Nobelpreis für Literatur ging an Al. S.," FAZ (9 Oct), 32.

2070 Spiegel, Nr. 42: "S.: Schützen oder Schaden," 236-42; & "Verbotene Texte der Kettenbrief: Spiegel-Report über die intellektuelle Opposition in der Sowjet-Union," 244-51.

2072 [sic] Bronska-Pampuch, W. "Das andere Russisch," Zeit, 42 (16 Oct), 17.

2073 Reich-Ranicki, M. "Der diesjährige Nobelpreis für Literatur ist Al. S. zugesprochen worden: Die zweite Regierung," Zeit, 42 (16 Oct), 17-18.

2074 Ströhm, C. "Ehrung für den verfemten: Nobelpreis für Al. S.," CW (16 Oct), 9.

2075 Pörzgen, H. "S., zum Verräter gestempelt," FAZ (19 Oct).

2076 Krüger, H. "Ein Schachzug im Kalten Krieg," Zeit, 45 (6 Nov), 29.

2077 Rostropowitsch, M. "Lasst S. in Ruh," NF, 204, pp. 1077-8. [Tr. of 305]

2078 Hartlaub, G. "Krebsstation mit Kulissen," DAS (22 Nov). (On TV performance of 8 & 10 Nov 1970)

2079 Voss, E. "Al. S.," NZZ, 568 (6 Dec), 51-52.

2080 Lehmann-Braun, E. "Fanfaren und Applaus für S.," FAZ (12 Dec).

2081 "Übergabe der Nobelpreise 1970," NZZ (12 Dec), 3.

2082 Aucouturier, M. "Der unbestechliche Zeuge," Weltwoche, 52/53 (24 Dec), 25. [Tr. from French?]

1971

2083 Gerstenmaier, C. "Der 'Fall' S.," pp. 175-83, 305-21, 369-71 in: Die Stimme der Stummen: Die demokratische Bewegung in der Sowjetunion. Stuttgart: Seewald Verlag, 1971. 395 pp.

2084 Schultze, S. "Krebsgeschwulst als Symbol," Rhein-Neckar Zeitung, 3 (16 Jan).

2085 Jeschke, O. "Natur, Mensch und Gesellschaft bei S.," Hochland, 63, iii, pp. 243-56.

2086 Bronska-Pampuch, W. "Dokumentation über den Nobelpreisträger Al. S.," _Zeit_, 11, p. 20.

2087 Hoffmann, F. "Hoffnung jenseits des Prinzips Hoffnung: Marginalien zur _Krebsstation_ von Al. S.," _Stimmen der Zeit_, 188, pp. 87-105.

2088 Schlewe, H. "Die Moskauer Zensur wollte 'Gott' klein schreiben: Al. S-ns neuer Roman 'August 14'," _Welt_ (23 Jun).

2089 "S-ns Schlachtbeschreibung," _Spiegel_ (5 Jul), 99-100. (On _Avg. čet._)

2090 Mehnert, K. "Das Hohelied vom russischen Soldaten: Al. S-ns 'August 14'," _CW_ (6 Aug), 17-18.

2091 Razumovsky, A. "August Vierzehn': S-ns neuer Roman," _FAZ_ (21 Aug).

2092 Pörzgen, H. "Ist S. vogelfrei? Das 'Piratenstück' in Moskauer Sicht," _FAZ_ (23 Oct).

2093 Heeb, F. "Die urheberrechtliche Stellung eines sowjetischen Schriftstellers im Westen," _NZZ_ (5 Nov), 73.

2094 Steiner, D. _Stern_ (Hamburg), 48 (21 Nov). (Article on S. family; tr. into Russian: 232)

2095 Stutz, **M.** _Deutsche Volkszeitung_ [late 1971 or early 1972]. (Article on _Avg. čet._; tr. into Russian: 233)

1972

2096 Bienek, H. _S. und Andere: Essays_. München: Hanser Verlag, 1972. 102 pp. (Have not seen this; the essay on S. possibly was published earlier [see 2036])

2097 Walden, M. "Offener Brief an A. I. S.," _Welt_ (23 Sep), _Die geistige Welt_, p. ii.

2098 von Lilienfeld, F. "Al. S.: Der Fall und das Werk," _Wissenschaft und Praxis in Kirche und Gesellschaft_, 9 (Sep), 365-75; 10 (Oct), 442-54.

Reviews of _August 1914_ (1971-1973):

Reviews dated between Oct 1971 & Jul 1972 are of the Langen-Müller (pirated) edition, _August neunzehnhundertvierzehn_ [see 1963]. All of the reviews after Jul 1972 concern the Luchterhand edition, _August vierzehn_ [see 1964], but some treat the Langen-Müller ed'n. as well (so indicated with the notation: [Both]).

2099 _Berner Tagblatt_, 248 (21/22 Oct 1972). (J. Amery: "Russische Tragödie: Al. Is. S.")

2100 _CW_ (29 Oct 1971), 9. (K.-U. Ebmeyer: "Der unbequeme Preis: Al. S.: Ein Opfer der Diplomatie")

2101 _CW_ & _Deutsche Zeitung_ (11 Aug 1972). (W. Werth: "Russlands verlorene Identität: S-ns 'August vierzehn' auf Deutsch")

2102 _FAZ_, 197 (26 Aug 1972). (P. Urban) [Both]

2103 _FNP_ (6 Nov 1971), 18. (R. Hartmann: "Der heimliche Historiker S.")

2104 _FNP_ (8 Sep 1972), 5. (R. Hartmann: "Der doppelte S.: Zweimal 'August vierzehn'")

2105 _Literaturspiegel 3_ (Messe-Ausgabe, 1972). (G. Oberembt: "Gerichtsnotorischer Bestseller")

2106 _MM_ (6/7 Nov 1971). (F. Meurer: "Wie ist der neue S.? Auf 765 Seiten: 'möglichst genau und ohne Phantasieflug'")

2107 _NN_, 210 (9/10 Sep 1972). (H. Bock: "Gleichnis einer Schlacht")

2108 NZZ, 20 (1973). (F. Ingold: "Korn und Leid: Versuch über S-ns 'August vierzehn'")

2109 RM, 35 (1 Sep 1972). (O. Roegele: "Der Preis der Feigheit ist das Böse")

2110 Osteuropa, 3 (Mar 1972), 215-219. (E. Pruck: "S-ns 'August 1914' militärisch gesehen")

2111 Schaffhauser Nachrichten, 205 (2 Sep 1972). (H. von Ssachno)

2112 Solothurner Zeitung, 234 (7 Oct 1972). (R. Hartmann)

2113 Tagesspiel, 8230 (8 Oct 1972). (G. Werth: "S-ns Krieg und Frieden")

2114 Tat (Zürich), 206 (2 Sep 1972). (K. Schauder: "Das wichtigste Thema der jüngsten Geschichte")

2115 Welt (28 Oct 1971). (G. Zehm: "Ein Epiker, wie es ihn seit Tolstoi nicht gegeben hat")

2115a Westermanns Monatshefte (Mar 1973), 92. (M. Neumann: "Tannenberg kein Thema mehr? S. in kritischem Kreuzfeuer: 'August 14'")

2116 Zeit (4 Aug 1972). (R. Drommert: "Respektabel, aber nicht kongenial: Ein Vergleich der beiden deutschen Übersetzungen") [Both]

2117 Zeit (4 Aug 1972). (K.-H. Janssen: "Gemeinsam singen sie die alten Chorale")

1973

2118 Ingold, Felix Philipp & Elisabeth Markstein, eds. Ueber Solschenizyn: Aufsätze, Berichte, Materialen. Darmstadt-Berlin: Luchterhand, 1973. ca. 450 pp. With foreword by eds.: "Vorbemerkung der Herausgeber"; "Chronologie"; "Literaturverzeichnis" and Index. Texts by S.: "Meine Biographie" & "Nobelpreis-Rede".
Contributions
Czeremis, K. "S. und Leo Tolstoj".
Hotz, R. "S. als christlicher Denker und Schriftsteller" [tr. of 1640].
Kasack, W. "Die epische und dramatische Struktur im Werk S-ns".
Koževníkova, K. "Ein Meister des Stils" [tr. of 1590].
Künzli, A. " Vom Nutzen und Nachteil der Wissenschaft für das Leben".
Lakschin, W. "Iwan Denissowitsch, seine Freunde und seine Missgönner" [tr. of 145].
Nicholson, M. "S-ns Ansichten zur Literatur".
Schmemann, A. "Der Russland-Mythos und August Vierzehn" [tr. of 385]
Strada, V. "Vom Iwan Denissowitsch zur Krebsstation". [Tr. of 2167?]
Tikos, L. "Stilistische Beobachtungen zu S-ns August Vierzehn".
Weinzierl, E. "Vom 'Sinn des Lebens' bei Al. S.".
Winokur, T. "Ueber Sprache und Stil von Al. S-ns Ein Tag des Iwan Denissowitsch" [tr. of 187].

2119 Ingold, F. P. & Ilma Rakusa, eds. Alexander Solschenizyn, Kirche und Politik: Texte, Zeugnisse, Materialien. Zürich: Die Arche, 1973. With bibliography, annotations, index. Texts by S., Esliman, Jakunin, Zeludkov, Karelin, Ioann S.-Francisskij & G. R. Smeman. [For some of the probable original texts, see: 315, 316, 317, 317a, 488 & 497]

For articles by Ingold & Markstein appearing only in foreign languages, see: 619, 683, 1907, 1918 (pp. 389-99) and 2406.

(17) Greek

Special source: Artemova (429), four items. Abbr. S.: Solzenitsyn.

Translations:

2120 Mia ēmera tou Iban Ntenisobits, tr. A. Sarantopoulos.
Athēnai: Etaireia Ellenikon Ekdoseon, 1963.
2121 Mia ēmera tou Iban Ntenisobits, tr. S. Eliade. Athēnai:
Ekdoseis Oskar, 1970. 344 pp. With introd. by Eliade. Contents incl. MD, Pasx. kr. xod & other items (poss. also 2127).
2122 Mia ēmera tou Iban Ntenisobits, tr. S. Patatze. Athēnai:
Ekdoseis Papyros [E. P. E.], 1970.
2123 Mia ēmera tou Iban Ntenisobits, tr. D. Kōstelenos. Athēnai:
Didymoi, 1970. 230 pp. [Tr. from Engl.]
2124 Stathmos tou karkinou, tr. A. Grana. Athēnai: Boukoumanēs,
1970. 2 vols. [RK]
2125 To spiti tes Matrionas. O agnostos tes Kretsetobka. Gia to
kalo tou agona, tr. G. Gerale. Athēnai: Ekdoseis Papyros [E.P.
E.], 1971. [MD, SK, PD]
2126 Synebe sto stathmo Kretsetobka. To spiti tes Matrionas.
Gia to kalo tes ideas, tr. D. Kōstelenos. Athēnai: Ekdoseis "Pel-
la", 1971. [SK, MD, PD]

Criticism:

2127 Michaeloph [Mihaijlov], M. "To spiti ton pethamenon tou
Ntostogiebski [Dostoevskij] kai tou S. (E phainomenologia tes
douleias)". [Appears on pp. 33-95 of one of the translations of
OD, prob. 2121 (Artemova's info. incomplete); this is a tr. of 2430]

(18) Hebrew. (Israel)
Special source: Judith Borsuk (see note below). Abbr. S.:
Solzhenitsin. (Other spellings noted, due to mistransliteration
or misspelling in original Hebrew: Solzenitzin & Solzenitzyn.)
Information from various sources has been revised to conform to
a single system of transliteration, suggested by Dr. Israel Naamani of the University of Louisville.

Translations:

2128 Yom Ehad B'Hayei Iwan Denisowic, tr. E. Porat & H. Peleg.
Merhaviya: Sifriyat Poalim, 1963. 240 pp. With afterword by N.
Shaham.
2129 Ba'Mador Harishon, tr. Bronislava & Avraham Ben Ya'akov.
Jerusalem: Schocken, 1970. 569 pp. [KP]
2130 Agaf Ha'Sartan, tr. Y. Sa'aroni. Tel Aviv: Am Ha'Oved.
462 pp. [RK]
2130a Ogust 1914 (10-21 B'Ogust L'fi Ha'Luah Ha'Yashan), tr. Y.
Sa'aroni. Tel Aviv: Am Ha'Oved, 1972. 519 pp.

Criticism:

All of the articles listed below except 2139 & 2140 were reprinted (by photocopy process) in the following Israeli reference work--a collection of critiques on new books--which was the
main source used: Leket Divrei Bikoret al S'farim Hadashim [ab-
breviated below as Leket]. The data on original publication
given below is that supplied by Leket--often incomplete. Research

110

was conducted by Judith Borsuk, an American student from Louisville, Ky., at the Jewish National University in Jerusalem.

2131 Perlis, I. "B'Ma'agal Ha'Tofet shel S.," La'Merhav (1969).
Repr.: Leket (Aug 1969), 15. [On KP]
2132 Bosem, H. "Sefer Hova," Ha'aretz (18 Feb 1970). Repr.:
Leket (Feb 1970), 8. [On KP]
2132a Mirsky, N. "Ba'Mador Harishon L'Al. S.," Ha'aretz (17 Apr
1970). Repr.: Leket (Apr 1970), 16. [On KP]
2133 Zehavy, A. "Ba'Mador Harishon L'S.," La'Merhav (29 May 1970).
Repr.: Leket (May 1970), 11. [On KP]
2133a Aran, D. "Sh'losha Madorim," Al Ha'Mishmar (12 Jun 1970).
Repr.: Leket (Jun 1970), 12. [On KP]
2134 Ostridan, Y. "Ba'Mador Harishon," Davar (3 Jul 1970). Repr.:
Leket (Jul 1970), 14. [On KP]
2135 Perlis, I. "Ba'Mador Harishon L'S.," Moznayim, 31 (1970),
148-150. Repr.: Leket (Jul 1970), 14-15. [On KP]
2135a Zertal, I. "Agaf Ha'Sartan B'Ivrit," Davar (27 Aug 1970).
Repr.: Leket (Aug 1970), 12. [On RK]
2136 Ben-Ezer, E. "Al. S.: Agaf Ha'Sartan," Al Ha'Mishmar (14
Aug 1970). Repr.: Leket (Aug 1970), 11-12. [On RK]
2137 Amos, Y. "Mishtar Nagua B'Gidul Mam'ir," Ha'tsofeh (1970).
Repr.: Leket (Aug 1970), 12. [On RK]
2137a David, Z. "Mashehu al Sefer Gadol," Davar (25 Sep 1970).
Repr.: Leket (Sep 1970), 15. [On KP]
2138 Selah, D. "Nigudim Ha'Mit'alim L'Shlemut," Kol Ha'am (16
Oct 1970). Repr.: Leket (Oct 1970), 7. [On RK]
2138a Mirsky, N. "Agaf Ha'Sartan L'S.," Ha'aretz (1970). Repr.:
Leket (Oct 1970), 8. [On RK]
2139 Yovel, S. "Yehudim B'Ba'Mador Harishon L'S.," Molad, 17
(1971), 548-52. [On KP]
2140 Grodzinsky, S. "S. U'Svivo," Moznayim, 32 (1971), 51-54.
2140a Zehavy, A. "Achzavah im Hofa'at Ogust 1914 L'S. B'Targum
Ivri," Y'diyot Ahronot (1972). Repr.: Leket, 8-9 (15 May 1972),
9. [Disappointed in Hebrew tr. of Avg. čet.]
2141 Frois [Freuss?], T. "Pirkei-Ha'Milhamah shel S.," Davar
(1972). Repr.: Leket, 12 '30 Jun 1972), 6. [On Avg. čet.]
2141a Ben-Ezer, E. "Ha'Roman Ha'Histori shel S.," Al Ha'Mishmar
(1972). Repr.: Leket, 13-14 (31 Jun 1972), 7-8. [On Avg. čet.]
2142 Shmeman, A. "Ahava P'kuhat Ayin," Davar (1972). Repr.:
Leket, 16 (31 Aug 1972), 6-7. [Tr. of 385 by A. (or E.) Z. (Hebrew initials Ayin Zayin)]
2143 Kaizer [Kaiser], R. "Ha'Inteligentsiyah shel Moskvah M'va-
keret et Ogust 1914," Ma'ariv (1 Dec 1972). Repr.: Leket, 22
(30 Nov 1972), 9. [Tr. of article that prob. appeared orig. in
Washington Post; subject is same as that in entries 1270 & 1271]
2143a Soker, R. "Ogust 1914: S'faro Ha'Hadash shel S.," Ha'tsofeh (2 Jul 1971). Repr.: Leket, 9 (30 Jun 1971), 8. [This entry out of chronological order]

See also 2128 (afterword) and related items: 913 & 931.

(19) Hungarian

Special source (in addition to national reference work): László
Wessely of Budapest. The full title of the periodical identified
below as Kortárs is: Kortárs: Irodalmi és Kritikai Folyóirat; the

111

journal Kritika is sometimes identified in ref. works as Critique.
Abbr. S.: Szolzsenyicin (common) or Szolzsenyicin (rare).

Translations:

2144 Ivan Gyenyiszovics egy napja, tr. László Wessely. Budapest:
Európa Könyvkiadó, 1963. With introd. by Tvardovskij. This tr.
appeared earlier in monthly review Nagy Világ (1963). Wessely's
tr-ns of MD & SK were also pub. in this periodical in 1963.

Criticism:

2145 Galambos, L. "Protestálok," Kortárs, 7 (Mar 1963), 370-72.
2146 "S. és a mai szocialista réalizmus," Kritika, 3 (Mar 1965),
39-46. Includes tr. (or orig. Hungarian text?) of article on OD
by G. Lukács [see 1971], with reply by András Diószegi.
2147 Fehér Pál, E. "Szolzsenyicin," pp. 235-52 in: Az új szovjet
irodalom, ed. János Elbert & László Kardos. Budapest: Gondolat,
1967.
2148 Juhász, M. "Az antiheros heroizmusa," Kortárs, 13 (1969):
v (May), 801-810; vi (Jun), 959-967.
2149 Lukács, G. Szolzenyicin regényei. Budapest: "Forum", 1970.
[Tr. of 2052 (or orig. Hung. text?)]

See also related items: 603 & 1580.

(20) Icelandic. Translation.

2150 Dagur í lífi Ívans Denisovichs, tr. S. Sigurđsson. Reykja-
vík: Almenna Bókafélagiđ, 1963. 176 pp.

(21) Bengali. (India) Translation.

2151 Ivan Denisovicher jibaner ekdin, tr. S. Mukhopadhayay. Cal-
cutta: David Maximillian & Co. [D. M. Library], 1965. 222 pp.
[Tr. from English]

(22) Malayalam. (India) Translations.

2152 Ivan Denisovich geevitathil ora Divasam. Trichur: Current
Books, 1963. [Tr. ?]
2153 A vitu, tr. J. Mundasseri. Trichur: Mangalodayam, 1967.
75 pp. [MD]

For other publications in India, see 509 (one of the ed'ns of
For the Good of the Cause) and 605 (critical article in Eng. pub.
in Bombay).

(23) Italian. (Italy, Switzerland, Yugoslavia)

Special sources: G. Grazzini's bibliography (see 2233) and M.
Mirella of G. Einaudi publishers (information about book reviews).
Abbreviations: S.: Solgenitsin (most common); other spellings
noted in about equal numbers: Solgenitsyn, Solzenitsyn, Solzeni-
cyn, Solženicyn, Solženitsyn, Solzhenitsin. Periodicals: CC:
Civilita Cattolica; CS: Corriere della Sera; CV: Città di Vita;
GM: Gazetta del Mezzogiorno (Bari); NA: Nuova Antologia; RC: Rus-
sia Cristiana.

112

Translations:

2154 Una giornata di Ivan Denisovič, tr. G. Kraisky. Milano: Garzanti, 1963. 208 pp. Introd. by Tvardovskij. Other ed'ns.: 1970. 199 pp.; 1971. 214 pp. (with commentary by G. Santi)

2155 Una giornata di Ivan Denisovič, tr. R. Uboldi. Torino: G. Einaudi, 1963. 174 pp. (Later ed'n.: see 2173)

2156 "La giornata di Ivan Denisovič," Panorama (Yugoslavia),12 (1963): serialized in issues viii through xii, pp. 20-21 in each issue.

2157 La casa di Matrjona. Alla stazione di Krečetovka, tr. C. Coïsson & V. Strada. Torino: G. Einaudi, 1963. 143 pp. (Later ed'n.: see 2173)

2158 "Signore, com'è facile vivere conte," Epoca (Nov 1967); Avvenire (12 Nov 1969); also in: Martin, A. Russia fede e realtà. Torino: S.E.I., 1970. ["Molitva"]

2159 Unita (4 Jun 1968). (S.'s letter of 21 Apr. 1968; also sent to LG [see 207]; Eng. tr. at 1285, pp. 148-9.)

2160 Il primo cerchio, tr. P. Zvetermich. Milano: A. Mondadori, 1968. 746 pp.

2161 Divisione cancro, tr. M. Olsúfieva. Milano: A. Mondadori (Il Saggiatore), 1968. 397 pp.

2162 "La stanca mano destra," CS (10 Jan 1969). [Tr. of 1573]

2163 "La mano destra," Ponte (31 Jan 1969), 3-6; Epoca (25 Oct 1970).

2164 "Racconti minimi" & "Processione di Pasqua," RC (Jan-Feb-Mar-Apr 1969); also in Dissenso e contestazione nell'Unione Sovietica. Milano: Istituto di propaganda libraria, 1970.

2165 "La candela al vento," RC (May-Jun 1969).

2166 "Come leggono Ivan Denisovič," Ponte, 12 (1969); RC (Nov-Dec 1970).

2167 Reparto C., tr. G. Dacosta. Torino: G. Einaudi, 1969. xxiv, 584 pp. With "Introduzione" by. V. Strada [prob. it is this which is Strada's contribution to 2118]. (RK)

2168 Per il bene della causa, tr. G. Crino. Roma: Tindalo, 1969. 153 pp.

2169 "La preghiera di S. e il paradosso delle voci clandestine," p. 57 in Poesie di vari, comp. & tr. Centro Studi Russia Cristiana. Milano: Istituto di propaganda libraria, 1970. ["Molitva"]

2170 Nell'interesse della cosa e altri racconti, tr. G. Spendel. Milano: Longanesi. 1970. 172 pp. [Prob. same contents as 520]

2171 Il cervo e la bella del campo. Una candela al vento, tr. M. Martinelli. Torino: G. Einaudi, 1970. 216 pp. [Olen' & Sveča]

2172 Per il bene della causa, tr. C. Coïsson, V. Strada, R. Uboldi & P. Zvetermich. Milano: A. Mondadori, 1971. 390 pp. (Contents: same as 520, plus OD)

2173 Una giornata di Ivan Denisovič, tr. R. Uboldi. Torino: G. Einaudi, 1971. 307 pp. (Also has MD & SK in tr. of Coisson & Strada: combined ed'n. of 2155 & 2157)

2174 Agosto 1914, tr. P. Zvetermich. Milano: A. Mondadori, 1972. 614 pp.

See also 2190 (has some letters by S.).

Criticism:

For books and articles in books, see 2181, 2184, 2190-91, 2232-34. Important articles in periodicals include the following: 2182, 2183, 2185, 2196, 2202, 2209, 2219, 2226-30.

2175 Zampa, G. "La nuova tattica sovietica," CS (25 Jan 1963).
2176 Sassoli, D. "L'Amara verità du libro di S.," Gazzetta del Popolo (Torino), 5 Feb 1963.
2177 de Rosa, G. "Una giornata di Ivan Denisovič," CC, 114, iii (1963), 144-49.
2178 Strada, V. "'Che cosa ci fu nel'37?'," Unita (22 May 1963).
2179 Abbate, M. "Scaffale," GM (28 May 1963).
2180 d'Aleo, V. "La casa di Matrjona," Paese Sera (12 July 1963).
2181 Strada, V. "Il diario di Nina Kosterina e i racconti di S.," pp. 145-48 in his Letteratura sovietica, 1953-1963. Roma: Ed. Riuniti, 1964.
2182 Strada, V. "In difesa di S.," Europa Letteraria, 5, xxvi (Feb 1964), 5-13.
2183 Lukács, G. "S.: Una giornata di Ivan Denisovič," Belfagor, 19, iii (Mar 1964), 257-74; also in his Marxismo e politica culturale. Torino: Einaudi, 1968. [Tr. of 1971]
2184 Lo Gatto, E. La letteratura russo-sovietica. Firenze-Milano: Sansoni-Accademia, 1968. [Have not seen this; probably includes note on S. if it is a new edition.]
2185 Castello, F. "Al. Is. S.: 'Il destino della scrittore non sacrà mai facile'," CC, 1 (1968), 8-19.
2186 Milano, P. "Un limbo sovietico: E senza speme vivemo in desio," Espresso (28 Jul 1968). [On KP]
2187 Baldacci, L. "S. ci guida nell'inferno staliniano," Epoca (4 Aug 1968).
2188 Bo, C. "Il primo cerchio," CS (7 Aug 1968).
2189 Milano, P. "S. continua: Dai lager di Stalin alla città del sole," Espresso (6 Oct 1968). [On RK]
2190 Tra autoritarismo e sfruttamento: Interventi di A. I. S. Milano: Editore Jaca Book, 1968 & 1971. 83 pp. Contents: Ital. tr. of 1604, 250, 261, 262, 266, 271, 272. (Translations: 1840, 2347, 2349, 2365-66)

1969

2191 Strada, V. Tradizione e rivoluzione nella letteratura russa. Torino: G. Einaudi, 1969. [Have not seen; prob. refers to S.]
2192 Chukovskaja, L. "La responsabilita dello scrittore e l'irresponsabilita della 'Literaturnaja Gazeta'," RC (Jan-Feb), 48-56. [Tr. of 278]
2193 Želudkov, S. "Pensieri sulla liberta intelletuale," RC (May-Jun), 52-60. [Tr. of 285]
2194 Perego, R. "'Reparto C.': La Russia dopo Stalin," Adige (Trento), 4 Mar.
2195 Abbate, M. "Reparto C.," GM (9 Mar).
2196 Strada, V. "Gli ideali di S.," Rinascità (Roma), 14 Mar. [On RK]
2197 Ripellino, A. "S. espulso dall'Unione scrittori: Il consiglio fraterno di suicidarsi," Espresso (16 Nov).
2198 Giusti-Fici, F. "Incartamento A. S.," Ponte, 12 (1969).

2199 Stevenson, B. "Rapporto sul caso S.," <u>Epoca</u> (7 Dec), 64-70.
2200 Maldini, S. "La giornata di S.," <u>Resto del Carlino</u> (14 Dec).
2201 <u>Unità</u> (ca. 20 Dec). (Article protesting exclusion of S. from Writers' Union; see 1867)

1970

2202 Mondrone, D. "Un drama sconosciuto di A. I. S.: 'Che la luce che è in te non sia tenebra," <u>CC</u>, an. 121, v. 2, iii, pp. 236-43.
2203 Tvardovskij, A. "Lettera a Konstantin Fedin," <u>Giorno</u> (1 Apr). [Tr. of 267]
2204 "Come si persequita uno scrittore," <u>Mondo</u> (29 Mar; 5 & 12 Apr). [Tr. of 262]
2205 "Evviva S.," <u>Mondo</u> (2 Aug). [From <u>samizdat</u>; have not seen this]
2206 "Il caso S.," <u>Sovietica</u> (Oct).
2207 Boffa, G. <u>Unità</u> (9 Oct). (Article in support of S.; excerpt in Eng. at 1285, pp. 212-213.)
2208 Cristini, G. "Ha denunciato ad alta voce terrore e delitti della stalinismo," <u>Avvenire</u> (9 Oct), 6.
2209 Silone, I. "David e Golia," <u>CS</u> (11 Oct), 13.
2210 Sormani, P. "Come ho visto S.," <u>CS</u> (12 Oct).
2211 Strada, V. "La polemica sul Nobel a S.," <u>Rinascità</u> (16 Oct), 19. (Excerpt in Eng.: 1285, p. 213)
2212 Vigorelli, G. "S. un Nobel scomodo," <u>Tempo</u> (24 Oct), 92.
2213 Sormani, P. "Perché fu scetto S.," <u>CS</u> (25 Oct), 5.
2214 Vinci, L. "S.: Fiducia nell'uomo," <u>Adige</u> (28 Oct).
2215 Vanozzi, G. "S.: Un problema per il marxista," <u>Rinascità</u> (13 Nov). [Letter]
2216 Abbate, M. "L'Ultimo S.: Una staffetta per il XXI secolo," <u>GM</u> (18 Nov).
2217 Josca, G. "S. non va a Stoccolma," <u>CS</u> (28 Nov).
2218 Lo Gatto, E. "Al. S.," <u>NA</u>, 510, pp. 361-68.
2219 Casolari, G. "La lunga giornata di A. S.," <u>Letture</u>, 12 (Dec), 807-34. (With bibliography)
2220 Croce, E. "Il primo cerchio," <u>Settanta</u> (Dec).
2221 Vigorelli, G. "Risposta alla 'Literaturnaja Gazeta'," <u>Tempo</u> (5 Dec). [See 224 & 222]

1971

2222 Dursi, M. "Due storie di pena," <u>Resto del Carlino</u> (Bologna), 12 Jan. [On Olen' & Sveča]
2223 Fattori, B. "Reparto C.," <u>Voce Adriatica</u> (Ancona) (2 Feb), 3 & 10.
2224 Reed, D. "Lettera a S.," <u>Fiera Letteraria</u> (21 Feb). [Tr. of 231]
2225 Mauro, W. "Per il bene della causa," <u>Mattino</u> (25 Feb).
2226 Lo Gatto, E. "S. e il 'realismo socialista'," <u>NA</u>, 512, pp. 158-93.
2227 Lo Gatto, E. "Al. S.: L'agosto dei quattordici," <u>NA</u>, 513, pp. 270-78.
2228 Chaix-Ruy, J. "Alienazione marxista nella narrativa di S.," <u>CV</u>, 26, pp. 373-86. [Tr. from Fr.?]
2229 Passeri-Pignoni, V. "La lezione di Al. S.," <u>CV</u>, 27, pp. 463-72.

2230 Mazzariol, F. "Una giornata memorabile di S.," Studium, 57, pp. 554-59.

2231 Abbate, M. "Il socialismo di S.," GM (26 Jun).

2232 Risalti, R. Momenti del realismo russo. Pisa: Libreria goliardica, 1971. 247 pp. (On N. A. Nekrasov, M. E. Saltykov-Ščedrin, L. N. Tolstoj & S.)

2233 Grazzini, G. Solženicyn... Milano: Longanesi, 1971. 322 pp. Bibliography, pp. 303-311.

1972

2234 Lombardo-Radice, L. Gli accusati: Franz Kafka, Michaíl Bulgakov, Aleksandr Solženitsyn, Milan Kudera. Bari: Di Donato, 1972. 413 pp.

2235 Ferrari, E. Calendario del Popolo (Apr). [Brief accusatory article on S.; Russ. tr. at 236]

See also 2167 (foreword by V. Strada) and another article by Strada at 2118 (possibly a translation of the former).

(24) Japanese

Special sources: Kim, Hak-Soo of Korea; also, several items taken from Artemova (429). The only possible transliteration of the spelling of S. in the Japanese kata-kana syllabary is: Sorujanitsuin. (But the internat. spelling Solženicyn is used below.)

Translations:

2240 Iban Denisobichi no ichinichi, T. Egawa. Tôkyô: Mainichi shinbun-sha, 1963 & 1970. 198 pp. (Also in 1970 this trans. appeared with a trans. of "Sud'ba čeloveka" in Šoloxov, Solženicyn. Tôkyô: Kôdan-sha, 1970. 384 pp.)

2241 Iban Denisobichi no ichinichi, tr. H. Kimura. Tôkyô: Shinchô-sha, 1963. 212 pp.

2242 Iban Denisobichi no ichinichi, tr. T. Ogasawara. Tôkyô: Kawade shobô shinsha, 1963, 1965, 1970. 230 pp.

2243 Kesareta otoko, tr. T. Ogasawara. Tôkyô: Kawade shobô shinsha, 1963. 228 pp. [SK & MD]

2244 Iban Denisobichi no ichinichi, tr. I. Sadao. Tôkyô: Kadokawa shoten, 1968. 234 pp.

2245 Iban Denisobichi no ichinichi. Kurechetofuka eki no dekigoto. Matoryôna no ie, tr. T. Egawa & T. Ogasawara. Tôkyô: Keisô shobô, 1968. 358 pp.

2246 Rengoku no naka de, tr. H. Kimura & R. Matsunaga. Tôkyô: Time-Life International, 1969. 2 v.: 347 & 330 pp. [KP]

2247 Gan byôtô, tr. T. Ogasawara. Tôkyô: Shinchô-sha, 1969. 2 v.: 297 & 236 pp. (Also 1971 ed'n.) [RK]

2248 "Kaze ni yuragu tomishibi--Nanji no uchi naru hikari," tr. S. Someya & G. Uchimura. Bungei (Oct 1969), 70-125. [Sveča]

2249 Matoryôna no ie, tr. T. Ogasawara. Tôkyô: Kawade shobô shinsha, 1970. 230 pp. [Prob. same as 2243]

2250 Iban Denisobichi no ichinichi. Matoryôna no ie, tr. T. Egawa. Tôkyô: Kodan-sha, 1971. 294 pp. [Also has SK, PD, ZK]

2251 Solženicyn shoshetsu shu, tr. Ogasawara. Tôkyô: Kawade shobô shinsha, 1971. 246 pp. [OD, SK, MD, ZK]

2252 Iban Denisobichi no ichinichi, tr. S. Someya. Tôkyô: Iwanami shoten, 1971. 219 pp.

2253 Shika to râgeri no onna. Kaze ni yureru tôka, tr. S. Some-ya & G. Uchimura. Tôkyô: Kawade shobô shinsha, 1970. 294 pp. [Olen' & Sveča] (This entry out of chron. order)
2254 Sen kyûhiyaku jû yonen hachigatsu, tr. T. Egawa. Tôkyô: Shinchô-sha, 1972. [Avg. čet.]

Criticism:

2255 Uchimura, G. Solženicyn noto. Tôkyô: Kawade shobô shin-sha. 1971. 227 pp. [Notes on S.]
2256 Lukács, G. Solženicyn, tr. H. Ikeda. Tôkyô: Kinokuniya shoten, 1971. 151 pp. [Tr. of 2052]

(25) Korean

Special source: Kim, Hak-Soo--translator and professor of Russian literature at Hankuk U., Seoul. The system of transliteration used is that suggested by Prof. Kim. (Another system is used by Index Translationum, which renders Kim's given name, for instance, as Hwag-Su.) A suggested transliteration of the Korean spelling of S. is: Soljenichin.

Translations:

2257 Ibandenisobichi-eui haru, tr. Hak-Soo Kim. Seoul: Sasang-gesa, 1963. 250 pp. (Also: Seoul: Donghwa, 1970).
2258 Ibandenisobichi-eui haru, tr. Hwa-Yeong Kim. Seoul: Jim-ungag [or Jimoongak], 1963. 276 pp.
2259 Ibandenisobichi-eui haru, tr. Dong-Hyen Lee. Seoul: Moon-ye, 1970.
2260 Nobelsang moonhak jeonjip, S. pyeon, tr. Hak-Soo Kim. Seoul: Singu, 1970. (Contents: "Oreun son" [Pr. kist']; "Sasu-em-wa lageri-eui eoin" [Olen']; "S. sopeum jip" [Krox. rasskazy])
2261 Am byong dong, tr. Wan Dong. Seoul: Jongeum, 1971. [RK]
2262 Cheon gubak sipsa nyeon palwol, tr. Hak-Soo Kim. Joong-ang Ilbo, 1971. 2 v. (First appeared serially in 4 supplements to the monthly Wolgan Joong-ang [Sep-Dec 1971]) [Avg. čet.]
2263 "Krechetovka yeok-yeseo saengin il," tr. Hak-Soo Kim: in collection titled Babi Yar. Seoul: Samjin, 1972.
2264 ["Matrenin dvor"], tr. Hak-Soo Kim. (Accepted for publi-cation by [Modern Women's Monthly], prob. Mar 1973.)

Criticism:

2265 Kim, Hak-Soo: author of the following articles:
"Ibandenisobichi-eui haru," Wolgan Joong-ang, 149 (1 Jan 1970), 138-144. [On OD]
"Jiseong-wa hanggeo-ro godok-han S.," Chosun Ilbo (18 Oct 1970), 4. [General]
"S.-wa Ibandenisobichi-eui haru," Jugan Chosun (18 Oct 1970).
"Jeonjaeng-wa pyonghwa-ye bigyeon-hal cheot yeoksa soseol," Joong-ang Ilbo (15 Sep 1971), 4. [Avg. čet. as historical novel]
"S.-wa Cheon gubak sipsa nyeon palwol," Chosun Ilbo (13 Feb 1972), 4. [S. & Avg. čet.]

(26) Lithuanian. (U.S.S.R. & U.S.)

Translation:
2266 Viena Ivano Denisovičiaus diena, tr. A. Pakalnis. Vil'njus: Goslitizdat., 1963. 191 pp.

Criticism:

2267 Visvydas, P. "Solženicyno byla tęsiasi," _Aidai_ (Brooklyn), 1971, pp. 180-82.

See also 879.

(27) Norwegian

Special source: Ingvild Broch, U. of Oslo. All periodicals listed are pub. in Oslo unless otherwise indicated. Abbr. S.: Solsjenitsyn or Solzjenitsyn.

Translations:

2268 _En dag i Ivan Denisovitsjs liv_, tr. N. Fredriksen. Oslo: Tiden Norsk Forlag, 1963. 202 pp.; Oslo: Den Norske bokklubben, 1970. 214 pp.
2269 _Det hende i Kretsjetovka; Ei krigsenke: To noveller_, tr. O. Rytter. Oslo: Norske Samlaget, 1964. 128 pp. [SK & MD]
2270 "Innsjøen Segden," tr. I. Ravnum. _Aftenposten_ (13 Dec 1969), 15. [Prose poem]
2271 _Kreftavdelingen_, tr. I. Broch. Oslo: Tiden. v.1, 1969 & 1970, 316 pp.; v. 2, 1970, 259 pp.
2272 _Ergo_, 3 (1970):
"Zakhar-Kalita," tr. I. Broch.
"Påskeprosesjonen," tr. I. Ravnum.
2273 "Min biografi," _Aftenposten_ (21 Jun 1971).
2274 _I første krets_, tr. I. Broch. Oslo: Tiden, 1971. 613 pp. [KP]
2275 _Til sakens beste (Noveller og prosa-miniatyrer)_, tr. I. Ravnum. Oslo: Tiden, 1972. (Contents: same as 520)
2276 "Nobelpris-tale," _Morgenbladet_ (6 Sep 1972).
2277 _August 1914 (1. Knutepunkt)_, tr. I. Broch, with R. Stokke & B. Valderhaug. Oslo: Tiden, 1972. 570 pp.

Criticism:

For books, see 2295-96. Important articles: 2278, 2280, 2287-88.

2278 Ustvedt, Y. "Fra Dostojevskij til S.," _Samtiden_, 74, x (1965), 598-608.
2278a Nag, M. [_Sovjetlitteraturen, 1917-1967_]. Oslo, 1968. [Information incomplete; see Danish tr. at 1611]
2279 Ravnum, I. "S. og det lukkede samfunns tragedie," _Aftenposten_ (13 Dec 1969), 15.
2280 _Ergo_, 3 (1970):
Ravnum, I. "En studie av Kreftavdelingen".
Nag, M. "En studie av En dag i Ivan Denisovitsjs liv".
2281 Bugge, N. "Al. S.--en moderne Gralsridder," _Morgenbladet_ (17 Aug 1970). [On KP]
2282 Hegge, P. "S.--en aktuell klassiker," _Aftenposten_ (9 Oct 1970).
2283 Ravnum, I. "S., Tolstoj og döden," _Aftenposten_ (9 Oct 1970).
2284 Brodal, J. "S.--Sovjetsamfunnets samvittighet," _Bergens Tidende_ (10 Oct 1970).
2285 Solumsmoen, O. "Stenene skal rope," _Arbeiderbladet_ (10 Oct 1970). [On RK]

2286 Kaltenborn, K. "S-ns siste," Aftenposten (13 Oct 1970).

2287 Braadland, A. "Religiöse motiver hos Al. S.," Frisprog, 21 (14 Nov 1970). [On RK]

2288 Ravnum, I. "To århundrer--én sennhet," Edda, 70 (1970), 207-214. [Dostoevskij & S.]

2289 Vetlesen, T. "'August 1914'--et mestervork, en utfordring til Kreml," Morgenbladet (9 Jul 1971).

2290 Timofejeff, A. "S-ns nye utfording," Morgenbladet (21 Aug 1971). [On Avg. čet.]

2291 Hegge, P. "Dantes arv--og Stalins," Aftenposten (2 Nov 1971). [On KP]

2292 Solumsmoen, O. "En troika av lögnere," Arbeiderbladet (20 Nov 1971). [On KP]

2293 Bugge, N. M. "S. og avmytologiseringen av det politiske univers," Morgenbladet (3 & 4 Dec 1971). [2 pts.; on KP]

2294 Ravnum, I. "Russiske Dantevisjoner," Aftenposten (29 Dec 1971). [On KP]

2295 Hegge, Per Egil. Melloman i Moskva. Oslo: Cappelens Forlag, 1971. [Swedish tr.: 2396; excerpts in English at 1492; see also articles in English by or about Hegge: 1172, 1196, 1200, 1432]

2296 Björkegren, H. Aleksander Solsjenitsyn: En biografi, tr. H. Krag. Oslo: Tiden, 1971. 154 pp. [Tr. of 2397]

2297 Udgaard, N. "S-ns bakgrunn brukt i kritikken av ham," Aftenposten (12 Jan 1972). [General]

2298 Udgaard, N. "S. avviser anklager i 'intervju'," Aftenposten (14 Jan 1972). [S. rejects accusers]

2299 Egeleand, E. "Russlands fiender," Morgenbladet (15 Jan 1972). [Russia's foes]

2300 Hagelund, K. "Aksjon mot S.," Dagbladet (3 Mar 1972). [Action against S.]

2301 Solum, K. "Livets prøvelser skaper hans styrke," Morgenbladet (28 Apr 1972). [Trials of life create his strength]

2302 Engelstad, C. "De intellektuelle og friheten," Aftenposten (27 May 1972). [Intellectuals & freedom]

(28) Polish

Special source: aside from basic Polish ref. works, received information about early translations of S. in Poland from Krzysztof Zarzecki, Warszawa. Abbreviations: S.: Sołženicyn. Periodicals: TL: Trybuna Ludu; ZL: Życie Literacke (Kraków); ŻW: Życie Warszawy.

Poland

All periodicals listed pub. in Warszawa unless otherwise indicated. For publications in the Polish language abroad, see next section.

Translations:

2303 "Jeden dzień w życiu Iwana Denisowicza," tr. I. Lewandowska & W. Dąbrowski. Polityka, Nos. 48-52 & 1-5 (1 Dec 1962-2 Feb 1963). [Serialized; trans. somewhat abbriged]

2304 "Zdarzenie na stacji Kreczetowka," tr. H. Broniatowska, pp. 229-90 in Słoneczna dolina. Warszawa: Państwowy Instytut Wydawniczy, 1964.

2305 "Dla dobra sprawy," tr. I. Szenfeld. Kultura (29 Sep 1963), 7-11. [PD]

2306 "Zdarzenie na stacji Kreczetowka," tr. H. Broniatowska & I. Szenfeld. Wiatraki, 21 (1963), 1-3; 22, p. 3; 23-24, pp. 2-3; 1 (1964), 2-3.

2307 "Zachar Kalita," tr. R. Kotowski. ŻL, 13 (1966), 1-5. [Artemova (429) gives tr. as R. Lasota; this seems to be an error]

Criticism:

2308 J[aruželski], J. "Wydarzenia literackie i polityczne: Korespondencja z Moskwy," ŻW, 277 (1962), 2.

2309 Łucki, M. "Dzień, którego zapomnieć nie wolno: Korespondencja z Moskwy," TL, 327 (1962), 6.

2310 Łucki, M. "Wokół powieści A. S-na: Korespondencja z Moskwy," TL, 333 (1962), 4.

2311 Triolet, E. "...o opowiadaniu S-na," Nowa Kultura, 51/52 (1962), 16; Polityka, 52 (1962), 12. [Tr. of 1680b]

2312 Jaruželski, J. "Nurt intelektualny: ZSRR," Przegląd Kulturalny, 51/52 (1962), 10.

2313 Jaruželski, J. "S. i jego otoczenie: Korespondencja z Moskwy," ŻW, 23 (1963), 2.

2314 Rudnicki, A. "Oczyszczenie: Niebieskie kartki," Świat, 36 (1963), 11.

2315 Redlich, J. "Obrona utworu S-na w 'Nowym Mirze': Korespondencja z Moskwy," ŻW, 284 (1963), 2.

2316 Žakiewicz, Z. "W kręgu wielkich tradycji," Twórczość, 10 (1963), 10.

2317 Kariakin, Ju. "Epizod współczesnej walki ideologicznej," Problemy Pokoju, 9 (1964), 80-85. [Tr. of 180]

2318 Gomolicki, L. "Spór o S-nie," Odgłosy, 10 (1964), 21. [The controversy concerning S.]

2319 Wieczorek, D. "O stylistycznej funkcji miejsca przydawki przymiotnej w języku polskim i rosyjskim (Na przykładzie tłumaczenia powieści A. I. S-na," Język Polski (Kraków), 5 (1966), 385-89. [Limited comp. anal. of stylistic function of position of adjectives in Polish & Russian, using OD as language sample (in tr. of Lewandowska & Dąbrowski [see 2303]).]

2320 Ličko, P. "Jeden dzień u Al. Is. S-na," ŻL, 21 (21 May 1967), 9. [Tr. of 1604]

2321 R. N. "'Literaturnaja Gazieta' o S-nie," ŻL, 28 (1968), 14. [See 207]

2322 Romanowski, J. [On Avg. čet.], WTK (26 Mar 1972). [Russ. tr.: 234; Eng. tr.: 1513]

Polish language abroad

Note that in Paris as well as in Warszawa is published a journal titled Kultura; all references below are to the Paris publication.

Translations:

2323 "Zdarzenie na stacji Kreczetowka," tr. L. Furatyk. Kultura, 7/8 [189/190] (Jul-Aug 1963), 5-53. [Artemova (429) gives tr. as J. Stempowski (=Stępowski); this is incorrect.]

2324 "Zagroda Matriony," tr. J. Łobodowski; in: We własnych oczach: Antologia współczesnej literatury sowieckiej. Paris: Instytut literacki (Biblioteka Kultury), 1963.

2325 "List do Zjazdu Pisarzy," tr. Z. Hertz. Kultura, 7/8 [237/238] (Jul-Aug 1967), 7-10. [S's letter of 16 May 1967; tr. from French text]

2326 "Prawa dłoń," tr. J. Łobodowski. Kultura, 12 [267] (Dec 1969), 31-40. [Pr. kist']

2327 "List otwarty do Związku Pisarzy Sowieckich," tr. Z. Hertz. Kultura, 12 [267] (Dec 1969), 41-42. [Tr. from French]

2328 Krąg pierwszy, tr. M. Kaniowski. Paris: Instytut literacki, 1970. v. 1, 400 pp.; v. 2, 384 pp. [KP]

2329 "Wiersze prozą," tr. I. Szenfeld. Kultura, 11 [278] (Nov 1970), 66-75. [The first 15 prose poems]

2330 "Modlitwa," tr. I. Szenfeld. Na Antenie (London), 11 (1970).

2331 "Procesja Wielkanocna," tr. M. Kaniowski. Kultura, 4 [283] (Apr 1971), 11-14. [Pasx. kr. xod]

2332 "List otwarty Al. S-na do K.G.B.," Kultura, 9 [288] (Sep 1971), 74-76. [Tr. from Russian]

2333 Oddział chorych na raka, tr. J. Łobodowski. Paris: Instytut literacki (Biblitek "Kultury"), 1971. 480 pp. [RK]

2334 "Niewygłoszone przemówienie (Z okazji przyznania nagrody Nobla za r. 1970)," tr. M. Kaniowski. Kultura, 10 [301] (Oct 1972), 3-18. [Nobel lecture]

Criticism:

2335 Mihajlov, M. "Martwy dom Dostojewskiego i S-na (Przyczynki do fenomenologii niewolnictwa)," tr. Tadeusz & Radmiła Lisiccy. Kultura, 9 [215] (Sep 1965), 3-33. [Tr. of 2430] This tr. appeared in Polish tr. of M.'s book: Tematy rosyjskie. Paris: Instytut literacki, 1966. [See Eng. tr. of this book at 586]

2336 Herling-Grudziński, G. "Literatura i rewolucja," Kultura, 7/8 [237/238] (Jul-Aug 1967), 3-6. (See pp. 5-6)

2337 Herling-Grudziński, G. "Realizm rosyjski," pp. 115-129 & "Godzina prawdy," pp. 129-138 in his: Upiory rewolucji. Paris: Instytut literacki, 1969.

2338 Kruczek, A. "Z sowieckiej prasy," Kultura, 6 [261] (Jun 1969), 101-102.

2339 Kruczek, A. "W sowieckie prasie," Kultura, 1/2 [268/269] (Jan-Feb 1970), 143-45. [On S.'s expulsion from Wr. Union]

2340 "Al. S.," Kultura, 11 [278] (Nov 1970), 65-66. [Biog. note]

2341 Chiaromonte, N. & G. Herling-Grudziński. "Dialog o S-nie," Kultura, 4 [283] (Apr 1971), 3-10.

See also 589 & 1689.

(29) Portuguese. (Portugal & Brazil)   Translations:

Only spelling noted for S.: Solzhenitzin.

2342 Um dia na vida de Ivan Denisovich, tr. Fernando de Melo Moser & Paulo Madeira Rodrigues. Lisboa: Guimarães Editores, 1963. 185 pp.

2343 Um dia na vida de Ivan Denisovich, tr. H. Silva Letra. Lisboa: Europa-América, 1963. 201 pp.

2344 A casa de Matriona, tr. J. Feio. Lisboa: Arcádia, 1964.

192 pp. [Prob. contains SK & PD as well]
  2345 O primeiro círculo, tr. M. Ramos. Amadora, Portugal: Ibis,
1969. 684 pp.
  2346 Pavilhão de cancerosos. Rio de Janeiro: Expressão e Cultura, 1969. Pt. 1, tr. S. Jambeiro, 398 pp.; Pt. 2, tr. A. Weisenberg, 300 pp.
  2347 Os direitos do escritor, tr. T. Netto. São Paulo: Docu-
mentos, 1969. 90 pp. [Tr. of 2190]

(30) Catalan. (Spain) Translations:

  2348 La Casa de Matriona. Tot sigui per la causa, tr. J. Güell.
Barcelona: Edicions 62, 1968. 167 pp.
  2349 Entre autoritarisme i explotació, tr. Xavier Fort & Bufill.
Barcelona: Edicions 62, 1970. 100 pp. [Tr. of 2190]
  2350 Miniaturas en prosa, tr. J. Güell. Barcelona: Edicions 62,
1971. 78 pp.

(31) Spanish. (Spain, Argentina, Chile, Cuba, Mexico)

  Special sources: José Ferrer Aleu & Mariano Orta Manzano, Barcelona, & Francisco del Carril, Emecé Editores, Buenos Aires; also,
4 items taken from Artemova (429). Spellings of S. noted (in
about equal distribution): Soljenitsin, Solschenitzin, Solyenitsin, Solyenitzin, Solzhenitsin, Solzhenitsyn.

Translations:

  2351 Un día en vida de Iván Denisovich, tr. I. Antich. Barcelona: Herder, 1963. 253 pp.
  2352 Un día en la vida de Iván Denisovitch, tr. J. Mercado & J.
Bravo. Barcelona: Luis de Caralt, 1963. 192 pp. Also: Barcelona: Círculo de Lectores, 1970. 174 pp.
  2353 Un día de Iván Denisovich, tr. I. Vicente. Mexico: Ed. Era:
1963. 177 pp. With introd. by Tvardovskij.
  2354 Un día de Iván Denisovich. La Habana: Editora del Consejo
Nacional de Cultura, Editorial Nacional de Cuba, 1965. ix, 163
pp. With introd. by Tvardovskij. [Tr.?]
  2355 El primer círculo, tr. Mariano [Orta Manzano] & Rafael Orta. Barcelona: Bruguera, 1968. 647 pp.; 1970. 891 pp. [Tr. from
Italian [see 2160)]
  2356 En el primer círculo. Buenos Aires: Emecé Editores, 1969.
578 pp. (Tr. by 3 members of permanent staff of Emecé, revised
by Irina Astrau)
  2357 Un día de la vida de Iván Denisovitch, tr. José Ferrer Aleu.
Barcelona: Plaza & Janés, 1969. 203 pp.; 1970. 155 pp. [Tr. from
French]
  2358 "Estudios y pequeños cuentos," pp. 55-68 in Literatura clan-
destina soviética, tr. V. Andresco. Madrid: Ed. Guadarrama, 1969.
[First 15 prose poems]
  2359 Cuentos en miniatura, tr. I. Astrau. Buenos Aires: Emecé,
1969. 179 pp. [Also has SK, perhaps more]
  2360 El Pabellón de los cancerosos. Santiago de Chile: Ediciones Ercilla, 1969. 500 pp. [Tr. ?]
  2361 Un día en la vida de Iván Denisovich, tr. A. Puig. Barcelona: Ediciones Grijalbo, 1970. 176 pp.
  2362 La Casa de Matriona. Santiago de Chile: Ed. Ercilla, 1970.

184 pp. (Also has SK & PD) [Tr. ?]

2363 Nunca cometemos errores: Un incidente en la estación de Krechetovka, tr. X. Fierro. Barcelona: Ed. Tusquets, 1970. 77 pp. [Though taking its title from "We Never Make Mistakes" (see 505), contains only the first of the two stories; prob. tr. from English.]

2364 El pabellón del cáncer, tr. Inés del Campo Ruiz. Madrid: Aguilar, 1970. 2 v. 450 pp.

2365 Entre el autoritarismo y la explotación, with "Una candela bajo el viento," tr. Melitón Bustamente & Francisco Fernández Buey. Barcelona: Ed. Península, 1970. 156 pp. [Tr. of 2190, with Sveča added, prob. also tr. from Italian (see 2171)]

2366 Los derechos del escritor. Buenos Aires: Signos, 1970. 96 pp. [Prob. tr. of French tr. of 2190 (see 1840)]

2367 La casa de Matriona. Todo sea por la causa, tr. J. Fuster & M. Oliver. Barcelona: Península, 1971. 152 pp.

2368 Por el bien de la causa, tr. J. Pomares, P. Giralt & R. Ibero. Barcelona: Ed. Bruguera, 1971. 348 pp; 1972 & 1973. 333 pp. [Contents: same as 520, plus OD; tr. from Ger. (see 1956)]

2369 Nudo I. Agosto, 1914 (10-21 de agosto), tr. Jóse Lain Entralgo & Luis Abollado. Barcelona: Barral Editores, 1972. 678 pp. [Tr. of pirated Ger. ed'n. (see 1963)]

Criticism:

2370 "Los criticos soviéticos juzgan a Iván Denisovich," Bohemia (Habana), 3 (1965), 36-7.

2371 Lukács, G. "Un día de Iván Denisovich," Union (Habana), 5, ii (Apr-Jun 1965), 120-132. [Tr. of 1971]

2372 von Ssachno, H. Literatura soviética posterior a Stalin. Madrid: Ed. Guadarrama, 1968. 424 pp. [Tr. of 1975]

2373 Míguez, A. "S.: De Iván Denisovich al Primer Círculo," Madrid (8 Mar 1969).

2374 Arbeloa, J. [On Un día], Pensamiento Navarro (Pamplona) (22 Jun 1969).

2375 Sanchez del Rio, L. "Al. S.: Premio Nobel de Literatura," Arbor: Revista General de Investigación y Cultura, 299 (1970), 85-87.

2376 Murciano, C. "S. o la integridad," Estafeta Literaria (Madrid) (1 Jan 1971).

2377 Perez-Minik, D. "La novela extranjera en España: S.," Insula, 26 (Jan 1971), 7.

2377a Digame (Madrid) (16 Mar 1971). [Has least laudatory of numerous articles on S. in Spanish press at this time.]

(32) Swedish

Special source: Hans Björkegren. Abbreviations: S.: Solsjenitsyn & Solzjenitsyn. Periodicals: DN: Dagens Nyheter; SD: Svenska Dagbladet.

Translations:

2378 En dag i Ivan Denisovitjs liv, tr. R. Berner. Stockholm: Arena, 1963. 191 pp.

2379 Två berättelser: Ett möte på Kretjetovka stationen. Matrjonas gård, tr. K. Johansson. Stockholm: Wahlström & Widstrand,

1963. 154 pp.

2380 Cancerkliniken, tr. E. Thomson-Roos. Stockholm: Wahlström
& Widstrand. v. 1, 1968. 259 pp.; v. 2, 1969. 218 pp. Revised
ed., tr. E. Thomson-Roos & S. Vallmark, 1970 & 1972. 480 pp.

2381 Den första kreten, tr. H. Björkegren. Stockhom: Wahlström
& Widstrand, 1969, 1970 & 1972. 520 pp.

2382 En dag i Ivan Denisovitjs liv, tr. H. Björkegren: Stockholm:
Wahlström & Widstrand, 1970. 131 pp.

2383 Högra handen och andra noveller, tr. H. Björkegren & others.
Stockholm: Wahlström & Widstrand, 1970 & 1971. 190 pp. [Con-
tents sama as 520]

2383a (18 Oct 1971). [According to a note in 1204, a letter by
S. appeared in Swedish press this date; probably this is letter of
18 Sep 1971 to Per Hegge (see 48).]

2384 Augusti fjorton (Gamla tideräkningen), tr. H. Björkegren.
Stockholm: Wahlström & Widstrand, 1972. 500 pp.

See also 534 & 538.

Criticism:

For books & important articles, see 2394, 2396-97 & 2406.

2385 Björkegren, H. "Uppseendeväckande rysk debutnovell," Stock-
holms-Tidningen (22 Nov 1962). [1st article in Swedish press]

2386 Vallmark, S. "S-ns cancerberättelse: En verklighet till
döds," DN (8 Nov 1968).

2387 Schildt, G. "En lycking manniska," SD (23 Dec 1968).

2388 Ahnlund, L. "Ett epos över vår tids resurser av ondska och
godhet," SD (6 Jul 1970).

2389 Björkegren, H. "En sanning som ser oss rakt i ansiktet,"
Expressen (30 Sep 1970).

2390 Ahnlund, K. "Storstilat diktarskap i mänsklighetens tjänst,"
(9 Oct 1970).

2391 "S.," Liberal Expressen, No. 11 (1969). [Information incomplete; source: Rothberg bibl. (569); may not be Swedish]

2392 Hallden, R. "En annorlunda Nobelpristagare," DN (10 Dec
1970), 4.

2393 Lindmarker, I. "Krusjtjev och S.," SD (10 Dec 1970), 5.

2394 Lukács, G. Solsjenitsyn, tr. R. Åhlstedt. Stockholm: Ra-
bén & Sjörgren, 1970. 111 pp. [Tr. of 2052]

2395 Lagerlöf, K. "Företräder Jarring Bresjnev eller oss?" Göteborgs-Handels och Sjöfartstidning (24 Sep 1971).

2396 Hegge, P. Solsjenitsyn kan inte komma, tr. J.-E. Mattson.
Stockholm: Wahlström & Widstrand, 1971. 111 pp. [Tr. of 2295]

2397 Björkegren, H. Alexander Solsjenitsyn: Biografi och doku-
ment. Stockholm: Wahlström & Widstrand, 1971. [Translations:
570, 1672a & 2296]

2398 [Announcement by V. Muberg], DN (12 Sep 1971). [Russ. tr.:
429]

2399 Harning, A. "Affären S.--en studie i kryperi och oheder-
lighet," Göteborgs-Tidningen (10 Oct 1971).

2400 Jangfeldt, B. "S.," Aftonbladet (11 Oct 1971).

2401 Ahnlund, K. "Ensam, stark," SD (15 Oct 1971).

2402 Lagercrantz, O. "S.," DN (20 Oct 1971).

2403 Falk, A. "S. är farligare," Expressen (30 Oct 1971).

2404 Braconier, J. "S.," Sydsvenska Dagbladet (7 Nov 1971).

2405 Linder, E. "Sovjet och S.," Göteborgs-Posten (7 Nov 1971).
2406 Ingold, F. "S-ns nya roman (Avgust četyrnadcatogo)," Credo (Uppasala), 1 (1972), 18-22. [Tr. of Ger. ms. by Ingold]
2407 Larni, M. [Comment on Shub's rev. of Avg. čet. (see 1461)], Norsen Flammen (Jan or Feb 1972). [Russian tr. at 233; this article was pub. without L.'s permission, according to Ž. Medvedev (see note at 1271).]
2408 Göteborgs-Handels och Sjöfarts Tidning (5 Oct 1972). [Has article on S., according to 495]

See also 1662.

(33) Turkish

Special source: two items taken from Artemova (429). Spellings of S. noted: Solyenitsin, Solzenitsin.

Translations:

2409 İvan Denisoviç'in bir günü, tr. N. Dalyancı. İstanbul: Ataç Kitabevi, 1965. 160 pp. Also: İstanbul: Altin Kitaplar-Yayinevi, 1970. 357 pp. (with other stories).
2410 İvan Denisoviç'in hayatinda bir gün, tr. Z. Özalpsan. İstanbul: İskender Matbaasi, 1965. 147 pp. [Vol. 1; for Vol. 2, see 2411] Also: İstanbul: Cem Yayinevi, 1970. 175 pp.
2411 Dava uğruna, tr. Z. Özalpsan. İstanbul: İskender Matbaasi, 1965. v. 2: pp. 147-211. [v. 1=2410] (PD)
2412 İlk çember, tr. H. Aslan. İstanbul: Özüpek Matbaasi, 1968 & 1969. 2 vols., 759 pp. Later ed'ns.: 1970, 1971. [KP]
2413 Kanser koğuşu, tr. Ö. Süsoy & G. Suveren. İstanbul: Altin Kitaplar-Yayinevi, 1970. 518 pp. [RK]
2414 13 numerali koğuş, tr. N. Erkurt. İstanbul: Kitapcilik Ticaret. v. 1, 1970, 374 pp.; v. 2, 1971, 349 pp. [RK; tr. from French]

Criticism:

2415 Batu, S. "S.: Kanserliler pavyonu," Varlik, 36 [750], pp. 24-25. [Info. from Artemova (429), who does not give date, but must be either 1970 or 1971]

(34) Ukrainian. (Germany) Criticism:

2416 Koševelivec', I. "A. Solženicyn--nobelivs'kyj lavreat," Sučasnist' (Munich), 2, ii (1971), 52-62.

(35) Yiddish. (U. S.) Criticism:

See 931 (rev. of August 1914 in Jewish Daily Forward). [For criticism and translations in Hebrew language, see entries 2128-2143a; see also 913]

(36) Macedonian. (Yugoslavia) Translation:

2417 "Na stanicata Krečetovka," Nova Makedonija, 20 (6 Jan 1963). [Info. from Roland (701) who does not name translator]

(37) Serbocroatian. (Yugoslavia)

Special source (aside from standard Yugoslavian bibliographies): Peter Rolland (see 701), several items. Abbreviations: S.: Solženjicin. Periodical: NIN: Nedeljne Informativne Novine (Beograd).

Translations:

2418 Jedan dan Ivana Denisoviča. Dogadaj na stanici Krečetovka. Matrjonina kuča, tr. Ž. Žujovič, A. Grdan & S. Durbabić. Beograd: "Kultura", 1963. 212 pp.

2419 "Dogadaj na stanici Krečetovka," Politika, 60 (23 Jan-7 Feb 1963), 1707-22. [From Rolland (701); tr. not named]

2420 "Matrjonina kuča," Vecernje Novosti, 11 (23 Jan-6 Feb 1963), 2908-20. [From Rolland (701); tr. not named]

2421 "Radi koristi stvari," in: Savremeni sovjetski pisci, v. 4 (1961-1963), ed. & tr. A. Flaker. Zagreb: "Naprijed", 1964. 372 pp. [PD]

2422 Odjel za rak. Rijeka: Otokar Keršovani. v. 1, tr. Ivan Kušan, 1968, 344 pp.; v. 2, tr. Ivan & Jakša Kušan, 1969, 288 pp. Also: 1970. [RK]

2423 U prvom krugu, tr. N. Šoljan. Rijeka: Otokar Keršovani, 1969. 555 pp.

2424 "Kako su primili 'Ivana Denisoviča'," NIN, 962 (15 Jul 1969). [Tr. of 14]

2425 Sveča na vetru. Jelen i logorska lepotica, tr. M. Jovanović. Beograd: Obelisk, 1971. 210 pp. Foreword by Jovanović: "Scenski prilog Al. S-na".

2426 Vatra i mravi, tr. M. Čolić. Beograd: Obelisk, 1972. 107 pp. Afterword by Čolić: "Fenomen zvani "S.". [Contents: Krox., PD, Molitva, Avtobiog. & tr. of 13, 14 & other letters]

Criticism:

Important articles: 2427, 2429-30, 2434, 2444, 2447-49.

2427 Car, D. "Jedan dan Ivana Denisoviča," Kolo, 1, iii [n.s.] (1963), 357-68.

2428 Zaharov, L. "Nova proza S-na i njegovi kritičari," Telegram, 4 (21 Dec 1963), 187.

2429 Zaharov, L. "S., njegov Ivan Denisovič i diskusija o obojici," Književnost, 78 (1964), 126-32.

2430 Mihailov, M. "Mrtvi dom F. M. Dostojevskogo i A. S-na," Forum, 3, v/vi (1964), 906-28. [Translations: 332, 586, 601, 1987, 2127 & 2335]

2431 Obradović, M. "Jedan dan Ivana Denisoviča," Trudbenik, 19 (16 Jul 1964), 33.

2432 Maksimović, M. [Rev. of 2418], Illustrovana Politika, 8 (1964), 27 & 41.

2433 Mihajlov, M. ["Lakšin i S."], Delo (Beograd) (Jan 1965). [Translations: 437, 1279, 1285, pp., 55-56]

2434 Trifković, R. "Od Babelja do S.," Izraz (Sarajevo), 5 (1965), 483-87.

2435 Bojović, I. "Fragmenty iz razgovora s Jevtušenkom," NIN (26 Sep 1965).

2436 [Excerpts of protocol of 22 Sep 1967], Vjesnik (Zagreb) (1, 2 & 3 Jun 1968). [See 262]

2437 Jovanović, M. "Pledoaje za etički socializm," Književne Novine, 20 (6 Jul 1968), 331.
2438 "Muki S.-na," NIN, 927 (13 Oct 1968).

Reviews of Odjel za rak (2422)

2439 Borba, 33 (12 Oct 1968), 284. (M. Danojlić)
2440 Dometi, 1, ii-iii (1968), 107-11. (M. Jeličić)
2441 Izraz, 24, xii (1968), 553-56. (R. Trifković)
2442 Student, 32 (5 Nov 1968), 22. (L. Jeremić)
2443 Telegram, 9 (8 Nov 1968), 445. (S. Mihalić)

2444 Lukács, G. "Jedan dan Ivana Denisoviča," tr. Z. Konstantinović, in: Eseji o književnosti. Beograd: Izd. Preduzeće "Rad", 1969. [Tr. of 1971]
2445 Bajalski, R., Ž. Bogdanović, D. Rančić & D. Simič. "Nobelovac S.," NIN (18 Oct 1970).
2446 F. K. "Nobelovac S.," NIN (1 Nov 1970). [Letter]
2447 Jovanović, M. "Etički socijalizam S.-na i njegov značaj u savremenosti," Savremenik, 33 (1971), 10-21.
2448 Jerotić, V. "U prvom krugu S.-na," Savremenik, 33 (1971), 22-6.
2449 Lukić, S. "Pred savremenošću i istorijom: A. S.," Savremenik, 33 (1971), 32-39.

See also foreword and afterword by translators at 2425 & 2426.

(38) Slovene. (Yugoslavia)

Special source: France Klopčič. Abbreviations: S.: Solženicin. Periodical: NR: Naši Razgledi. All periodicals listed are published in Ljubljana.

Translations:

2450 "En dan Ivana Denisoviča," tr. F. Klopčič. Serialized in weekly Tovariš: 50 (31 Dec 1962), 82-87 & 1-8 (12 Jan-3 Mar 1963): 52-57, 26-38, 26-39, 4-45, 42-47, 4-45, 38-43 & 37-40; with after ter word by translator: Tovariš, 8 (2 Mar 1963), 41-43. [Repr: 2452]
2451 "Matrjonina hiša," Večer, 19 (5-23 Mar 1963), 53-68 [+?]. [From Rolland (701); tr. not named]
2452 En dan Ivana Denisoviča in še dve noveli, tr. F. Klopčič. Ljubljana: Državna založba Slovenije, 1964. 227 pp. With afterword by Klopčič, pp. 219-227. (Also has: "Dogodek na postaji Krečetovki," 124-81 & "Matrjonina hiša," 182-218) Later ed'n.: see 2455.
2453 "Desna roka," tr. N. Mužič. NR (22 Mar 1969). [From Fr.]
2454 Prvi krog, tr. D. Železnov. Ljubljana: Mladinska knjiga, 1970. v. 1, 386 pp.; v. 2, 454 pp. [KP]
2455 En dan Ivana Denisoviča. Povesti, črtice, dokumentacija, tr. F. Klopčič. Ljubljana: Državna založba Slovenije, 1971. 342 pp. With afterword by Klopčič, pp. 331-340. (Contents same as first ed'n. [see 2452], with translations of the following added: PD, ZK, six of the prose poems, and: 238, 1604, 6, 248 [excerpt], 250, 261, 262 [excerpt], 266-67, 269, 271-73, 207, 216, 294, 1593, & 222.]
2456 Rakov oddelek, tr. J. Stanič. Ljubljana: ČGD Delo, 1970. v. 1, 258 pp.; v. 2, 221 pp. [RK]

Criticism:

2457 Kališnik, Š. "Dnevi Al. S-na," <u>Delo</u> (4 Jun 1964). [On <u>En dan</u>]
2458 Rupel, S. "En dan Ivana Denisoviča," <u>Borec</u> (7 Jul 1964), 427-28.
2459 "Preganjan in varovan," <u>NR</u>, 6 (22 Mar 1969).
2460 "Pariz o S-nu: Izključitvi A. S-na na rob," <u>NR</u>, 24 (Dec 1969).
2461 Vogel, H. "Konjunkturni S.," <u>Tedenska Tribuna</u> (6 Oct 1971).
2462 Železnov, D. "S. in Dimitrova," <u>Komunist</u> (15 Oct 1971).
2463 H. H. "Al. S.: En dan Ivana Denisoviča," <u>Delo</u> (4 Dec 1971).
2464 Rupel, D. "Tosočletje Al. S-na," <u>NR</u>, 23 [478] (10 Dec 1971).
2465 Klopčič, F. "Brez resnobe," <u>NR</u>, 24 [479] (24 Dec 1971).

Also see translator's afterwords by Klopčič at 2450, 2452 & 2455.

Index of Names

Alphabetization follows the English alphabet and ignores all accents and diacritical marks, including the Slavic haček, the German umlaut, the Polish barred L [Ł], and so on. Cyrillic names are Romanized using the transliteration system described in the introduction to this bibliography, p. xiii. Common Western spellings of some Russian names are listed as a form of cross-indexing. Russian émigrés publishing both in Russian and in a second language under the legal, Westernized version of their name are listed under both spellings of their name, with a note identifying the two names as belonging to one person.

1. Authors of books, articles, prefaces, forewords & afterwords.

Also listed are subjects of articles whose statements or writings about Solzhenitsyn are extensively quoted. Prior to the main alphabetical index is a list of unidentified pseudonymous signatures and initials.

A. C. 1806
A. F. [Cyrillic] 382
A. J. O. 1648
A. O. [Cyrillic] 359
Ayin Zayin [Hebrew initials] 2142
Byvš. student Rostovskogo universiteta 491
Čitatel' 240
C. J. 1841
C. M. 1695
D. G. 999
E. C. 1623
e. e. 642
F. K. 2446
H. H. 2463
Kenett 1791
L. D. 1693
L. T. [Cyrillic] 494
L. V. [Cyrillic] 463
M. B. 1859
M. P. 1761
M. W. 1824
[Očedvidec] 442
P. Me. 1940
P. R. 1805
R. 1441, 1454
R. F. 1630
R. M. S. 901
R. N. 2321
S. K. 1460
S. M. [Cyrillic] 499

S. M. M. 758
T. R. [Cyrillic] 481
V. I. [Cyrillic] 341
V. O. [Cyrillic] 422
V. P. H. 970
W. S. K. 896

Abalkin, N. 204
Abbate, Michele 2179, 2195, 2216, 2231
Adamovič, Georgij [same as Adamovitch] 340, 348, 383, 388, 454, 1918 (pp. 412-16)
Adrian [Anisimoff], Esa 1665-67, 1672
Afonin, L. 68
Afonskij, Georgij 415
Ahnlund, Knut 2388, 2390, 2401
Aleksandrov, I. 229, 1285 (pp. 228-9), 1556
Alekseev, M. 199, 1918 (p.204)
Alekseev, V. [same as W. Alexeev] 314
Alexander, James E. 977
Alexandrov. See Aleksandrov
Alexandrova, Vera 580
Alexeev, Wassilij [same as V. Alekseev] 536
Alvarez, A. 761
Améry, Jean 2099
Amette, Jacques Pierre 1854
Amory, Judy 899
Amos, Y. 2137

Bonavia, David 1377, 1385
Borel, P.-L. 1713, 1784, 1821
Borisov, K. 432
Borman, Arkadij 403
Borowski, Kay 1961 (afterword)
Bortoli, Georges 1703
Bory, Jean-Louis 1927a
Bose, R. 1699
Bosem, Hedda 2132
Bosquet, Alain 1891, 1930
Bouchine. See Bušin.
Bouilly, Jacques 1874
Bouketitch[sic]-Voutchetitch.
  See Vučetić.
Boukhanov. See Buxanov.
Bourdeaux, M. 632
Bowen, John 739, 748
Braadland, Aase 2287
Brablik, T. 1586
Braconier, Jean 2404
Bradley, Thompson 574, 583
Brady, Charles A. 888
Brandenburg, Anne 1643
Brass, Alister 832
Bratschi, Georges 1712,1746,1801
Brice, Jacques 1720
Brodal, Jan 2284
Broido. See Brojdo.
Brojdo, E. 63, 1918 (p. 128-9)
Bronska-Pampuch, Wanda 1991,
  2009, 2072, 2086
Brooks, Mary Ellen 625
Brovman, G. 82,143, 146,158,
  188-9,1538,1918(p. 201)
Brown, Deming 826
Brown, Edward J. 574, 578,
  588, 596, 640
Brown, Lloyd L. 1250
Brown, Marjorie L. 715
Brumberg, Abraham 1284
Bruni, Thomas G. 935
Brunsdale, Mitzi M. 928
Buchanow. See Buxanov.
Bugge, N. M. 2281, 2293
Bukhanov. See Buxanov.
Bukin, V. 113
Bukovskij, K. 166
Bulgin, Randolph M. 922
Bunke, Joan 911
Burg, David 498, 571, 1411
Burucoa, Ch. 1782
Bushin. See Bušin.
Bušin, V. 94,114, 148,1538,
  1918 (pp. 148-9)

Bushman, Irene 1364
Buxanov, Viktor 26, 88 [tr.: 503,
  544, 1285 (p. 5-9), 1303,1685,1918
  (p.104-09), 1967]

Cady, Richard 930
Callaghan, Morely 626
Čalmaev, V. 102,122,1278,1535
Calta, Louis 1125
Čapčaxov, F. 78,1918(p. 133-5)
Capouya, Emile 837-8
Car, Duško 2427
Carden, Patricia 738, 825
Carlisle, Olga 678, 1039
Carpovich. See Karpovič.
Carver, David 1285 (p. 195-6)
Casolari, G. 2219
Castello, Ferdinando 2185
Castillo, Michel. See del Cas-
  tillo.
Cathala, Jean 1681a, 1757
Cazenave, Pierre 1841
Chaix-Ruy, Jules 1870, 2228
Chalmaev. See Čalmaev.
Chamberlain, William H. 754, 771
Champenois, Jean 1704
Chapchakhov. See Čapčaxov.
Chavardes, Maurice 1903
Cheinis. See Šejnis.
Chevallier, Marjolaine 1878
Chiaromonte, Nicola 2341
Chicherov. See Čičerov.
Childs, James 954
Christesen, Nina 616, 648
Chukovskaya. See Čukovskaja.
Čičerov, I. 65, 1918 (p.129-30)
Cimerinov, R. 123, 509 (p.128-
  30), 1918 (p. 154), 1537
Čistjakov, inž. 281, 429
Clardy, John 628
Clarity, James F. 1089,1093,1096,
  1100-02, 1105, -18, -29, -34, -43,
  -99,1254,-67, -69
Clark, Luelle M. 882
Clive, Geoffrey 595
Cohen, E. F. 858
Cohen, Lynn Sneider 700
Cohen, Miriam 967
Čolić, Milan 2426 (afterword)
Connolly, Cyril 749
Conquest, Robert 1277,1312,1445,
  1448
Constant, Stephen 849
Cook, Bruce 823, 952

Cosgrave, M. S. 868
Cournot, Michel 1862
Cramer, Dwight 926
Crankshaw, Edward 808, 844,
  1366-67, 1437
Crespin, Raoul 1883
Cristini, G. 2208
Critchlow, J. 1435
Croce, Elena 2220
Crousse, Jean-Louis 1877
Čukovskaja, Lidija 291, 278
  [repr.& tr.: 428 (p.122-34), 429,
  440, 1285(p.172-6), 1918(p. 306-
  12), 2192]
Cuneo, P. K. 1351
Czeremis, Konstanty 2118

Daix, Pierre 1285 (p.212), 1673a,
  1683, 1716, 1827, 1841, 1898
Dalbey, Alice 929
d'Aleo, Vilma 2180
Dan'kov, I. 235
Danojlić, Mića 2439
Dar, D. 256 [repr.& tr.: 428
  (p.392-3), 429, 1285 (p. 90-91),
  1918 (p. 264-5)]
Dargent, Marcel 1835
d'Aubarède, Gabriel 1735
Davenport, Guy 801, 872
David, Z. 2137a
Davranches, J. 1819
Day, Dorothy 643
Debidour, V. H. 1777
de Fabrègues, Jean 1786
de Figueiredo, Antonio 1448
de Kerchove, Arnold 1770
del Castillo, Michel 1811, 1918
  (p. 327-43), 1933
del Rio. See Sanchez del Rio.
Dement'ev, A. 190, 1545
Demets, Gilbert 1646
Dennis, Nigel 813
Denoix, Pierre 1918 (p.423-25)
de Proyart, Jacqueline 1918 (p.
  436-490)
de Rosa, Giuseppe 2177
de Rosbo, Kerlero 1807
Descargues, Pierre 1747, 1802
Des Pres, T. 644
Deutscher, Tamara 679
Devalière, F. 1783
Dewhirst, Martin 1436
Dikušin, N. 190, 1545
Diószegi, András 2146
Djilas, Milovan 495, 574, 1014

Dolbier, Maurice 984
Domogackij, B. 339
Donatov, L. 338, 376
Donovan, Laurence 945
Dovhiy, W. 690
Dox, Claude 1820
Dremov, An. 142
Driscoll, James G. 1517
Drommert, René 2116
Droutse. See Druce.
Drozda, Miroslav 1579, -85, -91
Drozdov, I. 213
Druce, Ion 79, 1918 (p.135-7)
Dubinin, M. 419
Dumayet, Pierre 1826
Dumon, Marthe 1846
Dunlop, John B. 574 (article),
  687, 705
Duranteau, Josiane 1904
Dursi, Massimo 2222
Dutton, Geoffrey 1390
Dymchitz. See Dymšic.
Dymšic, Aleksandr L. 58, 105
  1918 (p. 127-8; 143-4)
Dynnik, Aleksandr 371
Džilas. See Djilas.

Ebmeyer, Klaus-U. 2100
Edmunds, Paul J. 1017
Eekman, T. 1622
Egeleand, Erik 2299
Egoryčev, Nikolaj G. 192-3, 1543,
  1918 (p. 201-02)
Ekman, Rolf 1661
El'cov, Igor' 463
Eliade, Stavrou 2121 (introd.)
El'jaševič, Arkadij 90, 1285(p.20)
Elkin, A. 211
Elliott, Janice 839-40
Ellmann, Mary 828
Emery, L. 1795
Emmanuel, Pierre 298, 1285(p.195)
Engelstad, Carl Fredrik 2302
Epstein, Joseph 990, 1014
Epstein, Julius 1249
Erëmin, D. 163
Ericson, Edward, E., Jr. 689
Erlich, Victor 574, 600, 685
Ermilov, V. 57, 74, 89, 1285(p.18-
  19), 1529, 1918 (p. 123-5)
Esam, Irene 614, 1369
Ešliman (Fr.) 2119
Esslin, M. 568
Eve, Martin 568
Evtušenko, Evgenij 2435

Grant, Louis T. 996
Grazzini, Giovanni 2233
Grebenščikov, A. 212, 1371
Grebenščikov, Vladimir I. 358, 360, 375, 642, 687
Green, Alan 1505
Greene, Graham 1512
Greenspun, Roger 1178
Grekov, L. 169, 1918 (p.185-6)
Gribačev, N. 222, 1955, 1593
 [tr.: 1876, 2060, 2455]
Griffin, Frederick C. 881
Griffiths, John 747
Grigorenko, Zinaida M. 303
Grigor'ev, A. I. 242
Grigor'ev, B. 205, 1918(p. 209-10)
Grigorev, Dmitry 703
Grodzinsky, Shlomo 2140
Grose, Peter 1042, -47, -53, -83
Grosvenor, Peter 1302
Grunert, Manfred 2032, 2053
Gubko, N. 93, 164, 1918(p.137-8)
Gudzenko, Aleksandr A. 125,1534
Guéhénno, Jean 1849
Guillet, M. 1787
Guissard, Lucien 1696, 1725, 1781, 1818
Gul', Roman 320, 322, 327, 398, 427a
Guščin, K. 324
Gustafson, Richard F. 710
Gwertzman, Bernard 1112, -13,-21, -27, -44, -48, -50, -52, -54, -58, -68, -72, -75, -82, -85, -92, -94, -95, 1403

Haedens, Kléber 1694
Haffner, Suzanne A. 572, 936
Hagelund, Karl Emil 2300
Hallden, Ruth 2392
Hamryluk, Vladimir 1779
Handler, M. S. 1037, 1048
Harari, Manya 610
Harning, Anders 2399
Harrington, William 902
Hartlaub, Geno 1992, 2010, 2078
Hartley, Lodwick 965
Hartmann, Rainer 1985, 2103-04, 2112
Hatfield, Harold 699
Hatzfeld, Genevieve 1878
Haugh, Richard 574
Havlíček, Dušan 1598
Haworth, D. 803

Hayes, Alexia K. & E. Nelson 943, 974
Hayward, Max 500 (intr.), 600, 1942 (intr.)
Hecht, Yvon 1710,-40,-90, 1841
Heeb, Fritz 1285 (p.159), 1401,2093
Hegge Per Egil 1200, 1432,-92,2282, 2291, 2295, 2396
Hehl, Werner 2001
Hendrikse, Huib 1628-29
Herling. See Herling-Grudziński.
Herling-Grudziński, Gustaw 589, 1689, 2336-37, 2341
Hermans, Marge 993
Hess, John L. 1179
Hilsbecher, Walter 2059
Hingley, Ronald 827, 848, 864, 983, 1294, 1312, 1414
Hoffmann, Fernand 2087
Hogan, William 989
Hollenbeck, Ralph 973
Holloway, David 906
Holmes, Alexander 1004
Holmes, Richard 1008
Holmesby, Sterlin 917
Holthusen, Johannes 1983
Honzík, Jiří 1575, 1590
Hood, S. 798, 834-5, 859
Hope, Francis 873
Hotz, Robert 1640, 2118
Howe, Irving 574, 728
Huber, Eduard 2057
Hughes, Catherine 878
Hull, David S. 741
Humphries, Gordon 618
Hutchens, John K. 885

Iampolskaia. See Jampol'skaja.
Ierunca, Virgil 1924
Il'ičev, L. F. 73, 84, 1285 (p. 19-20), 1528, 1530
Il'ičev, V. 75
Il'in, V. N. 341
Il'ina, Tat'jana 366, 373
Ioann S[an]-F[rancisskij], Ar- xiepiskop. See Šaxovskoj.
Ingold, Felix Philipp 1989, 1998, 2042,-67, 2108,-18,-19, 2406
Isaacson, Rose L. 897
Iswolsky, Helene 624, 647
Ivanov, Viktor 137,179, 206,1536, 1549, 1918 (p. 164-6)
Ivanova, T. 1586

Mixajlov, M. 117
Mixajlov, Mixajlo. See Mihajlov.
Mixajlov, S. V. 221a
Mixalevič, Anna 235
Mixalkov, S. 1593 [tr.:1876,
 2060, 2455]; 1955
Mkrtič, Mkrjan 235
Mohrenschildt. See von Mohr-
 enschildt.
Mojniagoune. See Možnjagun.
Mok, Michael 1514
Molčanjuk, N. 149, 1538, 1918(p.167)
Moltchaniouk. See Molčanjuk.
Monas, Sidney 719, 774
Mondrone, Domenico 2202
Monod, Martine 1732, 1825
Moody, Leo Carl 695
Moreau, Jean-Luc 1914
Morgan, Edwin 850
Morozov, Ivan V. 335
Morris, Bernard 755
Mort, Viktor 351
Moseley, Philip E. 724
Mossman, Elliott D. 976
Motjašov, I. 108, 118
Motyleva, T. 132
Možajskaja, O. 369-70
Možnjagun, S. 203, 1918 (p.203)
Muberg, V. 429, 2398
Muchnic, Helen 569a, 574, 593,
 622, 811, 862
Muggeridge, Malcolm 572
Murciano, Carlos 2376
Murray, G. E. 997
Murray, James G. 939
Murray, Michele 950

Nadeau, Maurice 1794, 1939
Nag, Martin 1611, 2278a, 2280
Nantet, Jacques 1759, -73, 1922-37
Natova, Nadežda A. [same as Na-
 dine A. Natov(-Popliuyko)] 445,
 682, 709
Neal, Roger 998
Nefedov, Nikolaj 402
Neiswender, Rosemary 536 (rev.),
 568, 569a, 722, 759, 775, 833, 869
Nejmirok, A. 413
Neumann, Michael 2115a
Newman, Myron 975
Nicholson, Michael A. 574, 1238,
 2118
Niebolsyne, Arkady 1918 (p.365-9)
Nivat, Georges 1676 (intr.), 1912,
 1915, 1918 (p.9 & 352), 1920

Nivat, Lucile 1912
Nol'man, M. 76, 1918 (p.129)
Nolmane. See Nol'man.
Nordmeyer, Barbara 2054
Novikov, V. 92
Nyssen, Hubert 1723

Oberembt, Gert 2105
Obolenskij, Aleksandr P. [same
 as Obolensky] 425, 569a, 642,
 704, 709
Obolenskij, Sergej 337, 386, 446
Obradović, M. 2431
Očadlíková, Miluše 1581
Oerlemans, J. W. 1631
Okuneva, I. 123 [tr.:509 (p.117),
 1285 (p.49), 1537, 1918 (p.153)]
Okunieva. See Okuneva.
Olivier, Daria 1769, 1841, 1910
Oljander, L. 235
Olson, Ivan 921
O'Malley, Michael 794
Opitz, Roland 1982
Ordjan, Guren 235
Orexov, V. 473
Orlova, Raisa 1918 (pp.370-81)
Orth, Samuel F. 706
Ošarov, M. 480
Ostridan, Yishayahu 2134
O'Sullivan, Robert 821
Ovčarenko, A. 130, 1918(p.158)
Ovtcharenko. See Ovčarenko.

Pál. See Fehér Pál.
Palante, Alain 1823
Pallon, V. 150 [tr.:1315, 1536,
 1918 (p. 167-9)
Palme, Olof 475, 1198
Palmier, Jean-Michel 1912
Panin, Dmitrij 496
Pankov, Viktor K. 116, 147, 152,
 210, 1918 (p. 169-70)
Paper, Herbert H. 1176
Parente, William J. 884
Parias, Louis-Henri 1850, 1909
Parkinson, Thomas 920
Parks, James P. 909
Parrill, William 1005
Parry, Albert 1116
Pascal, Pierre 1934
Pašin, Nikolaj S. [same as Nicho-
 las S. Pashin] 411, 574, 673, 1286
Passeri-Pignoni, Vera 2229
Pavlov, S. P. 101, 196, 1918 (p.
 141 & 202)

2. Translators, editors, compilers, adapters and directors of
 dramatic performances, dissertation directors and chairmen
 of symposia

Reddaway, Peter 572, 1290
Rees, Kurt 683
Reeve, F. D. 541
Rich, V. 1288
Robel, Andrée & Léon 1673a,-74b
Rodrigues. See Madeira Rodrigues.
Rolland, Peter A. 701
Ruiz. See del Campo Ruiz.
Rytter, Olaf 2269
Sa'aroni, Yosef 2130, 2130a
Sadao, Inada 2244
Samarin, A. 284a
Sarantopoulos, A. 2120
Sarv, E. 1649
Saville, J. 581
Sémon, Jean-Paul 1676, 1680
Shabad, Theodore 563
Sigurdsson, Steingrímur 2150
Silva Letra, H. 2343
Simmonds, George 583
Skelton, Geoffrey 619
Šoljan, Nada 2423
Someya, Shigeru 2248,-52,-53
Spendel, Giovanna 2170
Stanič, Janez 2456
Stavrou, Theofanis G. 536, 696
Stępowski, J. 2323 [note]
Stempowski. See Stępowski.
Stokke, Ragnfrid 2277
Strada, Vittorio 2172-73
Strom, Roland 589
Summerer, Siglinde 1942
Süsoy, Özay 2413
Suveren, Göntül 2413
Szenfeld, Ignacy 2305,-06,-29,-30
Tafel, Jaroslav 1566

Thomson-Roos, Eva 2380
Thorn[e]. See Torn.
Tikos, Laszlo M. 674
Timmer, Ch. 1615
Tinzmann, Ingrid 1943,-50,-56,-61
  1961
Tissot, Véronique 1675
Tkac, Raja Note preceding 238
Torn, Ljudmila 430
Trušnovič, Ja. 332, 437
Tyrmand, L. 589
Uboldi, Rafaello 2155,-72,-73
Uchimura, Gósuke 2248,-53
Valderhaug, Bjørn 2277
Vallmark, Sven 2380
van der Westhuijzen 1560
Vicente, Isabel 2353
von Block, Bela 502
von Holbeck, Mary 1945, 1956
von Ssachno, Helen 2053
Walker, James G. 519
Waszink, P. M. 1618
Weijers, Mons 1619
Weisenberg, Aurea 2346
Wessely, László 2144
Weyer, Iris 1957,-59
Whiting, Frank M. 696
Whitney, Thomas P. 503, 521, 540
Willemse, Cobi 1618
Willets, Harry T. 506, 508, 514
Žekulin, Gleb 707
Železnov, Dušan 2454
Žiglevič, Evgenija 495
Žujović, Zoran 2418
Zvetermich, Pietro 2160,-72,-74

3. Persons referred to in titles or mentioned in descriptive notes

Subjects of book reviews are not included. (Reviews of books
about Solzhenitsyn are listed immediately following the entry for
such books.)

Amal'rik, Andrej 1117, 1863
Andropov, Jurij, V. 46, 309,
  561, 1192
Babel', Isaak 1585
Bajaubaev, Ulmes 191
Barabaš, Jurij 123, 175
Beckett, Samuel 587, 1873, 1979
Bulgakov, Mixail 296a, 2234
Bunin, Ivan A. 380, 427a
Bunina, V. N. 427a
Burg, David 24, 485, 492; 50a
Burkovskij, B. 150-51, 1033
Čakovskij, A. 278, 281; 249a

Čalidze, Valerij N. 1158
Černouseva, Fridja Ivanovna 191
Chalidze. See Čalidze.
Courtenay, Tom 1475
Daniel, Julij 1041, 1089
Dante 642, 687, 804
Demičev, P. 253, 1284, 1331
Dollefeld, Theodore 1525a
Dostoevskij, F. M. 232, 420, 425,
  437, 586, 597a, 690, 605, 1906, 2127,
  2430; 601
Drommert, René 24
Dubrovin, A. 638
Dunaevskij, Ja. 128

146